The Alzheimer's Diaries

The Alzheimer's Diaries

Susan Elkin

The Book Guild Ltd

First published in Great Britain in 2022 by
The Book Guild Ltd
Unit E2 Airfield Business Park,
Harrison Road, Market Harborough,
Leicestershire. LE16 7UL
Tel: 0116 2792299
www.bookguild.co.uk
Email: info@bookguild.co.uk
Twitter: @bookguild

Typeset in 11pt Caslon Pro

Printed and bound in Great Britain by CMP UK

ISBN 978 1915352 293

British Library Cataloguing in Publication Data.
A catalogue record for this book is available from the British Library.

For Lucas and Felix Elkin, without whom
I would never have coped.

Introduction

Nick and I met at a church hall youth club in Forest Hill in early 1962 when I was fourteen and he was sixteen. A shared love of classical music drew us together almost immediately, first as friends and eventually as a couple. We married seven years later, living initially in a flat in south London and then in a house in Northamptonshire because Nick's job had relocated. After that, we lived in the same house in Kent for thirty-nine years before downsizing and moving back to our native south London in 2016. Along the way, we raised two sons who, between them, eventually presented us with four granddaughters.

Then it all went off track. Nick had always been 'sharp as a pin' to quote a horrified Kent neighbour when she learned of his problems. He'd been a fine, efficient administrator all his adult life too – both as an employee and later in my Susan-Elkin-as-Author business. But now, at about the time of our move 'home' to London in 2016, he started to be worryingly vague, forgetful and unreliable.

Devastatingly, he was diagnosed with Alzheimer's disease on 29 April 2017. He died in Lewisham Hospital on 20 August 2019, just two years and four months later. There were no underlying health conditions. Alzheimer's killed him. Quickly.

With his knowledge, understanding and permission, I charted his illness in blogs, which soon settled into a weekly pattern. Nick liked the idea for two reasons. First, he said that it was much easier for him if we told the world what was happening to him as the illness progressed, because people would make allowances when they met him. Second, he was very clear that being truthful and setting it all down as it really was, would, he hoped, help other people in a similar position.

This book presents the blogs in the order that I posted them. Thus, they diarise the progress of the disease and offer many thoughts, reflections and reactions as they occurred at the time.

It was a bit like writing a real-life soap opera as it unfolded and, in the end, many regular readers seemed to be eagerly awaiting the next 'episode'. People even apologetically told me that they 'enjoyed' (sort of) reading them. Sometimes, they said, that they laughed. I hope they have the same effect on you.

Part One

2017

8 June 2017

A third presence has arrived in my marriage. Until recently, it was him and me. But the man I married in 1969 and I are no longer a self-contained, private unit. Ms Alzheimer's – I think of her as a hideous, be-fanged, brain-eating monster – has come to live with us. Permanently. Symptom-slowing drugs might just keep her in the hall rather than the sitting room for a bit, but even that's not guaranteed.

The shock of learning that the person whose personality, mind (and body) I fell in love with over half a century ago is now steadily, inexorably and relentlessly going to fade away before my eyes, is a life-changer like no other. The death of parents was hard to bear, but it came nowhere near the horror of this.

Not that we're unusual (as if that makes it any easier). Nick is seventy-one. According to Alzheimer's Research UK, one person in fourteen over the age of sixty-five has dementia. And let me share something I've only recently come to understand. The word '*dementia*', from the Latin, literally means *out of mind*. It refers to a generic set of symptoms, like fever. A number of diseases cause it. Alzheimer's is by far the commonest. Two-thirds of dementia sufferers have Alzheimer's – that's about 600,000 in Britain at present. Numbers are rising all the time as the population ages.

As our consultant informed us while we sat numbly trying to absorb the enormity of our situation at her clinic last month, Alzheimer's is set to become the biggest killer in the next twenty years or so, outstripping, for example, cancer. "There is no cure," she said. So did the case worker who originally conducted an assessment at home several months ago. So does every website you look at. No one beats about the bush. Ms A is here to stay. She has to be lived with. Eviction is not an option.

Neither is driving. The hardest thing at this stage is that Nick has had to surrender his driving licence. Once the consultant saw the spatial awareness section of the cognition test Nick did (again) last week, there was no choice. She was very gentle (but firm) about it, observing that such conversations are the hardest part of her job.

Devastating as it was to have Ms A finally, unequivocally, named, her arrival has been gradual. Hindsight is a wonderful thing. There was disorientation during a holiday in Chicago ("Where's our hotel?" repeatedly.) in 2012. Last month, Nick got lost in a shopping mall in Kuala Lumpur and had to be restored to me by the police. He is unsteady on his feet, ponderous, struggles with simple clerical tasks and has lost weight. And as for his memory…

Well, we've all seen films such as *Iris*, *Still Alice* and *Away From Her*, not to mention reading powerful novels like Emma Healey's *Elizabeth is Missing* and Sally Hepworth's *The Things We Keep*. It's mainstream stuff. Over thirty-eight per cent of the UK population knows a family member or close friend with Alzheimer's. There are no secrets about where Ms A will eventually lead Nick – further and further away from the rest of us. The only unknown is how long it will take her.

So, while the consultant carefully advises us to set up lasting power of attorney as soon as possible – a practical but sinister issue with nasty connotations – we need to focus on the immediate future.

"Take him wherever he wants to go – now – while he can," says our elder son. "And let him have what he wants to eat – decades of 'sensible' abstemiousness don't seem to have done him much good!" says the younger.

So, grinning through the tears, I lay in vast quantities of chocolate biscuits. And fruitcake. Blow the sugar. If he likes it, he shall have it. (As long as he also eats the usual bucketload of daily fruit and vegetables – old habits haven't gone altogether.)

Asked if there's anywhere left that he'd like to go or anything he'd like to do – and we've already been fortunate enough to travel widely on some fabulous holidays over the years – Nick thinks hard. Yes, he'd like to hear the Vienna Philharmonic Orchestra on their home turf in the Musikverein in Vienna and, similarly, the Royal Concertgebouw Orchestra in Amsterdam. I've booked the latter for June and am working on the former for November. Susan-will-fix-it.

And at least it's peaceful now. I was angry with everyone and everything for months before Diagnosis Day. I suppose at some level my unconscious brain was trying to tell me that the whole thing was a wind-up and that Nick was putting it all on to annoy me. A counsellor would no doubt call it 'denial'. Now I have recognised the disease for what it is. And I've looked the hideous Ms A square in the face. I'm adjusting and I'm much better-tempered – despite the all-consuming sadness and fear.

Meanwhile, like thousands of other families who have to share their lives with the hateful, pernicious Ms A, we now, somehow, have to stop fretting about the future and live life to the full in the present. *Carpe diem*, every day as it comes and all that.

19 June 2017

Well, we've been to Amsterdam. Nick, the terrifying Ms Alzheimer's and I. I'm drafting this on the train heading home to London.

The toxic monster kept a fairly low profile for most of the three days we were away, but of course she's ever-present in the shadows. I'm continuously aware of her in the corner of my eye. She got at him, for instance, while I was snatching forty much-needed afternoon winks in our hotel room – eye off the ball for a few minutes. When I surfaced, Nick had showered, changed and was looking very dapper. "Are you going somewhere?" I asked.

"Well, I thought I'd better get ready for the birthday party," he replied.

I never ascertained whose birthday party he thought we were going to. It would be funny if it weren't so bloody tragic.

But of course there were lovely bits too, and for most of the time we've been able to have sensible adult conversations which more or less exclude the hateful Ms A, thank goodness. The whole point of the trip was to get Mr E into the Concertgebouw to hear the Royal Concertgebouw Orchestra on their own turf – a hitherto long-held ambition of his. We heard Radu Lupu play Mozart's *24th Piano Concerto* and then some pretty wonderful Strauss and

Wagner. Nick's eyes shone throughout and it was a tear-jerking sort of evening, in more ways than one.

Otherwise, it was difficult to know what to do with him, given that Ms A pecks away at him all the time so that he's perpetually tired. Ninety minutes in the Rijksmuseum (Rembrandt, Vermeer *et al.*) was all he could manage. And soon after that, we had to go back to the hotel to rest. A walk round the lanes and canals in the Jordaan area was really too much too, and crowds are always difficult.

I naturally walk at a moderately brisk pace – *allegro ma non troppo* perhaps. Because Ms A seems to drag him back as if he were carrying a couple of sacks of potatoes, Nick now walks at *lento.* That means that within a few hundred yards, a congenial walk becomes a tedious trudge. And that was what happened in Amsterdam's lovely Vondelpark. I found myself doing a lot of hand-holding – not out of romantic affection (although of course that's still there) but rather as you hang on to a child as a means of anchoring him or her. And I find the slow pace very wearisome. If I let go, I inevitably walk ahead, Nick drops back and then I look round and he's out of sight in the crowd. It happened repeatedly in Amsterdam. I'm turning into an anxious, protective mother hen – oddly, much more so than when I had young children.

Always slight of build and pale of complexion, Nick now looks quite frail – an adjective several friends have used lately. And that means that when we're out and about, most people are helpful and considerate – giving up seats on public transport and being patient in restaurants when he dithers, for example. I keep "My husband isn't very well" up my sleeve as a trump card but haven't so far needed to play it very often. People can see how things are.

It fills me with desperate sadness to watch the physical decline, though. He still automatically reaches for the larger of our two small wheeled suitcases – then finds he can't lift it across that ridiculous 'gap' even wider on some continental trains than British ones. So I have to do it, and he hates that.

He also feels the cold more than he used to. One of our days in Amsterdam was chilly. "Perhaps I'll buy a jacket. I could do with a new one." I told him, not very seriously, that what he needed was a nice warm hoodie, and to my astonishment, he went into a GANT shop and bought one. Nick! In a hoodie! Who says that leopards (especially demented ones) don't change their spots?

28 June 2017

One of my bitterest regrets is that Ms Alzheimer's managed to worm her nasty way into the car quite so early in her tenancy. Nick was firmly told to surrender his licence immediately upon diagnosis. And that's a distressing, demoralising blow when you're only seventy-one and have driven expertly all over the world. I'll never forget the exemplary way in which Nick sailed confidently onto and along a desperately confusing eight-lane motorway in Atlanta, for example.

About five years ago, Ms A (although I didn't recognise her at the time) nipped off the ability to park. This man who'd been driving thousands of miles a year since his early twenties suddenly couldn't judge where other parked cars, kerbs, walls and posts were. Not that he hit any of the aforementioned, but there was no competence or confidence and a great deal of shunting forwards and backwards and driving round the block looking for a bigger space. And the joke – I do try to hang on to a sense of humour – is that this least macho of men wasn't driving a massive Mercedes or SUV. For years, he had Fiat Pandas, with reverse parking sensors on the last one.

For a long time, we'd arrive in, say, a multi-storey car park and he'd ask me to park his car – and it was worse if he was driving my car, which is a little bigger. I used to giggle to myself that this stereotype-confounding behaviour must look extraordinary to anyone watching. "Hee hee hee," I'd say. "He can no longer park. Ha ha. What a good job I'm pretty damn good at it," I'd crow. Of course, I should have been thinking seriously about why he couldn't do it rather than laughing, and I'm ashamed of that now.

But he seemed to be okay when out on the road, so I didn't, in all honesty, give it much thought, although he often didn't seem to be able to remember where destinations were, and both our sons had long said that their dad seemed to have become a very slow driver.

Then came that dreadful diagnosis and the spatial awareness cognition test. One of the tasks was to copy a drawing of two interlinked figures of eight on their sides. Our youngest granddaughter, aged 2, would probably have made a better job of it than her grandpa did. Ms A has definitely made off with his sense of shape and space. And although that doesn't matter much if you bruise your thigh on a piece of furniture or even scrape a post in a car park, out on the open road it could be life and death. Thank goodness the accident was waiting to happen rather than having already occurred. The following morning, I downloaded the licence surrender form and made him sign it and post it. And a few days later, we sold his car – a clean break seemed best.

It is, however, still very hard for Nick. From the passenger seat in my car, he sees mad drivers doing the most unthinkably dangerous things (especially in London where we now live) and says, "Look at that. I've never done anything as stupid as that in my entire life, but he's allowed to drive and I'm not."

I reply patiently: "Look, no one has said there's anything wrong with your driving. It's simply that you've been declared medically unfit to do it." Unconvinced, he just grunts.

In another mood, he'll say, "They stopped me driving just because I couldn't draw a silly diagram. I've never been any good at drawing. What has that to do with anything?" And I explain over and over again (many of our conversations are verbatim repeat efforts these days) what spatial awareness is and why it matters.

Worse, I get: "If only we hadn't let those bloody women into our life then everything would still be normal." He doesn't mean Ms A either. He is thinking of the consultant, the nurse who is our first port of call at the euphemistically named 'Memory Clinic' and the occupational therapist. Almost daily, I tell him, as patiently as I can, that he has an illness. And he'd still have it whoever we consulted or agreed to talk to. "Loathe, hate and despise the illness if you like – but you can't blame people who are merely trying, as compassionately as they can, to do their very difficult jobs," I remind him.

Meanwhile, he worries that he can't help me as he always used to. And I really do have a lot to do – a business and home which I now have to run more or less single-handedly, plus the 'caring'. He used to pick me up in the car, share the driving, run errands, do the shopping, and much more.

Ah. Did someone mention shopping? I've bought him one of those big square wheeled shopping trolleys – much cheaper to run than a Fiat Panda. We are less than a mile from two excellent supermarkets. So I've put him in charge of fruit and vegetables (and now have all the bulky stuff delivered) – reminding him that exercise is meant to be vital in the management of Alzheimer's. As long as he has a clear list, he can manage that perfectly well at present. And it makes him feel both independent and useful. A tiny one in the eye for hateful Ms A for a bit.

5 July 2017

I've always been a positive, outward-looking, glass-half-full, don't-let-the-buggers-win kind of person. And, of course, there are a few pluses. I'm discovering – even in Nick's Alzheimer's diagnosis – an occasional flash of light in the gathering darkness. Clouds, silver linings and all the rest of it. Here, in no particular order, are ten of them:

1. **Better sleep** Ms Alzheimer's perpetual prodding at Nick's ailing brain makes him very tired. So he sleeps like a baby. And that means that I (sometimes) rest more easily too. For two people who have struggled with moderate insomnia for years, this is a bit of a bonus.

2. **Family** When our sons were growing up, we often despaired at their behaviour and attitudes and blamed ourselves – as most parents do. Now in their forties, both with families and busy businesses to run, they are astonishingly, generously, movingly supportive, kind, competent men, and we are deeply appreciative. We must, without knowing it, have done something right when they were young. The four or us are, I think, closer than we've been for a long time too, and we've always been fairly strong on family stuff. Then there are their partners and ex-partners, all

cheerfully on board when we need them. The help is practical, thoughtful and makes me, in particular, realise that I am definitely not alone with Nick and the foul Ms A.

3. **Wonderful friends** Since I started writing these blogs, literally hundreds of people – some we know very well and others whom we know only slightly – have expressed concern, offered help and sent love. I feel more supported and fortunate than at any other time in my entire life. Thanks, Folks. Great to know you're there.

4. **Chocolate biscuits** What a lot of lovely varieties there are out there. For decades, we abstemiously forewent them. Now they're back on the shopping list because I let Nick have exactly what he fancies to eat. And it would be rude not to join him, wouldn't it? The biscuits in the M&S 'Extremely Chocolatey' range are our favourites.

5. **Learning curve** For years, we've been a team with complementary skills, and Nick has done most of our 'admin'. Now that he struggles with that, I'm having to develop new skills rapidly. Life is suddenly full of firsts. In the last week alone, for example, I have taxed my car from scratch and cracked online business banking with a fiddly fob thing.

6. **Safety awareness** I now notice steps and other hazards in a way I never have before. Because Nick is shakier on his feet than he used to be, I am constantly saying, "Mind this" or "Watch that." Of course, you should never be casual about safety, whatever your circumstances, so I regard my heightened awareness as a gain.

7. **Time to stand, stare and share** Suddenly the simple things seem good. Sometimes, it's enough just to stroll in the park

or listen to and watch the parakeets in our south London garden. Yes, I know it's not PC to like the latter, but we're not and we do.

8. **Getting things in proportion** There is nothing like a diagnosis such as the one we're living with to make you sort out what really matters. Things I might once have got very uptight about – such as whether the garden gets weeded or getting exactly the right sort of pre-show snack (he still comes out theatre-reviewing with me) – are suddenly revealed as the trivia they are. Not worth fretting about. Better to focus on things like remembering to hug him and tell him how much I love him.

9. **Sympathy for others** I hope (but it may be a vain hope) that I've always been kind to everyone who needs it, but I am, by nature, brusque, impatient and always in a hurry. And I'm sure I've often ridden roughshod over vulnerable people. I'm now conscious that I can very easily spot other people who are dealing with intractable problems in the same way as we are. My becoming even slightly more empathetic and sympathetic can only be a good thing.

10. **Education** I've learned to spell Alzheimer's.

13 July 2017

Well, that bitch, Ms Alzheimer's, certainly knows how to scupper sense of time – as in whether today is Tuesday or Sunday and whether we're doing what we discussed last night or dealing with some future arrangement mentioned in passing.

My lovely man now frequently asks me what day of the week it is. Last Sunday, we were due to pick the cherries from a tree in a Kent orchard – Rent a Cherry Tree is an annual Christmas gift from my sister. On waking (early on the alarm clock), I asked him what we were going to do. "Aren't we going to a funeral?" he replied. Well, I'm learning to read the surreal workings of his impaired brain now. Nick was thinking of a memorial service we were due to attend forty-eight hours later. My mistake was to have chatted about it at what must seem to him the 'wrong' time.

Time and its complexities is one of the last abstractions a child conceptualises. It's no good telling a two-year-old, in September, that we're all going to Granny's for Christmas. If he or she takes it in at all, there will be misunderstandings. 'When' is much harder than 'where'. And parents of young children know that instinctively. It isn't, I suppose, therefore surprising that time is one of the first things to go when the brain is regressing. It reminds me of Martin Amis's 1991 novel *Time's Arrow,* in which the protagonist is living his life in reverse, speeding back towards the womb, getting younger as he goes.

Meanwhile, I have to find practical ways of dealing with it. So I have a new policy. Each night, I say: "This is what you (or we) are doing tomorrow, and I'm not going to tell you about anything beyond that because you'll get in a muddle." He smiles gratefully. Then we go through it again in the morning, when he may or may not remember some, part, or all of it.

It's another slant on 'take every day as it comes', but it's far from easy because it destroys (bloody Ms A) much of the fabric of normal discourse and the kind of chatty conversation that has been part of our lives for decades. If I find myself trotting downstairs from my office and saying "Good news! I've got press tickets for *Fiddler on the Roof* in Chichester next week" or "We're going to lunch with the family on Sunday" or "I'll have to leave you a snack on Tuesday night because I'm working," I have to bite it back. Such bits of information are toxic. Within hours, they bounce back at me, garbled and misunderstood.

And I resent that a lot because I'm a communicator – forthcoming and informative by nature. Both as teacher and journalist, I have always been a disseminator – of stuff, at all levels. Having to desist from sharing quite ordinary things feels horrible. It means conversation isn't quite spontaneous anymore. Jolly hard.

19 July 2017

This week, I put Nick in charge of ordering three items by phone from a mail order catalogue – something he would have done without a second thought only a few months ago. On this occasion, it's a good job I hovered, because he could remember neither the name of our road (we moved here ten months ago) nor the postcode. Fortunately, the saleswoman at the other end of the phone was very patient and understanding.

In short, things aren't getting any better. The truth, of course, is that degeneration is clear – exactly as all the medics, media and everyone else confidently and bleakly predict. Our elder son said a week or two ago that he thought his father was worse on Saturday than he had been on the previous Tuesday. This condition is a one-way street. Ms Alzheimer's is here to stay, and the foul fiend is very determined.

So Nick needs to try a cholinesterase inhibitor drug as soon as possible. Yes, I know such drugs do nothing more than slow the advancement of the symptoms for a bit. I also know that they don't suit everyone. The side effects can be pretty unpleasant for some people. Moreover, Nick has a slow heart beat (first either of us knew about it and no, he has never been an athlete), so there has to be a second opinion before a prescription decision can be made.

Enter the NHS with all its desperately slow, bureaucratic inefficiency. Nick was deemed to need a twenty-four-hour ECG monitor to check his heart rate over time. For some unfathomable reason, you are not allowed to make appointments in hospitals – as you would at the dentist, the vet, the hairdresser or the garage which services your car. No, you have to wait until someone deigns to send you a take-it-or-leave-it slot. Who on earth dreamed it up? It's an absurd system which must lead to hundreds of no-shows and cost the NHS (actually the taxpayer, aka you and me) a huge amount of money. We're always being told that the NHS is strapped for cash. I'm convinced that they could at least dent that a bit if they just exercised some common sense occasionally and recognised that this is 2017, not 1947.

Another gripe is this entirely nonsensical (and costly) letters-in-the-post business. Why on earth can't they email like the rest of the world? And spare me that facile data protection stuff. It's just an excuse to do things in the most cumbersome, least convenient possible way.

To make matters worse, they 'lost' our referral, which means that had I not sought the help of two people in the know who pushed on our behalf, we'd still be waiting for the ECG appointment – indefinitely. Finally, two and a half months after diagnosis, Nick got the test done last week and now we wait for the next stage.

I have just rung and asked if I can make an appointment for Nick to see the consultant so that we can get the ball rolling. No no no. You can't do that. Silly me. You have to wait until you're 'offered' one. Why? I'm not trying to jump the queue. I know these things take time. But surely we could all operate like twenty-first-century grown-ups – with diaries?

I've always been a tooth grinder – at this rate, I shall have no teeth left at all by Christmas.

26 July 2017

It's deeply ironic that Nick should be succumbing to an age-related disease at this moment in his life. He finally became an orphan less than three years ago. Well, we knew that losing your last parent was the ultimate marker in attaining adulthood, but we didn't expect Ms Alzheimer's to arrive on the scene almost before the 'funeral baked-meats' were cold.

My father-in-law, George Frank Charles Elkin, died in October 2014, just a few weeks short of his ninetieth birthday. And I am deeply thankful that he didn't live another year or two to see his only child succumbing to Ms A, because it would have been a hideous reversal of how things are meant to be. George didn't have Alzheimer's. He was pretty deaf towards the end and a bit forgetful but perfectly sensible most of the time. He was just old.

When his father died, Nick was sixty-nine. They were separated by just twenty years. Back in 1944, George, nineteen, knew that the army, which had just conscripted him, was about to send him to the Far East for a long stint. So he married his teenage sweetheart quickly while the going was good. A weekend's leave a few weeks later meant that by the time George actually set sail for the Pacific Rim – where eventually he had to help deal with the aftermath of

Japanese atrocities – his young wife was pregnant with Nick. He learned he was a father when the baby was a week old and didn't actually see his first and only progeny until over a year later.

How, after all that, they ever settled down to become a proper family still astonishes and impresses me, but they did. Nick's parents celebrated their diamond wedding just before her death in 2004. George lived another ten years, most of them good ones. We took him on holiday several times with all of his grandchildren and great-grandchildren, for example.

Now the reason I mention all this here is that something very odd happened when George died. Nick had never seemed to me to be in the least like his father in appearance, manner or outlook. If there were family likenesses at all, it was his mother's father and brother that Nick resembled. Well, you know how the Buddhists believe that when someone dies, the soul is immediately reborn in another creature, human or animal? It was almost as if I was watching a version of that. From the moment that George breathed his last in Medway Hospital, Nick turned into him.

Logic, education and common sense tell me that it's just the strange vagaries of genes combined with the influence of the demonic Ms A. But it feels disconcertingly uncanny when I hear George's voice coming out of Nick's mouth. The sound is slightly raspy and often higher-pitched than it used to be. Nick also now makes exactly the same sort of (negative) remarks that his father would have done in precisely the same tone. And that's new. When we were flying home overnight from Kuala Lumpur recently, he thought the aircraft was 'messing about' and that the pilot had turned off the engine. I had to explain that we were cruising at 35,000 feet somewhere over Russia and that we'd be at Heathrow in five hours or so. "Huh!" he said contemptuously, in George's voice. "You've got more faith in British Airways than I have." If he were a mimic on a talent show, I'd give him full marks. Then there's the slow, trudging walk and small steps, all George could manage in his late eighties – if I catch Nick out of the corner of my eye, it's like seeing a ghost. I do double takes all the time. And as for that silent hovering when I'm working…

What happened to those twenty years, the generation that separated Nick from his father, then? Gone. No wonder he frequently tells me that he feels he has been cheated of at least ten years of life.

3 August 2017

That bloody fiend, Ms Alzheimer's, has taken up residence in my dishwasher – like a slug which has crawled obscenely up the waste pipe.

Nick was King of the Dishwasher. It's a gender thing, he used to tell me fondly as he expertly stacked plates and cutlery therein and, an hour later, fussily put every item away in its accustomed place. And woe betide me if I dared put so much as a washed mug in the cupboard or a knife in the drawer, because it would never be up to Nick's standards. Men are good at dishwashers. Women are not, I was told. He passed the same wisdom (or something) on to both our sons too. Elkin men are dishwasher chaps. Impede them at your peril.

Well, for decades, I've acquiesced in this sexist nonsense because I am very busy and it was one less thing for me to do. I'd delegated it, and if he chose to lord it over me on this one issue, then fine. Get on with it, mate.

But now, of course, it's different. Nick can rarely remember whether the machine has run or not, so I often have to remove a dirty cup or plate which he has popped in to sully the clean things which are drying. He can no longer stack it logically either. Setting it to go and/or finding the tablet to put in the plastic compartment isn't easy either. He unwraps the ready-to-use ones and leaves the cellophane on the ones you're meant to undo. And if he tries to empty it when the cycle is finished, many things get put in the wrong place. I might find the cat's dishes with our own plates and basins or tea mugs in with saucepans. Things I need in the kitchen disappear too, and I sometimes search for days.

Yes, I see Ms A's gloating face every time I open the dishwasher door. "Yoo-hoo, I'm in here too now," she crows. And I have to keep telling myself that I must never complain. It's the illness, not him. It was hard to remember that, though, when – as this week – I exasperatedly found a ruined bag of expensive best-quality oranges in the freezer instead of the fridge and had to remove a pile of dirty dusters from the tumble dryer. Although the latter is in a different part of the house, Nick had forgotten and mistaken it for the washing machine.

She has long, pernicious tentacles, does Ms A. And I'm afraid I grumble at her victim all the time. How can this orderly man I've lived with for nearly fifty years suddenly be unable to put the cutlery away competently or not know where his clean socks are? It seems so ridiculous. What I feel instinctively and from long habit is at total variance with what the medics say and what, incredulously, I see happening every day. I wish I were more saintly and could just keep quiet but...

9 August 2017

When I was a child, whimsical adults would talk about benign fairies coming at bedtime to scatter sleepy dust on us. How sweet. Well, hateful Ms Alzheimer's is certainly armed with pocketsful of sleepy dust but it's no blessing. More like a malevolent curse.

Nick, until recently an active, quite energetic man, is now tired all the time. If he sits down, he nods off, and that's despite also sleeping well all night. Take, for example, the night last week when Berlioz's *Damnation of Faust* was on at the Proms. Nick and Dave the cat repaired purposefully to the sitting room to listen to it. Now, I have to say that Dave is not a very discerning music lover. He's as happy with Elvis as Wagner, just as long as he's got a warm, cuddly, relaxed human being to lean against. And he certainly had it during said Berlioz. When I popped downstairs from my office half an hour later in search of a sustaining cup of tea, I glanced through the sitting-room door to see them both fast asleep. Chin uncomfortably on his chest, Nick wasn't hearing a single note of Berlioz's masterpiece.

The same thing often happens these days at live concerts, plays and films – and that would have been laughably unthinkable even two years ago. As a reviewer, I sometimes see two shows on one day – typically a matinee following by an evening performance. I wouldn't now dream of asking Nick to accompany me on such a long day because I know he'd find it unbearably exhausting. Frailty, thy name is man. Especially if Ms A has got at you.

Then there are shows which entail a long journey home. The later it gets, the more tired he becomes, and sometimes, anyway, I'm allocated only a single ticket. I've lost count, for example, of the number of times this year I've driven solo home from Chichester pounding along all those As and Ms – A27, A24, M23, M25 and A22 – with only late-night Radio 3 for company. In another life, I would have stayed at the Premier Inn in Chichester and driven home in the morning but am now uneasy about leaving Nick at home overnight. I have two double show days coming up actually in Chichester – so that's the problem compounded.

It's desperately sad, too, to watch Nick – a lifelong reader – struggling to read books through his fatigue. He has had the same two books, which he also carries around the house during the day, on the bedside for around three months. He reads a page and then the book falls from his hand as his head droops in sleep. I suspect – although I haven't asked the question and don't really want to know the answer at the moment – that he can't actually remember what he's already read when he picks up the book. It reminds me of the weak teenage readers I used to teach in secondary schools who would come to class with the same 'private reader' all year – until I intervened and told them to give up and get something short, easy and doable to build confidence. It's a very different situation when reading ability is declining because you've got Ms A chewing away at your brain.

I first noticed this uncharacteristic somnolence two years ago when we were on holiday in Arizona. Every night after dinner, we'd return to our hotel room to read for a couple of hours – me seated at the in-room desk and Nick on the sofa. Within a few minutes, I'd glance over my shoulder and he'd be asleep. At the time, I just thought it was mildly amusing – the desert air and all that. Little did I know. I seem to have watched him – still only seventy-two – age twenty years in just a few months.

Well, this disease is a one-way street. He isn't likely to get any livelier – although the medication he's due to start next month could, just possibly, stop him getting any sleepier for a bit. Meanwhile, the hardest part is the poignancy of his saying, quite often, that he hopes to be better soon. If only. The bitter truth is very hard to accept, especially when you're the person it's happening to.

16 August 2017

Sod you, Ms Alzheimer's. Time for some positive thinking. Whatever you say and do, there are still, at the moment, plenty of things Nick continues to do quite happily. Here are ten of them. He can still:

- walk the mile from our house to Beckenham alone (and come home safely) and do a job when he gets there – provided he doesn't have more than one purpose. So he can take a parcel to the post office, buy some biscuits in M&S or get his hair cut – but not more than one of them. If he tries to do both X and Y, one or other will be forgotten.
- remember routes – provided he's known them for a long time. Driving from Elephant and Castle to Waterloo the other day, I was thrown by an unexpected road sign and turned the wrong way. "It's okay," Nick said, quick as a flash, "there's a roundabout round the next bend. Then you can peel off to the right towards Waterloo Bridge." Spot-on.
- recognise everyone we know and greet them by name, although it was very funny the other day when our second granddaughter popped her head unexpectedly round the dining-room door

where we were breakfasting. (Her dad has a key and had come to do some work in the house, but we weren't expecting his lovely daughter.) She was wearing dark glasses and her father's company uniform and for a moment neither of us recognised her.

- enjoy a favourite meal and eat very well. It's a joy to see him enthusiastically tucking into, say, sautéed potatoes and fried eggs. He also eats things that he's always refused to touch in the past, such as tomatoes and beetroot – bit of a bonus from the cook's point of view.
- trundle his old chap's trolley to the supermarket and buy most of what's required reasonably efficiently – provided it's a fairly short list and he can go at his own *adagio* pace. I now have all the bulky stuff delivered and send him just to choose, for example, nice apples.
- quote poetry and songs he learned as a child such as *The Boy Stood on the Burning Deck, Ozymandias* and some filthy ditty he learned in the Scouts in which 'Venus' rhymes with 'penis' – well you can't expect callow, pubescent youth to have mastered the finer points of poetics.
- do lots of household tasks – provided they are very clearly explained and assigned one at a time. "Can you go and collect the windfall plums and put them in the compost bin, please?" or "How about you vacuum cleaning the inside of the car?" are fine, but it's no good asking him to do first one and then the other in the same conversation. It's very much like dealing with a child on the autism spectrum. In fact, isn't it about time someone researched the similarities between autism and Alzheimer's?
- get me a cup of tea. A non-tea drinker himself, Nick has twice in the past week got out of bed while I'm still sleeping off the previous night's show and subsequent late-night review and

returned with a mug of tea. Bit heavy-handed with the milk and not all that hot because he moves pretty slowly, but I'm touched that a) he thinks of it and b) still makes a reasonable fist of doing it.

- get a lot of pleasure from a walk round the park. It's a simple thing but he likes seeing trees, wildlife, flowers, children having fun and all the rest of it. There's a circular walk round Beckenham Place Park we do fairly often and this week, we revisited Horniman's for the first time since we moved back to our native south London last year. It all helps with fitness too, which is meant to be a way of helping to distance Ms A.
- make me laugh. Quite often, there's a flash of how he used to be. He'll come out with some silly pun or a chunk of WS Gilbert (who had a witty comment on almost everything) and we giggle together. Long may it last.

23 August 2017

If something happens to me or to someone close to me, I thirst for information. When I was pregnant with my first child, I borrowed library books which detailed every stage of the nine months. When my mother was diagnosed with glaucoma (which is hereditary), it was hot foot to a medical encyclopaedia. And as for when my father got Guillain-Barré syndrome and was months, paralysed, in Intensive Care, you can imagine how well informed I became.

Inevitably then, I have read a great deal about Alzheimer's in recent months. Knowledge is power (sort of), and at least I can look the loathed Ms A straight in the eye if I know the awful facts. And that makes me feel a bit stronger, if nothing else.

There is, I have now noticed, some sort of news story about Alzheimer's in the newspapers almost daily. I have collected a fat file of cuttings. Alzheimer's research, incidentally, is scandalously underfunded.

An analysis in 2012 (reported in *BMJ Open* in April 2015) found that from a combination of government and charitable funding, only £90m was spent on Alzheimer's research in Britain that year. £544m went to cancer research in the same period – six times as much. And this is against a background of Alzheimer's being described as 'the defining disease of the baby boomer generation', or as our consultant put it cheerfully: "Alzheimer's is set to be the leading course of death over the next twenty years."

A University College London study confirmed all this in July by estimating that more than 1.2 million people will have dementia by 2037 – it's around 850,000 at present. For years, (younger) people have been saying rather crossly that my generation is the most fortunate in history – we haven't fought a war, we've bought houses whose value has escalated, we had free education and all the rest of it. Now, it seems that our luck has run out. With a vengeance.

Anyway, back to those cuttings. The point I was rambling round to is that given that Alzheimer's research is so woefully and disproportionately underfunded, there seem to be an awful lot of reports about – some interesting, some ruefully hilarious and some just statements of the bleeding obvious.

I laughed a lot, for instance, on 20 July at the *Telegraph* strapline '*A-levels and healthy hearing cut risk of Alzheimer's*'.

"There!" I said to Nick over our breakfast muesli and fruit. "I always said you should have worked harder for your A-levels!" Then I read the piece. It referred to a (different) University College London study which found, among other things, that people who stayed in education beyond age fifteen have an eight per cent less chance of developing Alzheimer's. Grades and certificates are nothing to do with it. Well, he remained in full-time education until he was twenty-one, so that's another one to cross off.

Last week, a study at McGill University, Canada noted that Alzheimer's can start twenty years before the patient, or anyone else, is aware of it. And one of the earliest signs can be anosmia, or loss of sense of smell.

It is at least two decades since Nick and I were driving along a country lane in Kent on a summer's day with the windows down. Then we passed a beautiful blue field of flax and I said, "Oh, what a wonderful smell!"

"What smell?" he asked, puzzled. I was utterly incredulous, because it was an aroma of bowl-you-over strength. Then we realised that his sense of smell had pretty much gone, and ever since then, we've had to be careful about pans on the stove, toast stuck in the toaster, and so on, because he cannot smell burning – or anything else. I have to do the smelling for both of us, we've joked. Would it have helped if we'd known that this was actually the top of a very nasty, slippery downward path? Probably not.

Then, only this week, *The Times* (on its front page) announced that gum disease increases the risk of Alzheimer's by 70%. What this boils down to is that researchers from Chung Shan Medical University in Taichung, China have established a link between poor dental hygiene and the dreaded Ms A.

Pause for a gulp of disbelief. Nick has been a mildly obsessive teeth-cleaner – a three-times-a-day-with-the-brush-man – all his life. And, of course, he has seen a dentist regularly and, in latter years at least, rarely needed any treatment. So that's yet another tick for the N/A box.

Over and over again, research finds that factors such as a Mediterranean diet, not being overweight, refraining from tobacco, maintaining healthy blood pressure help to prevent Alzheimer's. Well, maybe they do, but it really isn't what we want to hear at the moment.

Nick is a man of slight build who has always weighed less than ten stone and never been anywhere near overweight. He accepted a Woodbine from another boy in the Scouts when he was twelve, hated it and has never smoked since. His blood pressure has always been fine. We both became vegetarians in the late 1970s, initially for health but also for ethical reasons. Nick has, therefore, been eating large quantities of vegetables, fruit, legumes and nuts every day for forty years. He's always been a willing walker too. And he has a beer with his dinner three or four times per week and no other alcohol. What more could he possibly have done in pursuit of what these researchers piously call 'a healthy lifestyle'? More hollow laughter.

Then there are books. It was Nick himself who read a feature about Joseph Jebelli's book *The Pursuit of Memory: the Fight Against Alzheimer's* and asked me to buy it. Jebelli is a neurobiologist who graduated from UCL and now specialises in Alzheimer's research at the University of Washington, Seattle. His interest in the disease was triggered by watching his grandfather succumb to it.

Well, I haven't yet been able to get my hands on this book because Nick has been struggling though it for three months. Alleyns School in the misguided 1960s taught him no science, and he says he finds some of Jebelli's explanations hard to understand. It is meant to be a mainstream book, however, so I shall reserve judgement until I've read it myself.

What I have read, though, is *Memory's Last Breath: Field Notes on My Dementia* by Gerda Saunders. Someone on Twitter drew my attention to this and introduced Gerda to these blogs of mine. Gerda is a South African-born academic and has lived for many years in Salt Lake City where she worked until her retirement as an academic at the University of Utah.

She was diagnosed with Alzheimer's in 2010 just before her sixty-first birthday. Gerda's book is a delightful blend of her own thoughts and experiences – often very down-to-earth and personal – and fascinating, intelligent reflections on the nature of memories and how we shape them. Since Nick and I have known each other since I was fourteen, I'm now pretty sure that many of the things we fondly remember are simply memories of memories which we've created together. It's an entertaining, informative, thoughtful and brave book which helped me, a little, to understand how it really feels to have a cloudy brain as opposed to observing someone else with one.

The single truth to deduce from this plethora of reading matter? There is no justice or mercy in nature.

30 August 2017

Money is becoming a problem in the household I share with Nick and the loathed Ms Alzheimer's.

Don't squirm. This is not a fundraising appeal. I have worked flat out all my adult life – often doing several jobs at once – lived within my income and always saved a bit. Nick has worked just as hard, for many years, as a mind-blowingly efficient househusband between bouts of employment as an education administrator. In latter years, he has also run my writing business – doing just about everything except the writing, although he's now fully retired from it, thanks to Ms A. The result of all these endeavours is that we can pay our bills and afford the occasional takeaway curry. We're not wealthy (whatever that means), but there's certainly no need to pass the hat round.

No. Our money worries relate to something else. Nick is finding it increasingly difficult to manage it – whether it's the notes and coins in his pocket or funds in the bank. When we went to Malaysia in March, he bought some *ringgits* in advance – as you do. It was a wad of notes which we put carefully in one of the pockets of his man-bag. For most of the first week we were away, he told me several times a day that he was very worried because he'd lost that money or perhaps left it at home. Each time he mentioned it, I showed him where it was. It was a conversation that went round and round like a stuck gramophone record. Back in Blighty, we've had exactly the same issue with the little bank bag of coins he carries with him – he frets continuously that he's lost it. He hasn't.

We've always had separate bank accounts – plus one joint one which pays for household stuff, now entirely managed online by me. This means that I don't know – and have never cared as long as there was enough day-to-day money for what we needed or wanted to do – the details of his savings accounts, ISAs, and so on. Well, assisted by our very practical elder son, we have now been through all the muddled files. And I've lost count of the number of accounts we've found with small forgotten sums in them. We've closed most of them now and tided everything up. Nick, meanwhile, just looks on, bemusedly, saying things like "Well, I didn't know I'd got that", as if it were someone else's affairs – which I suppose in a way it is. The man who only two or three years ago had impeccably orderly paperwork (he's never really trusted online banking) which told him, literally, to the penny exactly what was where, has gone. In his place is a financially helpless old chap with Ms A on his shoulder, sneering. And I try to shake my fist at her rather than breaking down and howling at the misery of it. I don't always succeed.

Not, obviously, that this is all bad. It's much better to find little bits of money you didn't know you had than it is to uncover the horror of debt you weren't aware of. Always look on the bright side. Or try to.

When I was a child, we knew several old ladies who 'went funny in the head'. Then, eventually, when their relations had to sort out the house, it was quite common to find hundreds of pounds hidden away and forgotten – like squirrels with their acorns. Well, a couple of generations later, we all use cash much less, but money is still something that dogs a diseased mind. I suppose it's because we were taught from infancy that it is very important and must be kept carefully and safely. These days, there are debit and credit card issues too. Nick keeps his in a wallet in his man-bag (I could write a whole blog about that bag – and perhaps I will), frequently telling me in a panicky voice that he's lost this card or that. Then I look and find it in the accustomed place. Another worry dispelled – for half an hour, anyway.

It's the stress and anxiety that worrying about all this causes him that is the saddest thing. Money worries of any sort are deeply debilitating. I have activated the enduring power of attorney (now known as a lasting power of attorney or LPA) which Nick signed in the early 1990s and have a stash of certified copies ready to register with banks. I'm reluctant, though, to take away from Nick all control over his money until I really have to. He's been grown up for a long time, and I have to maintain the illusion for as long as possible. To do otherwise is to hammer yet one more nail into the coffin containing his independence. Difficult balance.

6 September 2017

One morning last week, Nick strode (yes, strode – not shambled, shuffled or trudged) into my office. He'd been to Beckenham, on one of his single-target excursions to take a package to the post office. Now, in Beckenham, the post office is within WHSmith, where, on his own initiative, he had stopped off and bought a couple of packets of the plastic propelling pencils we both like. It's an old joke that neither of us can ever find one because they're so gregarious that they like to hold meetings in my handbag or violin case. "I'm rationing you to two of these new ones," said Nick with an assertive twinkle. "If I let you have any more, you'll only eat them." It was, for a few moments, as if I had my husband back – the man who could run a business, manage files, administer the household as well as being someone I could, and often did, lean on heavily to keep everything running smoothly. Ms Alzheimer's was nowhere to be seen. She was banished. There we were, just the two of us – grinning at each other. Equal partners.

Of course, it didn't last. This disease doesn't go away. There is no such thing as 'remission'. If you've got it, you've got it. A few days later, we came in from a reasonably constructive, congenial afternoon's gardening to find an alarming, growing puddle on the kitchen floor. Nick did a lot of hand-wringing and negative muttering while I got down (a long way down) to mopping it up and phoning our plumber son for help. Eventually, flat on my stomach on a very wet floor, getting soggier by the minute – having pulled all the kick panels off – phone glued to my ear, I ascertained that the waste pipe had separated from the outlet under the sink. An hour later and, with verbal guidance from the family plumber, I had effected a temporary fix. Shall I add plumbing to my ever-growing CV? Maybe not. The reason I mention this incident here is that throughout the damp drama, Nick simply hovered, looking anxious and vaguely relieved that someone was dealing with it. Ms A was definitely in the kitchen with a vengeance. I hope she got horribly wet feet. And a nasty chill.

Every day, at least one person kindly asks me how Nick is. Most people are terrifically supportive and sympathetic, by the way. There's not a lot they can do in practice, but the warmth helps. I just answer, "Well, up and down. Good days and bad days... you know? You just have to take each day as it comes." They then commend me for coping with it all so positively. As if I have a choice. The pencils followed by the plumbing are a good couple of illustrations of just how yo-yo-like life with Ms A really is. You have to go with the flow and hope it won't be literally across the kitchen floor.

Four months after the meeting at which we were given the devastating diagnosis, Nick has just had a follow-up appointment with the consultant. At last he now has some medication. There were delays because of a couple of minor medical issues, now successfully negotiated. The drug is called Memantine – in case you're interested in the technicalities – and he's on an escalating dose over four weeks. It's helpfully categorised as an 'anti-Alzheimer's medicine' (and there was I thinking it was a cold cure – silly me) and is supposed to work on the receptors in the brain that deal with memory. "Some people find it useful," said the consultant cautiously. Well, it's early days, and this week he's on only a quarter of the target dose, but the lack of side effects thus far is encouraging. And maybe, just maybe, it will help to lessen Ms A's grip a little, at least in the short term.

A few more pencil days and rather fewer plumbing days would be good. But I'm not holding my breath. Hope has to be tempered with realism when you have Ms A in residence.

13 September 2017

Sometimes I feel that our marriage is over. Something else has replaced it, although I can't quite put my finger on what. Have I really morphed in just a few months into a Joyce Grenfell-style nursery manager-cum-hearty carer?

Take the night last week when Nick staggered off to the bathroom in the early hours as usual. When he opened the bedroom door on his way back, the room was flooded with light. "Can you just turn the bathroom light off, please?" I said.

"But there are people in the bathroom," he replied, glancing back anxiously over his shoulder.

Well, I couldn't help wondering just who these imaginary 2am revellers occupying our bathroom might be in the fog of a demented mind, but I needed to be practical. "No, there's no one in the bathroom. Turn the light off, please," I said in my best grown–up, kind (I hope) but no-nonsense voice. I could hear myself going straight into dispassionate, assertive classroom mode without an ounce of wifeliness. Yet another thing Ms Alzheimer's has stolen.

In a long, committed marriage, when both partners are well and thinking straight, there is a lot of shorthand communication. A raised eyebrow, a joke shared via a glance, a knowledge of each other which goes hundreds of miles beyond sex. That depth of integration which is what earlier forms of English (in the 1611 *Bible* for instance) really meant by 'knowing'. It means you sense things about each other and understand things which may never have been discussed. It's the marital dynamic which people who have serial relationships or who remain single or have part-time partners can never get their heads round. On a very trivial level, I've never forgotten, some years ago, a quasi daughter-in-law being astonished when I sent Nick off to settle the bill in a restaurant using my card. "But surely he doesn't know your pin number?" she asked. Yes, he did. And he knows almost everything else about me too. There are no secrets. It's called trust.

Then along comes Ms Alzheimer's, in her perniciously determined way, and puts her oar in. Of course, I still trust him implicitly but it's no longer an even thing. He has no choice but to trust me more than ever – I even have power of attorney over his bank account, I make sure he takes the right pills and that the house is securely locked when we go to bed at night. Every day, he arrives in my office with papers which have just come in the post, about, say, the burglar alarm or a magazine subscription, muttering, "I'm worried about this," only for me to say tartly, "Well, you needn't be. I've already dealt with it."

We now have daily briefings – which take me back to one school I taught at in which the head required all staff in the staffroom for a few minutes before registration to be told what was what for the day. It's very institutional and formal. I tell him, for instance, that the cleaner is coming at 10.00 and/or I am leaving to review a show at 4.30 and/or he has an optician's appointment at noon – all of which is also on a large calendar in the kitchen. Retention is poor. Last Sunday, we had (or rather I had, and delivered it as a *fait accompli*) planned to go to Ightham Mote, a National Trust property in Kent. We'd talked about it for several days. I reminded him at breakfast time then raced about doing various domestic and professional jobs which needed to be done before we left. At 10.30, I said, "Right, let me just put some make-up on. Ten minutes and I'll be good to go."

In reply, I got a very distracted "Are you going to tell me where you're going and when you'll be back?"

Well, of course I know that he's not going to go trying his luck with another woman or waltzing off to the Caribbean with our savings. That sort of trust is rock solid. But the day-to-day unreliability militates against trust at other levels and is hard to live with – the doors left unlocked, the forgotten bag in a coffee shop, the items on the shopping list he omits to buy and dozens more ordinary things which I took for granted for nearly half a century. In practice, I have to issue constant reminders about where to put things, what to do and where to go. And I have to remind myself continually that I am not Joyce Grenfell and I am not running a nursery class, although the similarities are hideous.

And one of the worst things is coping with the decline of real, intuitive communication – Shakespeare's 'marriage of true minds'. A friend who lives in Australia and is in a very similar situation commented recently, "I feel so angry. This is not what I signed up for." I know exactly what she means, but I try very hard to be resigned, practical and loving rather than angry. If only I always succeeded.

20 September 2017

When dementia first starts to nibble, it's tiny things such as slight slowness of speech when you're tired or suddenly deciding that perhaps you do like cooked cheese after a lifetime of insisting that you don't. Then as suspicions that the many-tentacled Ms Alzheimer's may really be lurking in the wings develop, everyone tells you that you must get a diagnosis. "Then you'll have access to HELP," runs the received wisdom. We heard that many times from many people.

So that's what you do. You see your GP, who refers you to the local hospital's 'memory service' – a hilariously inapt euphemism. It should, of course, be called the 'Dementia Department'. I suppose they have their reasons for this coy refusal to call a spade a spade.

The process is tortuous. There's a home visit from an assessor who asks the 'client' (yes, really) who the prime minister is and tests spatial and cognitive skills with funny little drawings. They're rather like the ones Nick and I both remember from the LCC Eleven-Plus intelligence test – for the record, we both passed when we were 10. I very much doubt that Nick would now. Then she talks to the consultant, who orders a brain scan at King's College. A couple of false starts precede the appointment with the consultant, who finally delivers the dreaded, scan-based diagnosis.

Four months after that – almost a year after we initially saw the GP – comes another appointment at which symptom-lessening (maybe) pills are prescribed.

Our – or rather Nick's – diagnosis appointment was 29 April. "Nothing changes," said the consultant, valiantly denying the self-evident truth that everything does. Instantly. One minute you're a chap who can't always lay his hands on his car keys and the next you're an Alzheimer's patient. It's a death sentence – although the timescale prognosis is very vague. There's no chemotherapy or anything with any hope in it for Alzheimer's patients. It is penetratingly clear that the three of us – Nick, Miss Alzheimer's and I – are heading downhill towards '*second childishness and mere oblivion/ Sans teeth, sans eyes, sans taste, sans everything*'. Good old Shakespeare. He'd seen it all.

I can't help thinking about all this 'help' and 'support' which is cracked up to be so indispensable. The trouble is – that if you've always been capable, competent and independent – allowing these professionals into your life feels very intrusive and alien. "Monstrous regiment of women," mutters Nick under his breath more than once. The line between 'supportive' and 'bloody patronising and interfering' is a potentially narrow one.

When the occupational therapist came to our house, she wanted to check the staircase and see what Nick could and couldn't do. Well, at the moment, he can do most things except work the locks on the external doors. And he's a bit shaky on our stairs, which are steeper than the ones in the house we moved out of last year. She proposed an additional hand-grab at the top of the stairs – which has turned out to be useful. Our youngest granddaughter, aged 2, hangs on to it carefully as she ascends the stairs too. She, of course, will get better at stairs, unlike her grandpa, who won't.

The OT's suggestion that we leave the outer door open was a non-starter, though. It runs totally against the Metropolitan Police's security advice. Before she came, I was terrified she'd upset

Nick with crass, tactless suggestions about karaoke and bingo at a day centre but, to her credit, she got the measure of us very quickly. She soon worked out that he'd be more comfortable at a Mahler concert at the Royal Festival Hall than in an old people's club – although she can't, obviously, organise the former.

On the other hand, some of the information leaflets she left me were aimed at the lowest level of ignorance. Yes, I know how to present information simply and in bite-sized chunks. I was a teacher for thirty-six years, for goodness' sake.

Other Alzheimer's professionals are a different story. One, in particular, is probably trying very hard to be clear and inclusive but her manner comes across as gluily patronising. And, I am a working professional with a diary and a lot of commitments. I cannot cancel a working day in the Midlands, arranged for months and involving a lot of other people, just because she decides that's the day she wants Nick and me to meet the consultant. It's called the memory service because they are, one presumes, giving us some sort of service, not issuing us with orders.

The consultant herself is refreshingly different. She is quite prepared to talk to me as a fellow professional in a different line of work. She is also, once you come face to face with her, prepared to make appointments by negotiation at mutually convenient times. We all sat in her consulting room and got our diaries out. Very grown up.

So this whole notion of help and support is a mixed blessing. Yes, it's good to know that you're not alone – but then we never were. We have a terrific family and many warmly generous friends. There is very little (apart from the pills) that we need at present that we can't generate from our own networks. And I could certainly do without being told bossily, "This really is very important, Mrs Elkin. It concerns your husband's health. Surely you could rearrange your work and attend this appointment?"

28 September 2017

It is vital, if you can, for the three of you to take lots of interesting holidays when you're a couple plus Ms Alzheimer's. She might bite less viciously if her victim is exposed to lots of mind-enhancing experiences. Or so they say.

At the time of writing, we are just coming to the end of a week in an upmarket holiday camp in Greece – a huge five-star hotel, a marble temple to tourism hewn out of a beautiful hillside on the east coast of Corfu. It's the sort of place hundreds of people come to in search of skin cancer as they fry themselves all day every day on sun loungers like rashers of bacon on a grill. And the piped music consists of Frank Sinatra, Pavarotti, the Beatles and Mozart pops, which tells you something about the, mostly British, clientele.

Anyway, although it's not quite our usual style, I thought it would be a good place for a rest and in many ways it has been. We don't do the sun worship thing – but I like being able to get a decent daily swim – we've each read several books and eaten lots of nice food which I didn't have to cook. I miss the car, though, because it would have made sense to explore more of the island. But I'm not comfortable driving a left-hand drive car on the 'wrong' side of the road. Day trips by coach? Well, they start before 8am and don't get back until 7pm, and there's no way Nick and Ms A have the stamina to cope with that, so that wasn't an option either. So we confined ourselves to just a couple of very pleasant outings by taxi.

I was curious to know how they – Nick and his partner-in-illness – would manage the flight. They were, thank goodness, fine, probably because it was only three hours. They've had problems with the hotel, though. Because we're on a steep hillside, there are steps everywhere. "When I look down, it's as if the steps are coming up to meet me and I'm terrified," he says, clutching the rail, taking one step at time, moving at the speed of a slow loris and looking about ninety-seven.

Then there's stepping manfully up to the bar to order hot drinks or beers, as chaps do. And then being totally unable to remember our room number – about twenty times in the course of the week. The bar staff quickly sussed the situation and would say tactfully, "You go and sit with your wife over there, sir, and I'll bring your drinks over to you." That meant, bless them, that they could check the room number with me without making a fuss about it.

Leaving our room was usually a bit of an adventure too as I led the way to breakfast or dinner. "Where are we going?" he'd ask mildly.

In general, though, the pundits and medics do seem to be right. Nick has been relatively bright this week. The change of scenery, plus getting my undivided attention twenty-four seven, has allowed him to relax, and he reports that his brain feels 'less foggy'. Holidays probably really are good for the three of us.

Next time, I must pack for Nick, though, or at least oversee his suitcase. Ms Alzheimer's, silly bitch, managed to get him to Greece without a toothbrush or razor and with too few shirts for the week. All remediable but daft. And avoidable.

Next time? Well, yes, of course we shall holiday again. But it's quite tricky to decide what would work best. We both loathe the idea of cruising, English-speaking tour guides or anything which reminds me of a school trip. We've always done our own thing in our own way and taken some pride in that. It's much less straightforward now.

We love city breaks, especially in the US. That needs stamina, though, because you tend to be out and about on your feet all day. We once spent a whole week walking the streets of Manhattan, and I guarantee we've seen bits of it that not one other tourist in a hundred has.

"Can't we go back to the States?" he asked quite incisively this week.

"Well, if we did, where would you like to go?" I responded cautiously, well aware that there's a lot of *carpe diem* in this.

"Washington. And we could stay in that nice place I loved so much," he said immediately. He meant Georgetown, although he couldn't remember its name. Okay. If he's reasonably chirpy though Christmas and New Year, I'll book it for the spring and hope Ms A, curtailed by pills, copes with the jet lag better than the last time we went long haul. Only seven hours… not like flying to the Pacific coast, after all.

We've always liked self-catering in cottages in Britain too. Perhaps we should do more of that. At least I can take the car so that we're independent, and Nick can take his hateful companion for a lie-down when he needs to – without having to negotiate with chambermaids and hotel routines.

Note that in all of this, it's me making every decision and arrangement. Not so long ago, I had a husband who could and did book a holiday after discussion about where we were going. He'd sort flights, accommodation, car hire, insurance, currency, visas and all the rest of it – an administrator through and through. All I had to do was organise my professional work around the chosen dates and pack a suitcase on the right day. How I hate you, Ms Alzheimer's.

4 October 2017

Not so long ago, Nick and I – we are decent children of the cap-doffing 1950s after all – would leap to our feet to allow an elderly or infirm person to sit down. We'd help people in wheelchairs through doors and parents with buggies on and off trains. They were in need. We weren't. Now the boot is firmly on the other foot, and I'm increasingly conscious of 'the kindness of strangers' as Tennessee Williams put it. It's yet another position which Ms Bloody Alzheimer's has forced us into.

Take the big brawny Brit who was immediately behind us as we all disembarked an easyJet flight last week from the rear of the aircraft down steps onto the tarmac. I was juggling two quite cumbersome cabin bags and the man heard me say to Nick, "I'll go in front. Hang onto that rail, now."

He stepped alongside and said with exquisite courtesy and kindness: "Would you like to hold my arm with your other hand, sir?" Thus, Nick was assisted to ground level quite regally.

Almost daily, people watch me levering him onto buses, trains and the Tube with one hand. They then obligingly vacate the nearest seat so that I can pop, swing or push Nick into it. There isn't supposed to be anything wrong with him physically, but he has quickly become quite shaky on his feet and is certainly not safe trying to keep himself upright in a crowded, rocking vehicle. I suppose that as brain cells become diseased or get knocked out, it affects every part of the body and takes different Alzheimer's patients in different ways. Most people, when we're out and about, can see the situation immediately, so they do what they can to help.

When we went to see *Dunkirk* recently in a cinema we hadn't been to before, Nick – as always – needed the loo halfway through the film. He took himself off and I thought nothing of it. I don't (yet?) need to escort him to the lavatory. Or so I thought. Well, I was absorbed in the film and didn't actually notice how long he'd been gone until he arrived back at his seat next to me, led by another paying punter who'd happened to pop out at the same time. Of course, Nick had got lost in the highways and byways of an old cinema, converted to multiscreen with lots of samey stairs, doors and foyers. It's a good job, come to think of it, that he remembered the name of the film we were watching. Otherwise, he and Ms A could have ended up in *Spider-Man: Homecoming*. I wonder if he'd have noticed the difference? Anyway, it was another example of a nice chap spotting a problem and dealing with it without a fuss. He even waved cheerily to Nick at the end of the film.

I think, if I'm honest (and goodness, how I try to be – euphemisms and dissembling just don't help), that Nick must actually look much frailer and seem vaguer than he or I realise. Even close family and friends are used to it, and we're all too close to it to be able to monitor the downward progress accurately. Complete strangers, on the other hand, can instantly see a poor old codger who may need help. That's all they see too. They're not superimposing it on a remembered image of how he used to be or any sort of presumption about how he is now. That's why people are generally very patient with him in shops and cafés when it takes him ages to find and count out the right money. Sometimes, he can't explain what he means, realises he's 'lost', smiles and hopes someone will bail him out – and usually somebody does. Thanks, folks.

4 October 2017

We hear a great deal about terror, ruthlessness and violence in the world these days. I'm writing this just a couple of days after the Las Vegas shootings. Yes, all of that is mind-blowingly dreadful. But it's news because, thank goodness, it's unusual, even in today's troubled, turbulent times. Closer to home, the vast majority of people are very kind, even to complete strangers – nothing unusual about it at all. And that's something very positive. Well worth hanging on to.

11 October 2017

On Sunday, I was at the Brighton Dome to review a Brighton Philharmonic Orchestra concert – a routine and regular professional job for me. Nick was with me and we seemed, as things turned out, to have left Ms Alzheimer's at home for once.

Before the concert, I spotted Gavin Henderson – Brighton man, sponsor of one of the BPO principal players, senior arts administrator and Principal of the Royal Central School of Speech and Drama. I've known Gavin for some time and had spoken to him on the phone only a few days earlier on a different matter. So, naturally, I scooted across to say hello. He was with another man whom I also recognised and exchanged pleasantries with.

When I got back to Nick, I said: "Gavin was with Nicholas Chisholm and—"

Before I could finish my sentence to explain that Nicholas is now BPO chairman, Nick had flashed back. "Yes! He used to be head of the Menuhin School, and you once went down to Cobham to interview him." This from a man who a few hours earlier didn't know what day of the week it was and had completely forgotten that we were going to Brighton. Alzheimer's is indeed a mysterious, patchy disease.

Perhaps Nick was getting into his stride for the concert, because music certainly seems to bring out the best in him. I've noticed before that it seems to keep Ms A briefly at bay. The Brighton concert – Schumann, Tchaikovsky and Brahms – certainly put him in a very upbeat mood.

Last week, we were at the Merry Opera Company's staged Verdi *Requiem* at St James's Church, Piccadilly. Well, the 'staging' is a bit odd but the singing is fabulous, and Nick's eyes shone from beginning to end – something I hadn't seen for months. Ms A was definitely on leave for a couple of hours that night.

Everyone knows that music affects the brain in general and the memory in particular. That old 'they're playing our song' cliché has a lot of truth in it. For us, since you ask, it's the Brahms *B Flat Piano Concerto*. Then there's the way certain sorts of music have been proved over and over again to benefit children's learning and development – the so called 'Mozart effect'.

And it's good, when Ms A is thumping on your door, to remember happy times. She doesn't like those and sulks. Good!

Nick has always been a bit of a classical music geek – pompous with it, in his poseur youth, of course, but much mellowed now, I'm pleased to report. I came to classical music in the first instance largely through playing and singing it at school. Some of the first things we did together as teenaged friends was to share music, usually on his primitive 'Hi-Fi system' (remember those?) and, when we could afford it, go together to concerts – mostly at the Royal Festival Hall or Proms. I can only have been about fifteen when he introduced me to Stravinsky's *Pulcinella* and lent me a record of the Brahms violin concerto – wonderful pieces, both of them. What a gift! And, obviously, it's something we've gone on enjoying together for the intervening half a century or so.

Whenever we hear something at a concert or on Radio 3 that we've known almost all our lives, I can see the music bashing Ms A on the head and triggering good memories in Nick. Music also makes him think – it's as much an intellectual experience as an emotional one if you listen properly – and that's very good for him too. It even seems to help him to remember other things I would have expected long since to have dropped off the hard drive in his brain. It must be at least fifteen years since I made that trip to the Menuhin School to interview Nicholas Chisholm.

18 October 2017

I am now a carer. Or so they tell me. Thanks, Ms Alzheimer's, you bitch. You have forced something onto my CV which I never sought and for which I have no qualifications, scant experience and nil inclination. I loathe, detest and abhor the c-word with a vengeance.

Nonetheless, this is the position fate and Ms A have strong-armed me into, so I have no choice but to knuckle down and get on with it. Nick is increasingly dependent on me for more and more 'services'. I am, for example, his chauffeuse. This week, he has told me first that he'd now be frightened to drive up hills and second, on a different occasion, that he still can't understand what all the fuss was about and of course he'd still be perfectly okay driving. I tried not to comment but...

I am also his secretary – arranging his appointments and ensuring that he gets there. Every day, I find for him the things he's 'lost' (he hasn't) and administer his pills. I lock the house when we go out or at night and manage the burglar alarm. These days, I also do the laundry and shopping (mostly online) – all things he used to do. And these are just examples.

Well, no one is indispensable, of course, but it has occurred to me recently that this caring malarkey is quite a responsibility. Supposing I become ill and can't look after him? It's all very well my dear clergy friend (we were at school together) telling me with warm wisdom in her eyes: "You would find a way." I'm not in with her loving God and am bleakly convinced that there is no benign presence in the sky on hand to bale me out if things go belly up. It behoves me, therefore, to stay as well as I possibly can.

I've always been pretty fit, actually, and have never had a serious illness, but there's always (inevitably?) a first time. Vegetarian food, never using the car for journeys of under a mile, taking the stairs, not smoking and going very easy on booze have paid off for me, so far, although the same lifestyle doesn't seem to have done much for Nick.

Two things have recently given me pause for thought.

First, I caught the worst cold I have had in decades while we were on holiday in Greece last month. For three full weeks, I felt really unwell – first the streaming, then the blocked sinuses and pain all over my head, then the residual... well, I'll spare you the revolting details. Suffice it to say, it was so tenacious and unpleasant that I really did begin to wonder if I'd got something worse than a cold.

Second, I phoned a relation who is eighty and usually bounces about playing bowls and attending energetically to his garden. "I've had pneumonia," he told me lugubriously, adding that he was so weak, he'd collapsed trying to climb the stairs to bed and was hospitalised overnight. That was three weeks earlier and he'd been told to allow at least another three weeks to throw it off completely.

Alarm bells. I pretend to be twenty-two but the truth is that I am no longer in the first flush of youth. Suppose that were me? How on earth would Nick cope? He might manage to make me a cup of stewed tea with too much milk in it and he'd feed the cat, but beyond that he wouldn't be able to look after me, and the household would collapse about our ears. I expect one of our long-suffering and wonderfully loyal sons would do his best, but they both have demanding businesses to run in cities sixty miles away from us.

18 October 2017

I've always been a bit chary of vaccines after a nasty experience with one in the 1980s. But I have to be grown up now – thanks to the arrival of Ms A in my household. Last week, I took myself off to the practice nurse and asked for both the flu and pneumonia jabs. "Oh yes, we do recommend them for carers," she said brightly, thereby rubbing salt into the wound of my incredulity. Me? A carer? No, you've confused me with someone else. I'm a journalist, author, bloody good former teacher, wife, mother and grandmother, but I never volunteered for that c-word thing.

25 October 2017

Alzheimer's is an unpredictable business. Last Friday, I left the house at noon to interview an author in north London. Then I went to Jermyn Street Theatre to review *Anything That Flies*. Because it's a short, ninety-minute show, I was home just after 10pm. That means that Nick and his unloved, ever-present companion, Ms Alzheimer's, were alone to do their own thing for ten hours. There's nothing unusual about that, of course. I have to work and at the moment he's perfectly okay at home. He can assemble simple food for himself quite capably, although I don't now leave him at home overnight on his own.

Usually, I come in to find Nick and *Catus Domesticus* asleep on the sofa pretending to listen to Schumann or Elgar. Not this time. During my absence, Nick had brought in all the washing – big load – from the garden and sorted it. He'd collapsed the rotary line neatly and put the cover on – having claimed for weeks to have been utterly baffled by the new one I'd bought. Indoors, he'd neatly stashed underwear, and so on, in the airing cupboard and ironed and hung up the shirts and blouses to air. He'd even put the iron and ironing board away in the right place. As if that weren't enough, he'd found a pair of shoes I'd dumped without discussion in the kitchen, intending to deal with them later. He'd polished them.

As a performance, it was almost as good as the one I'd seen at Jermyn Street Theatre. And I was astonished. Ms Alzheimer's was evidently having a day off. Of course, a couple of years ago, Nick would have done all this and more. Neither of us would have thought anything of it or commented. We used to be a team. Now, he often spends whole days simply reading his Kindle or nodding off over newspapers, completely forgetting simple tasks we've talked about. Friday's achievements therefore seemed very surprising, although ten hours is a long time and I suspect he worked very slowly. I said something to the effect of "Goodness! You've been busy. Thank you" – with a grateful hug.

He replied cheerfully: "Yes, I was very pleased with it too. I've felt really quite well today." The sad, tragic even, thing is, of course, that we've reached a stage where we have to get excited and congratulatory about a bit of routine ironing. Not so long ago, some of my Twitter followers would regularly tease me, and by extension, Nick, about his dedication to, and expertise in, ironing. Those were the days.

Even when Ms A is backing off a bit and Nick is saying things like "I feel a bit of a fraud – everything seems almost right at the moment," there's the tiredness to deal with.

Now that we have our 'new' (we've been here thirteen months) house more or less as we want it inside, I'm trying to sort the garden. So, several times recently, after a few hours' essential desk work, I've put on old clothes, repaired to the garden and got busy with clipping, nipping and unearthing the detritus, such as car batteries and bricks, which our eccentric predecessor saw fit to bury in the flowerbeds. Well, it wouldn't occur to Nick and Ms A to go out and start gardening independently, but if they see me out there with a rake or hoe in my hand, they find a pair of dirty-jobs trousers and wander out to join me.

Then he tries to be helpful and is – provided I issue very clear instructions. One task at a time. I find myself saying things like, "Go and get the small saw from the big shed. It's on the third shelf down on the right." It might take him ten minutes to find it and I might have to repeat the instruction but eventually he's by my side with the requisite tool and I say, "Saw this branch off – just here, please." He quite likes cutting bits off trees. It brings out his inner George Washington. Thus, our gardening can be quite congenial for an hour or two.

But Ms A soon starts leaning on him and heavy weariness sets in. I can see him visibly flagging. "Why don't you clean up and go and lie down for a bit," I say. Next time I see him, when I come in from the garden myself, he'll be fast asleep on the bed as if it were two in the morning.

The variability is curiously unsettling. Yes, it's wonderful to have my Real Husband – the one who lovingly cleans my shoes without being asked – back for a few hours, but it's hard to adjust when he's so different so soon after. Take each day as it comes? Much easier to say than to do.

1 November 2017

We're old-fashioned, Nick and I. Most days start with a sit-down breakfast during which we don't talk much. It's newspaper time. We both like proper paper copies and we still have them delivered early in the morning, exactly as our parents and grandparents did.

Well, so far, Ms Alzheimer's doesn't seem to have touched Nick's reading ability or appetite for the printed word. One breakfast time recently, there was suddenly an excited grunt from across the table as he pounced on something. So I looked up. The strapline in *The Sunday Times* magazine, which I read upside down, was '*Do [sic] this couple have the cure for the Alzheimer's Time Bomb?*' and then '*They think so*'.

I could also see a photograph of a very serious-looking man and woman in white coats. "I bet they come from California," I said sceptically, because most whacky ideas about health, medicine and cures fly sunnily across the Atlantic from the Golden State. So he read on a bit before confirming that I was right. Dean and Ayesha Sherzai, both neurologists, work at Loma Linda University Medical Centre. It's sixty miles north of Los Angeles and the town is dominated by the Seventh-day Adventist Church whose vegetarian members don't smoke, drink or use caffeine, but they're keen on exercise.

Later, when Nick had finished reading it, I read the piece myself. And all the time I was doing so, I was thinking about the late, great John Diamond. He was a journalist, married to Nigella Lawson, who died of head and neck cancer, aged forty-seven in 2001. He wrote most movingly about his illness both in *The Sunday Times* and in two books. I remember him crossly telling readers to stop sending him cranky miracle cures. If, he wrote, drinking three litres of beetroot juice a day or sitting in a cold mud bath flavoured with turmeric (or words to that effect) would see off cancer, then the whole of the medical establishment would be seizing on these ideas and be busily curing everyone's cancer. But they're not.

Diamond was right, and exactly the same thing applies to Alzheimer's. If the Sherzais really had found a cure, then it would be being applied worldwide – it wouldn't be just a couple of thousand words in *The Sunday Times* magazine. As journalist Ben Doyle, who wrote the piece, reminds us bleakly, by 2050, an estimated 155.5 million people will have dementia. It is therefore urgent, to put it mildly, that we find a cure PDQ. No economy is going to be able to cope with it unless something gives.

The Sherzais have studied thriving Loma Lindans (all that healthy Seventh-day Adventism pays off, apparently) and compared them with their chronically unhealthy neighbours in nearby poverty-stricken San Bernadino. Their conclusion is that lifestyle changes can prevent ninety per cent of Alzheimer's cases and even reverse its effects in some existing patients.

Well, that's a pretty dramatic claim, given that most doctors (including our consultant in south London) say that the condition is incurable. So what lifestyle changes are the Sherzais advocating?

It's more or less the same formula that you read for just about every other illness – avoid processed foods, sugary drinks and cakes and biscuits, not to mention alcohol. The Sherzais also condemn processed meat, red meat, chicken and cheese, so that means adopting a more or less vegan diet. At the same time, they recommend an active lifestyle, getting a good night's sleep, doing puzzles, having an active social life and practising some form of meditation, such as yoga, preferably in the open air.

All a bit disappointing really. I'm sure you've heard it all before, as we have. Not particularly way out or 'Californian'. It's sensible advice for healthy living, although many people would find the veganism a bit difficult. But are we really to believe that living like this could cure Alzheimer's? I can almost hear John Diamond's refuting voice of reason and common sense.

And, anyway, Nick has been doing most of this all his life. Fat lot of difference it has made. Ms A is with us, anyway – with a vengeance. There are good days and bad days, but her grip is gradually tightening.

Am I going to buy the Sherzais' book *The Alzheimer's Solution* (Simon and Schuster, £14.99)? No. Am I going to clutch straws by attempting to push Nick from vegetarianism to veganism and denying him his beloved cheese and scrape of butter on his toast? No. Do I have any faith at all in any miracle cure which is unacknowledged by almost every medical practitioner? No.

Would I like to see Nick in full health and Ms Alzheimer's dead and rotting in the gutter outside? Oh yes... but it isn't going to happen, whatever Californian neurologists may argue.

8 November 2017

Wrath. Anger. Fury. I do them all every day. Expertly. And it's all very well St Paul, a single gent who didn't have to live with Ms Alzheimer's, telling the Ephesians – many of whom would have been married – to resolve their quarrels before bed. I bet some of them were jolly irritated. "What does he know about it?" I can hear them muttering down a couple of millennia.

Of course, if your life, marriage and home is invaded and occupied by Ms A, then you simply have to learn to put up with rubbish, recycling, food waste and garden stuff being put in the wrong bins. And it's infuriating. Then there are the items on (very short and simple) shopping lists which are ignored, drawers and cupboards left open and things being 'put away' in all the wrong places. You know it's all going to get worse, too.

Add to that what's said or not said. When you've been asked the same question – such as "Is anyone coming today?" – four or five times, it's hard to answer with calm patience and equanimity. Nick would really, in his heart of hearts, like me to give up work and everything else I do so that I'd be continuously available with kindness, cups of coffee, chocolate biscuits and various other forms of sweetness and light, but that is not on the cards, I'm afraid. If I didn't work, I wouldn't be me, and then where would we be?

The frustration is dreadful. I explain over and over again that, for example, a company's coming to collect some rubbish this afternoon. Or that I have two tickets for a show tomorrow so we'll both go. I do my utmost not to make a fuss when my best (almost new) omelette pan is burned out because Nick tried to make himself an omelette and walked away from it.

Then there's speed. Or lack of it. I have always been a fairly nippy mover when I'm walking along a street or round the house, for instance. And I've had a rule for decades whereby I don't use the car if it's less than a mile. I routinely take stairs instead of escalators as a way of trying to get some exercise as I go along, and all that sort of thing. Until recently, Nick was the same. Now he does everything very, very slowly, and I'm constantly looking over my shoulder to see where he is. If I hang on to him, it's like taking a very reluctant dog for a walk.

I automatically went bounding down the long staircase from the new platforms at London Bridge the other day. And then had to wait for two full minutes at the bottom until he had cautiously negotiated every step. I should have put him on the escalator, of course, but didn't, for a moment, remember how things now are. Then I get stressy and remind myself that when I plan these excursions, I now need to allow an extra half-hour from the time we leave home. And the awful and devastating truth is that these days, it's actually much easier and better all round if I go on my own.

I try very hard not to let any of this show. But, of course, after a bit, human nature bursts forth and I blow up like a volcano about something really trivial. Then, like Etna, I'm inclined to smoke and smoulder for days. My personal tectonic plates are pretty volatile. Let not the sun go down upon your wrath? If only. Ms A, meet St Paul. St Paul, meet Ms A.

At the weekend, Nick was upset because I'd done my Etna thing about something very minor that he'd forgotten to do. "I try bloody hard to look after you, be there for you, do everything else that has to be done and keep smiling, but it's an uphill struggle," I snarled.

"Well, you're failing," he said. Great.

Then, the next day, a bit diffidently: "If I could remember what I said that upset you, I'd apologise." Well, in the end, the sheer ridiculousness of life with Ms A made us both laugh.

PS. *Sunday Telegraph* (5 November) had a strapline about a 'vampire cure' for Alzheimer's. A leftover from Halloween, or is 5 November morphing into the new 1 April?

15 November 2017

We've been discharged by our consultant. No, that isn't the royal we. The three of us – Nick, Ms Alzheimer's and me – are in this together for the long haul. The three of us have seen Dr Latha Velayudhan three times. She's satisfied that Nick is tolerating, maybe even benefiting from, his medication and that all is as well as it's likely to be.

So, from here on, we are to be 'managed' by our GP. That means we fill in a form when the pills run out and collect the prescription the next day – signed by someone at our practice whom we've never met. We are assured, though, that we can make an appointment with Doctor Latha if at any point in the future we feel we need to see her.

I am very impressed indeed by Dr Latha, who has done a great deal of Alzheimer's research, has written 'papers' and devised an app to help people like us. The coyly named Lewisham Memory Service is one of several places she works. She is pleasant, friendly, practical and, above all, recognises that we are intelligent, reasonably well-educated people who definitely don't need to be patronised or spoken to entirely in monosyllables. It's the little things that highlight this. She runs her own diary so that if another appointment is to be made, we all look at our diaries and fix one, completely bypassing all the usual NHS bureaucratic nonsense. She routinely shows us to the main door of the building herself too, as if we are respected visitors.

At the last meeting – and it feels more like a meeting than a medical consultation partly because we three sit in a computer-free meeting room at a circular table – Dr Latha asked Nick if he would agree to help with research if needed for any studies. He agreed, although it might mean extra scans and monitoring. And I might have to be involved in this, if it happens, as carer/observer. Well, that's fine. The research sorely needs to be done. If they don't find a way of holding back the Alzheimer's tide within the next generation, the economies of most Western nations will implode.

I asked Dr Latha – who clearly knows her stuff – to run the dementia statistics past me. We were speaking in the week of the cheerful announcement that Alzheimer's has overtaken all other diseases as the UK's leading cause of death. In money terms, though, is it really as bad as the press constantly tells us?

"It costs £23 billion per year to take care of these people," said Dr Latha soberly. I queried that to make sure I hadn't misheard a nought or two. "Yes, £23 billion," she confirmed, "and that's more than cancer, diabetes and cardio-vascular disease all added together."

But – and here's the real scandal – when it comes to funding, Alzheimer's research gets only around a third of what's in the pot. The other sixty per cent or so goes to cancer, diabetes and cardio-vascular disease.

Well, of course we need research into all the diseases which kill people, but I think there's a strong argument for sharing out resources in approximate proportion to the size of the problem. Or, is there a perception that Alzheimer's patients are (usually) old anyway so they matter less? Chilling thought, but I suspect I've hit the nail on the head.

Dr Latha then asked me if I would be willing – on an occasional basis – to take part in funding consultations when money for research is being allocated. They need carers and patients, apparently, to tell them what sort of research might be useful and what wouldn't. Of course, I said yes.

I honestly don't think that anything which emerges from any sort of research is going to help Nick directly. It is almost certainly too late for us. Ms Alzheimer's already has him firmly in her clutches. We might weaken her hold very slightly with pills for a while, but there isn't going to be any kind of new discovery which will enable us to shake her off.

But we have to think of future generations. Anything we can do now which might save others from finding themselves where we're heading now is worth doing. And, anyway, doing something positive and constructive does actually make you feel better. Moping doesn't help.

22 November 2017

When Nick first started to lose things Big Time – keys, credit cards, phone, rail card, wet wipes, pens and all the rest of it – I issued him with a handbag, a neat grey canvas cross-body job. Our elder son and his wife refer to it as his 'man-bag'.

"Right," I said, "it's easy. You keep all your everyday bits and pieces in here. You never leave the house without it, and you keep it with you at all times when you're out. Problem solved."

If only it were. I'd reckoned without the cunning of busy Ms Alzheimer's. For a start, the bag has lots of compartments and he struggles to find things inside it. He likes, for instance, to keep his coins in a polythene bank bag. On at least six occasions, I've been told, mournfully, that he's lost them. Of course, I then go through the bag and produce said coins like a chinking rabbit out of a hat. But that doesn't help if he's in the Co-op buying a loaf of bread on his own – the sort of small errand I'm determined he'll go on doing for as long as humanly possible.

Moreover, that bag has been left at home, in people's houses, in restaurants and in the car more times than I can remember. It is little short of miraculous that it has never been permanently lost. But people are awfully good. Several relatives and friends have very kindly put themselves to considerable trouble to return it to him when it's been left in their homes. Waiters scamper helpfully after him in restaurants – or look after it carefully until he returns for it. And so far the car has not been broken into.

Of course, we all remind him all the time, but we're none of us infallible. Sadder, really, is the anxiety it causes Nick. "I think I've left my bag at home," he'll often say from the passenger seat in the car when we're a few miles on our journey.

"No, you haven't," I reply. "It's next to mine on the bag seat under our coats." He and Ms A, have, of course, completely forgotten what they did when leaving the house. But she has got at him and he has started to fret and worry.

These days, in restaurants and coffee shops, I usually put his bag and mine together on my side of the table. I know I shan't forget mine so that ensures that his is safe. But once or twice during every meal, he'll say, "Have you got my bag? I don't know where it is." I'm used to that now, but it still seems pretty tragic if I pause and allow myself to think about it.

When I grumble at him about his carelessness, he will sometimes point out that it's different for women, most of whom carry bags from childhood so the habit is deeply ingrained. Man-bags – although now pretty widespread – are a relatively recent thing that have come in with laptops and tablets. He's right, of course – I've been carrying a handbag since I was about 11 and it's as much a part of me as my knickers or shirt. Glued to me, in fact. Twenty-five years of teaching in some very challenging secondary schools with known criminals in many classes taught me to keep my bag always within a few inches of where I was and never to allow it out of my sight. Bag awareness is second nature. In the same way, I'm a Londoner through and through so don't put my bag down in a public place and walk away from it, even for a few seconds, unless I'm with a trusted companion.

It would seem that if a man doesn't carry a bag for the first fifty years of his life, it is probably too late to learn such behaviour, especially if Ms A is pecking away at him like a malevolent woodpecker.

29 November 2017

I loathe watching Ms A polluting Nick's mind with her filthy confusion. "I'm getting very worried…" he said to me this week. Pause while he struggled for the right words to express what he wanted to say, and I paid full attention because this could be important. "…about the company accounts."

He meant the accounts for my writing business, Susan Elkin Ltd, for which he used to do all the administration. "It's fine," I said. "Nothing to worry about at all. I got the accountant to do the whole job earlier this year and paid his bill. He'll do the next lot too. You just have to accept that you're fully retired now. Drink your coffee and talk to the cat."

"Am I?" he said, still puzzled. "Fully retired? So I don't have to do anything?" And so it goes on.

I try, of course, to find things for him to do. It's not good for anyone's brain or mind to have nothing to focus on. At this time of year, there are shows and concerts I'm involved in either as reviewer or, occasionally, as performer. This week, for example, he seemed to enjoy the *Messiah* I played for and later this week he's coming with me to review *Rapunzel* at Chickenshed Theatre in north London. But more often than not at this time of year, I do these things solo and leave him with only the cat (who certainly earns his keep) and his CD collection for company.

Then there are jobs in the house. Very simple things such as pegging out a basket of washing or sweeping up some leaves are fine. But I was almost heartbroken when the other day Nick snatched up the nearly empty pepper grinder (he likes lots of black pepper on everything because he has no sense of smell and little of taste) after dinner. Bent over my crossword in a vain attempt at a five-minute respite, I could hear cupboards being opened and closed in the kitchen accompanied by attention-seeking humphing and tutting. So I got up and found the peppercorns for him. Then I looked up to see him, sitting opposite me, trying to shovel the peppercorns into the grinder with a teaspoon. Of course, he wasn't succeeding. Had he completely forgotten what a funnel is and what it's for? Cue for me, rather unkindly, to snatch the grinder, do the ten-second job with a funnel in the kitchen and fetch the broom to sweep the spilled peppercorns up off the dining-room floor. And no more crossword. Welcome to the frustrations of life as a threesome – him, me and her.

She was very present when last week's supermarket delivery arrived too. I'd had a last-minute morning review job (children's show) poked into my diary, so I wasn't at home at the time. I'd left careful instructions, though. "The delivery guy will give you a little bag of frozen stuff. Put that straight in the freezer. Leave everything else and I'll sort it when I get in." I got home early afternoon just in time to rescue the yoghurt, coleslaw, pasta and various groceries from the freezer before they froze solid and were ruined. Of course, I was jolly cross as well as incredulous and, worse, Nick was very upset when he realised what a silly thing he'd done. And that's the hardest part – trying to cut through my own frustrations to understand just how bloody awful it must be not to know what a funnel is or what should and shouldn't go in the freezer. Lots of hugs required.

When we arrived at the *Messiah* concert, on my way to the 'green room' (bit makeshift in a parish church), I deposited Nick on an audience seat next to a friend. "How are you?" Friend, who happens also to be a retired GP so he's more attuned than most, asked Nick carefully and kindly.

"Oh, up and down," said Nick lugubriously. And I suppose that just about sums it up for both of us.

A recent *Daily Telegraph* headline made me grin ruefully: '*Being married may reduce dementia risk*'. Well, sorry, UCL, who led a study of fifteen earlier studies and 800,000 people, it hasn't worked for us. We've been married forty-eight years and counting.

6 December 2017

Alzheimer's, they tell us, is progressive brain cell death. Over a course of time, the total brain size shrinks because the tissue has a diminishing number of nerve cells and connections. Funny, says she hollowly, how uncompromisingly blunt everyone is about Alzheimer's, while cancer, which kills far fewer people, is still often delicately euphemised.

So that revolting vulture, Ms A – actually, that comparison is an insult to vultures, which do at least wait until their dinner is dead – is picking off Nick's brain cells one by one. Given that every Alzheimer's patient lives with his or her own version of Ms A, then I suppose the effects are bound to vary between individuals, depending which particular cells have been killed.

I am noticing two things in Nick which I suppose are down to lost brain cells, although I've not seen either of them mentioned in Alzheimer's literature.

The first is the ability to spell. Now this is a man who was exhaustively drilled in spelling in a funny little private primary school, almost a dame school recast for the mid-20th century, and then by the legendary Dr Giles at Alleyns. He's always been a sharper speller than I, despite my many years of English teaching. If you were stuck in a crossword wondering whether 'aplomb' has a double p, whether there's a second h somewhere in 'Chekhov' or how to spell 'mnemonic', Nick would have been your man. Not any longer.

Last week, I said, without thinking, "Can you add Weetabix to the cumulative shopping list over there, please." When I later noticed that he'd carefully written 'Wittabix', I really did have to swallow hard to get rid of that lump in my throat. He wrote a note for our son asking him to check a 'wonkey' (like 'donkey'?) electrical connection the other day too, and there have been other instances. So whichever bit of the brain it is that's responsible for spelling, it's on the way out, courtesy of Ms A.

It seems to be an unravelling of education, as if the learning process is reversing itself. Children will have a stab at writing words they don't know how to spell – usually because they've never seen or noticed them written – and come up with a phonetic approximation such as 'Wittabix'. Now I see a man who's coming full circle, increasingly unable to spell words he's had under control since he was five or six years old. He's sliding backwards. How accurate Shakespeare's 'second childishness' is as a description of senility.

The second thing I find odd, but which presumably is down to the demise of a different set of brain cells, is the increasing inability to finish a job. Nick now never closes any of the dresser drawers when he takes out cutlery or a tablecloth. He'll start to put his laundered clothes away, then wander off and leave half of them on the bed. He rarely switches the bathroom light off or puts the yard broom away after using it, and so it goes on.

They're trivial things in themselves. And some people behave like this all their lives, which must drive those who live with them bonkers, but in Nick's case they're new. I presume this behaviour indicates that his short-term memory is cutting out very quickly and it used not to. He doesn't, after a few minutes, remember what he'd started doing, so of course he forgets to finish it. It's handy to have Ms A to blame, because I could get very irritated otherwise. As it is, I just finish every little job I see left undone – countless times every day. Mostly, he doesn't even notice. I do try not to comment but I'm afraid I'm human…

12 December 2017

On Sunday, I played (violin) in a little Christmas concert in Folkestone alongside my sister, a fellow fiddler. We had made complicated arrangements for her husband, who is much older than us; Nick, with Miss Alzheimer's attached; and Jean, an elderly friend of my sister's. They were to come to the venue from her house by taxi. There was an afternoon rehearsal and so, as performers, we had to be there much earlier.

Despite our misgivings, it all went according to plan, thank goodness. By the time our three audience supporters took their seats halfway up a steeply raked auditorium, I was sitting in my playing position on the stage. So I watched Nick. Jean, who is in her eighties, but 'with it' and well, had him carefully by the hand. She was facing him and walking gently, kindly and tactfully backwards while he shuffled towards her. Eventually, Jean got him into his seat. From where I was sitting, he looked like a helpless, lost old man. It was as if I was seeing him afresh, and it wasn't nice.

I don't understand, incidentally, why he now takes short steps, which make his gait look old and hesitant – there is nothing wrong with his knees or hips. It must, I suppose, be something to do with those knocked-out brain cells that are affecting walking confidence, especially in confined spaces.

There's nothing like Christmas – when you tend to do the same things every year – for assessing progress, change or deterioration over the preceding twelve months. When we did that same concert a year ago, Nick drove three people from my sister's house to the venue and then took over from me halfway home to London because I was tired. And of course he also got himself in and out of his theatre seat effortlessly and chatted confidently to people he knew. What a difference a year with Ms A has made.

The Christmas card-writing ritual was another rather pitiful exercise. For forty-eight years, we have sat down on either side of the dining table with the list, address book, stamps, pens – and an appropriate CD, such as *Messiah*. And last year was no exception.

But this time Ms A was firmly and squarely perched on the table like some kind of evil harpy getting fatter as she feasts on Nick's brain cells. "You write this one to Bill and Deborah," I said. Now, Deborah, a relation of mine, has been part of Nick's social circle for over half a century. He started to write. Then, painstakingly, letter by letter, asked me how to spell her name. I gulped and helped him, although we had to bin one card he'd messed up. Then he wrote one to his own cousin. I had to read out the address and spell Faversham, where she lives.

Realising what was happening, Nick then understandably got very upset along the lines of "I can't even do the simplest thing anymore," and, in this situation, there isn't an answer to that. In the end, I hugged him and said, "Okay, let's have a hot drink to cheer ourselves up. Then I'll write the cards and you put the stamps on." I'm left hoping that the cards we sent to friends in Australia and continental Europe had the right value on them. Sorry, folks, if they don't arrive. I did my best.

On the plus side, Christmas also brings time with family, which he always enjoys – partly, I think, because he feels less threatened and more confident when surrounded by people who know him well and understand where he is and what he's up against. He's also always better when I'm there and not going anywhere because he knows, like a child with his mother, that whatever goes wrong, I'll sort it out. So he worries less. And for a few days before and after Christmas, I shall be out working less than usual, so that will probably help to allay Ms A, or at least the havoc she wreaks, a little. Maybe.

20 December 2017

A phone call telling us about a Cardiff University project called Alzheimer's Disease Genetics invited us to take part in the research as promised. It was all painstakingly (laboriously) explained to us verbally and sent to us in writing. The eventual upshot was the arrival last week of, let's call them Leila and Naomi, who work at King's College, for a long information– gathering/sharing session. It took most of a morning with the two of us working with the two of them in different rooms at our home.

I answered dozens and dozens of questions about his family and changes I've noticed in his behaviour, attitude, mood, comprehension, etc. Nick was, meanwhile, doing cognitive and other assessments in the dining room. Predictably, he couldn't remember much to tell me about it afterwards, except to say fairly cheerfully, "I had to do that copying thing with the squiggles again. And of course I messed it up as usual."

The first thing that really interests me about this work is that the aim of the project is to identify environmental, biological and genetic factors which influence the progression of Alzheimer's disease and other neurodegenerative disorders. Yes – genetic. I did a double take too. For a very long time, medics have been telling the public that late-onset (that means at age sixty-five+)

Alzheimer's is not hereditary, although early-onset forms of the disease are. We've been personally assured of this several times by our consultant and others in the last few months too – and that's information I've been relieved to pass on to our sons.

Now, I gather, this project in Cardiff has found twenty genes which are related to Alzheimer's and, by implication, staff there are beavering away in search of more. So much for a disease that is not inherited then?

Leila and Naomi, who went off with blood and DNA samples (his, not mine) as well as huge sheaves of info, have ten sets of research interviews to do. We were their fifth. Others like them are doing similar groundwork all over the country, and then it all goes to Cardiff for analysis. We've been promised newsletters and so forth to keep us up to date with activities and findings.

If it is eventually established that genes are partly or wholly responsible for allowing Ms Alzheimer's to devastate people's lives, then surely – in time – there is hope that ways will be found of blocking whatever triggers this horrible illness. Gene therapy and all that. It isn't, at this stage, going to be any help to us, of course, but it comforts me a little when I think what the future might hold for our sons and grandchildren.

27 December 2017

Ms Alzheimer's is an especially unwelcome presence at Christmas, but our first festive season with her recognised in our midst has been and gone without too much angst. There was confusion about what day of the week it was and which days were actually Christmas Eve and Christmas Day, but otherwise it went fairly smoothly, largely because I was around all the time to troubleshoot. And as Christmases go, it certainly had its moments.

The best one was at our younger son's on Boxing Day. It's a delight for both Nick and me to have all four of our granddaughters (ranging in age from nineteen to two) in one room, and given geography, logistics, jobs and education, it doesn't happen too often. But there we all were ripping open presents, yelping in delight, chatting, catching up and eating too much in a homely Brighton sitting room.

Then the younger children, excited about a download of action songs someone had found for them, decided that they simply had to do the Hokey Cokey with their dad. So he moved some chairs to create a tiny dance floor and I stood up to join them – unthinkingly assuming that Nick would remain *paterfamilias* on the sofa where he'd already sat most of the day opening his old codger's presents such as a Down Your Way calendar and Very Warm Gloves.

But one of our quasi daughters-in-law and the elder granddaughters weren't having that. Much kinder and more thoughtful than I, they helped him to his feet and held his hands in our little circle. So the Hokey Cokey turned into a whole gathering activity – amidst lots and lots of laughter, because we must have looked awfully silly. And I had to throw myself into it with an undignified level of energy because I was so moved to see Nick opposite me, trying very hard, feeling loved and enjoying himself but looking an awful lot older and frailer than he did this time last year. Had I not forced myself to concentrate hard on hopping about, I would have broken down and howled.

Our younger son thinks the Hokey Cokey should be a new Elkin family tradition and is already looking forward to a repeat run at his brother's house next year. And I'm sure his daughters will be up for it. As for me, I dare not think a whole year ahead and reflect on what the ever-present and increasing invasive Ms A will be allowing us to do by then.

Part Two

2018

3 January 2018

Janus, who gave his name to January, was the Roman god of beginnings, gates, transitions, time, duality reflections, doorways and endings. He is traditionally depicted as having two faces: one looking forward and one back. Time, then, for a few Janus-like reflections.

2017 was quite a year. In April, Ms Alzheimer's moved in for good. Well, I suppose she'd been here for a while actually, but it was on 29 April – Diagnosis Day – that we were told firmly, finally and unequivocally that Nick's brain scan showed that he has Alzheimer's. A stop-you-in-your-tracks game changer, to put it mildly. Eight months on and we are, in a rickety-rackety kind of way, learning to live with Ms A – as we must.

During the same period, we've done a lot of pretty radical work to the house we bought in autumn 2016, which has meant dozens of tradesmen busily but disruptively working their magic on our premises and, every morning, a rather plaintive question from Nick: "Is anyone coming today?"

We also had a couple of pretty fabulous holidays – first in Malaysia, where Nick really wasn't well for much of the time, and then in Corfu, where he seemed much more 'with it' and gave me hope that perhaps the medication really is having some effect.

Meanwhile – busy working arts/education journalist that I am – I have seen 109 theatre shows and been to twenty-five classical music concerts, mostly to review. Recurrent tiredness means that Nick doesn't come to quite as many of these with me as he once did, but he's been to a good few. All the Alzheimer's advice tells you to do as many brain-stimulating activities as you can and theatre is good for that. So is the Polygon in *The Times,* which he does most days. He used to do the Codeword too, but dastardly Ms A seems to have destroyed that little pleasure.

Goodness knows there has been anger, sadness and frustration during the last twelve months, but we also laugh, which feels like the sun coming out and Ms A retreating temporarily into the shadows.

So that's what we have to focus on as the new year gets underway – laughing and counting our blessings. After all, we have each other, two brilliant sons and their equally brilliant families and a nice home in a very convenient location as well as half a century of shared happy memories. Without those things, dealing with Ms A would be an awful lot worse – and it is for many people.

And I've said before, people are very kind. For example, one night last week, I overheard the lifelong friend, almost another sister, who stays with us twice a year, gently helping Nick run his bath because he'd momentarily forgotten which tap was which and how the bath and shower taps relate to each other. Then there are people who leap to their feet on trains so that he can sit down, or patiently assist him in shops when he takes an unconscionably long time to find his money and organise his purchases. There's nothing like illness for bringing out the best in people and making you pause for a bit of blessing counting – especially as one year gives way to the next.

2017 was rich in Alzheimer's cure/prevention stories too. Almost every day, for the last eight months, during which I've been especially attuned, there's some sort of medical research report which makes the national media. Most of them come down to eating whole foods and getting plenty of exercise because it seems to work for mice. And that's pretty irritating because Nick has always lived like that. He and I were eating whole grains, pulses and nuts with lots of vegetables and fruit on a daily basis before most of the researchers were born.

Then, on New Year's Day, I read (in a small *Daily Telegraph* side panel) about a University of Lancashire study. It found that a 'triple receptor drug' created to treat type 2 diabetes helped – in more of those unfortunate mice at any rate – to reduce memory loss and the hateful amyloid plaques which are what Ms A really is. The scientists who published their findings in the journal *Brain Research* argue that their 'very promising outcomes' could bring new hope to thousands of Alzheimer's sufferers.

I wonder… Onwards and upwards into 2018.

10 January 2018

I've been thinking about tablecloths. As you do on a dank, damp, dark January afternoon. Nowhere in any of the Alzheimer's literature have I seen it mentioned, but Ms Alzheimer's has certainly hooked her claws into our napery.

Perhaps we're old-fashioned (okay – we are), but we've always used a tablecloth at every meal. Said item is then folded up and put away in nearby drawer in the dining room when not in use. The clean ones live in a different drawer.

In recent months, I've noticed that Nick can no longer manage tablecloths. "Shall I lay the table?" he'll say as he has done for forty-nine years when he can see dinner, lunch or whatever (I'm the family chef) is nearly ready.

"Yes, please," I reply and then, out of the corner of my eye, watch him confusedly trying to get the wretched thing onto the table.

When we're on our own, we fold the cloth and cover half the (rectangular) table. When anyone else is with us, it goes over the whole table. The folding and the lining up – an oblong cloth which is larger than the table, I now realise – is a basic form of applied geometry. And geometrical concepts rely, at least partly, on spatial awareness – one of the things Ms A is attacking ruthlessly so that

Nick can, for example, no longer drive or point towards central London or Kent accurately. Who would have thought it would affect table-laying as well?

In the dining room (contiguous with the kitchen in our house), it can take him as long as ten minutes flapping, laying, relaying and frustratedly trying it out in different ways to get the cloth neatly on the table. Often, it's all rumpled and lopsided even when he's finished. And clearing away afterwards is worse because once the cloth is shaken he can never work out how to fold it.

In practice, of course, I try now not to let him do it at all because it is irritating and upsetting in equal parts for both of us. What usually happens is that – if, as I too often am, I'm in a crosspatch mood – I snatch it from him and quickly do the laying or folding with an impatient tut and toss of the head. If I manage to be kinder and gentler, I pop the cloth on before he appears or fold it up after a meal while he's still drinking his coffee so that he doesn't get the chance to fail.

The same thing happens, incidentally, with sheets. The ones we use on our wonderful six-foot bed are ten foot square. And – not having arms as long as Roger Hargreaves's *Mr Tickle* – there is no way I can fold them on my own. Nick no longer understands how to help me without very detailed instructions along the lines of "Hold this corner in your left hand… lift your right hand to shake the creases out… fold towards me, etc." A year or two ago, we would have done the job collaboratively, quickly and wordlessly, probably while chatting about something different.

I find it very interesting – when I can detach myself from the tragedy of it enough to make objective observations – to watch the concepts of space and geometry unravelling. His declining brain presumably now won't allow him to visualise the shape and size of the table in relation to the cloth. And that's a very obvious, minor everyday thing, so goodness knows what other more important faculties the same decline is affecting in a less evident way.

In very young children – our youngest granddaughter, Libby, who is three, for example – you watch these concepts developing steadily, and there was a lot of stuff about Piaget's work on perceptions of volume when I trained as a teacher in the 1960s. Once Ms A moves into your life, the process goes into reverse as you head back towards infancy. At present, if Nick and Libby try to set the table together, they're about even in the tablecloth stakes. But their brains are changing in opposite directions. Within weeks, she'll be streets ahead of him and saying knowingly, "I'll do it for you, Grandpa."

17 January 2018

Alzheimer's research hit a bit of an impasse last week. Pharmaceutical giant Pfizer announced that it's pulling out of it. It seemed, at first glance and from where I'm standing – alongside Nick and the ever-predatory Ms Alzheimer's – pretty damned negative.

But read beyond the headline. It's still not good news but, in fairness, you can see Pfizer's point of view. Their aim has been to find and develop a drug which will make a real difference. In the last fifteen years, ninety-nine per cent of clinical trials have ended in failure. So – objective thinking and all that – it's hardly good business to throw any more money at it. And it isn't just Pfizer either. Eli Lilly in the US and Roche and Merck in Europe have all seen their 'breakthrough' Alzheimer's drugs fail at the final testing.

Scientists and commentators are beginning to hint that we may be getting ahead of ourselves. We simply don't (yet) understand the connections in the brain. Received wisdom – all the way back to the eponymous Dr Alois Alzheimer who, in 1906, conducted an autopsy on a patient with memory problems and observed sticky clumps between the dead and dying cells – cites amyloid protein as the culprit. But, it seems, drugs to combat these clumps of amyloid don't work, so is the cause actually something else? Back to the drawing board, a mere 111 years later. Some are saying that we need to return to basic brain research because we still don't understand the workings of a normal brain well enough to be able to work out what happens when dementia sets in.

Other scientists take an preventative line. They want to find ways of identifying the disease a decade or two before its symptoms start to show, because perhaps then the amyloid could be destroyed or dispersed with drugs in good time. The theory is that once the patient has become forgetful, clumsy, sleepy or whatever, the disease has already taken hold and it's too late to do anything about it.

Or perhaps they should focus on why – if it has – amyloid has built up in Nick's brain but not in mine. What are the factors that allow it to happen?

And where does it all leave Nick – a statistic in a huge, horrifying downward spiral. He is one of 850,000 dementia sufferers in the UK. Most of these have Alzheimer's. One person in ten over sixty-five has dementia and one person in three if you are fortunate (or should that be unfortunate?) enough to live to be over eighty-five. The current cost to the UK economy is £26bn per year. Obviously, the figures are rising continuously.

This is unsustainable. If they don't soon find some sort of drug to alleviate Alzheimer's effectively, then within twenty years we shall have voluntary (or maybe even involuntary) euthanasia for economic reasons. Ethics and morality will be luxuries that we, and other developed nations, won't be able to afford.

I'm sure the efficacious treatment (or the hideous alternative) will come too late to make any difference to us. Nick and his 849,999 fellow sufferers simply have to cope with life as best they can for as long as they can. There are drugs at the moment, but medics don't seem to have much faith in them. They just keep telling you firmly that the disease is incurable. Nick is prescribed memantine, which might – or maybe it's my wishful imagination – be making him a little more alert.

It's a horrible disease but, as I keep telling Nick, things could be a lot worse. He is still physically pretty good and can walk about and climb stairs, although he's much slower than formerly. Nothing hurts and there is no prospect of invasive surgery or debilitating treatment as would be the case with, say, cancer. And, after all, research hasn't stopped altogether. My glass is half full.

24 January 2018

Much ado about light bulbs in this household recently. Back in the days when Mr and Mrs E were able to manage their own lives and act on their decisions without a fuss, light bulbs were not an issue. Now that we have Ms Alzheimer's living with us, they are.

Light bulbs used not to be on my job sheet. He bought the ones we needed, made sure we had spares and fitted them as required. And I, of course, took it completely for granted. It's different now. So I have acquainted myself with lumens, found out what they mean in terms of the wattage I grew up with, and bought bulbs for every room in the house that we moved into sixteen months ago.

But I didn't get it quite right. Some are too bright and harsh. Others are so dim that you can't see to read a book. Then I had an idea. I said: "While I'm busy writing this review, could you do a little job for me? Please swap the centre light bulb in the sitting room with the one in the spare bedroom." I really don't think I could have expressed it any more clearly. And it's really vital, I'm sure, that Nick is allowed to feel there are helpful things he can still do.

When I looked up from my work half an hour later, I could see – through my office's glass door – that he was on the landing, removing the light bulb. Very carefully and earnestly on a small set of steps, he was trying (but failing!) to be useful. When I raced out to see what was going on, I found he had taken the centre light bulb out in our bedroom and the dining room too, with the result that I then had no idea which bulb was where anywhere in the house. I sorted it in the end, of course – by doing it myself on the steps but it took a while.

It was a worrying indication of the uncomprehending fog that Ms A has generated in Nick's poor, tired brain. He had, I fear, no real idea what I had asked him to do but didn't want to say so. He simply had a vague idea that I wanted light bulbs swapped, so that's what he was doing – more or less at random. It is, for anyone whose brain is functioning normally, almost impossible to imagine how this muddy muddle must feel to the victim of this horrible illness.

31 January 2018

My paternal great-grandmother lived on until I was sixteen. Throughout my childhood, I watched my grandparents carefully and lovingly looking after his mother even when she was difficult (which was often). A few years after her death, her son, my grandfather, succumbed to throat cancer. Cue for us all to rally round and be there for him and his widow, my beloved grandma, who lived on into her nineties and my forties.

Although we weren't quite so local by then, I used to visit Grandma every couple of weeks and speak to her on the phone weekly. And she would come to stay with us regularly. Meanwhile, our own boys were growing up and willing and able to be involved. In fact, with strange generational symmetry, our eldest son was sixteen when my grandma, his great-grandmother, died, exactly as I had been.

Since then, inevitably, all four of our parents have died (most recently, Father-in-law in 2014) and again as a family we have all – in our different ways – been there to support each other through illness, sadness, loss and loneliness, quite often tempered, of course, with jokes and laughter. My father used to tease his grandmother rotten – no one else could have got away with it – but by golly, he loved and looked after her. And I saw exactly the same pattern in our sons as their own grandparents gradually ailed.

It's like a baton in a relay race. One generation observes how the previous one does it and then takes it forward. Or at least that's how it seems to have worked for us – over and over again.

And now that Ms Alzheimer's has staked her claim on Nick, it is our turn to be supported and looked after. I'm sure our sons, partners and children (our oldest granddaughter is nineteen) have talked about it quietly among themselves, because I see kindness and astonishing acts of support all the time, despite the fact that no one lives particularly close.

The 'boys', who have, between them, enough practical professional skills to staff an entire building company, have each done an enormous amount of work in the house we downsized into sixteen months ago. And they've been on hand to advise almost continuously. I'd never have got it sorted out and created the lovely home it now is without the pair of them.

So I want to go on a music course in May. "Just send me the dates," says our elder son, who means he will come and stay with Nick and Ms A while I'm off duty. When the arrangement I'd made collapsed, he willingly agreed to do likewise next month while I visit a friend in Yorkshire too.

Then there's the week in April when Nick and I will be away on holiday. No sooner had I booked than I discovered that I couldn't get *Catus Domesticus* into the cattery, which had the effrontery to be fully booked. "Oh, don't worry," says elder son immediately. "I'll base myself in your house and work from there." That's yet another week away from his own family, although I hope his wife will join him for a London weekend with shows, and so on. It also means we get a house sitter as well as a cat minder. And, I expect, odd jobs will be done in our absence. Hero! I shall make sure there's plenty of beer in the fridge.

We have decorators in at present. "I'll pop up in the morning between jobs and take that radiator off the wall," said younger son last week, casually referring to a sixty-mile Brighton/London trip. "I don't want the decorators messing about with it." And he and his partner (who have a very young family) cheerfully put up with us taking over their house every time I review a concert in Brighton, which happens frequently. His long-suffering partner never complains if our son comes to us to do a job which overruns so he ends up staying the night either.

In short, life is not always easy these days, but we are very blessed in our fantastic children and their families, and that's an inestimable bonus. People in the know often say, "I hope you're getting the support you need." They mean from health services, voluntary organisations, social services, and so on, and I know that such things will be there when we need them. At present, yes, we are getting a terrific level of support – all home-grown. And I am learning to feel deeply grateful and accept it with grace while never taking any of it for granted.

Thinking about the past and watching the patterns repeating themselves over the generations, I've come to the conclusion that it's a case of reaping what you sow. Or doing as you would be done by. I'm not sure, though, that cantankerous old Great-Grandma ever said thank you. I do. Often. And my goodness, I mean it.

Then this week came a light bulb moment of a different sort, courtesy of a *Daily Telegraph* story. It was the first Alzheimer's research report I've read which made any personal sense at all. A UCL/King's College London study of 3,400 civil servants over thirty years has established that in some people, retirement triggers dementia. Use it or lose it seems to be the message, and they don't mean word puzzles and sudoku.

Nick was made redundant (by a new-broom CEO) in 1992 from a busy job as education officer for a professional body. It took him routinely all over Britain and, on one occasion, to the Far East to meet his institute's students. He was very busy, focused and dynamic. When the axe fell, he was in his late forties.

It wasn't, in the early 1990s, an easy age at which to start again. There were a couple of short-term contracts but nothing more. So, for many years – until Ms A arrived – Nick worked in my growing writing business. He did accounts, invoices, filing, admin (booking hotels, rail tickets, etc., on my behalf, for example) and some of my more straightforward information-gathering research and interviews. He also ran the domestic side of our life like clockwork so that for decades, I never ironed a shirt, changed a bed or bought a potato.

It was, however, all home-based and not – I suppose – the intellectual stimulation that going out every morning, besuited with briefcase, and working with lots of other people had been. Some would say that, effectively, he retired before he was fifty.

Could it be that over twenty years at home has triggered the arrival of Ms A at a relatively young age? Nick was seventy-one when he was diagnosed last year. We shall never know. But, as far as I'm concerned, it vindicates my own decision (made long ago) that, while I can possibly manage to work at all, I am most definitely not going to retire. My friends, many of whom seem to be having a lovely time doing not a lot, disapprove with a passion. But we're all different and I am certain that this is the right thing for me in my situation. I often say, flippantly, that's it's work which keeps me sane. Perhaps it's truer than I realise.

7 February 2018

The government – which, just occasionally, does something useful – has announced a proposal to change the eligibility criteria for the Blue Badge scheme to include people with non-physical conditions. They mean people like Nick, who has to drag Ms Alzheimer's with him wherever he goes, along with autism spectrum folk and other groups. It would give us access to disability parking.

The Blue Badge scheme, which has been running since 1970, has a framework set by central government, but local authorities are responsible for its administration and enforcement. And there's the rub. Their interpretation of the rules varies, so whether or not you get a Blue Badge can be a postcode lottery.

Of course, you can see why some councils are reluctant to issue too many badges because the scheme is open to abuse, given how little parking there is everywhere for everyone these days.

Parking, moreover, is an income stream for councils. They're already supposed to recognise non-physical conditions, but many LAs employ 'mobility assessors', who are concerned only with whether or not the applicant can walk. And I shall probably be shot down in flames for suggesting that if the councils were to offer incentives to their assessors for finding most applicants ineligible then it would help to sustain the level of parking revenues – but that won't stop me mentioning it.

Well, soon, maybe, it will all be better. Jesse Norman, Parliamentary Under Secretary of State for Transport, declares in her preface to the consultation document that '*The Government believes that the Blue Badge scheme should not discriminate in principle between physical and non-physical conditions*'. Consultation runs until 18 March. Fingers crossed that we get the proposed changes and that local authorities don't scupper it.

So why would a Blue Badge help Nick? He can still walk reasonably well, after all, although he's slower than he was and inclined to shuffle in crowds and confined spaces because he's frightened of falling or being pushed over. He's also very nervous and cautious on staircases. Otherwise, mobility isn't really an issue at the moment.

Alzheimer's is a complex, ill-understood disease and – as these blogs often observe – does unaccountable things to brain function, and that, obviously, affects the whole body because the brain is the body's central computer. Here's one odd but highly inconvenient thing: By the time Nick's addled brain tells him he needs the loo, there isn't a lot of time to get to one.

If I drive him into, say, a large motor service station and have to park a long way from the building, it can be – er – rather difficult for him to trudge the distance when 'urgency' is biting. If, to make it easier for him, I drop him at the door, by the time I've parked and walked across to find him, he could well be wandering round the service station puzzling about where I am. And that's tricky, especially at busy times when these places are crowded, because we both get panicky, which probably isn't good for either of us. If I could park in a disabled space near the door, none of this would arise.

It would be easier in some town centre car parks too. Take the very large, busy one beside Chichester Festival Theatre. Nick, who sometimes comes with me, usually needs to get into the building quickly when we arrive at the end of our seventy-mile journey, but the only parking space I can find is typically 500 yards away. We don't often take the car to a supermarket (deliveries are a great thing!) these days but when we do, he'd be much better offloading himself as close to the entrance as possible.

The Blue Badge 'belongs' to a person, not to a vehicle, so Nick would be able to take the facility with him if he was in someone else's car – with either of our sons, for instance – when all the same potential problems are present.

Would I be tempted to abuse the system by using it when Nick is safe at home and I'm out by myself? Definitely not. Let me assure the London Borough of Lewisham – which would, if the changes go through, be responsible for assessing Nick for eligibility – that after a long time in the car, I actually welcome a walk across a car park to stretch my legs. I am neither lazy nor any sort of cheat. I'm also lucky enough to be firing healthily on all cylinders. So if Nick were *chez nous*, so would the Blue Badge be.

Now let's see some humane, commonsensical changes in the assignment of Blue Badges. Soon, please.

14 February 2018

Last week, we – Nick, Ms Alzheimer's and me – went to Chickenshed ('theatre changing lives') in north London to see *Monolog*, directed by Lou Stein. To do that, we have to travel from London's 'Deep South' to Cockfosters at the northern end of the Piccadilly Line, and it's a bit of a hike, involving car, two trains and two walks each way – although the show was very interesting and well worth travelling for. And I have long been an admirer and supporter of Chickenshed's diverse inclusivity.

Anyway, on this occasion, I decided it would be a good outing for Nick. It's a welcoming venue and I thought it would be a nice change for him – and it was. It made me realise, though, that travel is getting ever more difficult. I now have to allow at least an extra half an hour for loo stops (at the garage next to Cockfosters Underground, for example, and at Charing Cross station both ways, as well as several times at the theatre and in the restaurant we got a bite in before the show). Then there's the trudging gait. I can walk from Charing Cross to Leicester Square Tube in five minutes. With Nick, it takes a quarter of an hour.

He had to ask me several times during the journey where we were going and why, too. And, rather poignantly, I can often see him not knowing but not asking (I do know him rather well, after all) in case I tell him off or snap at him. When we saw *Of Mice and Men* at Marlowe Theatre, Canterbury recently, Nick actually grinned at me because he recognised that the dynamic between George and Lenny has so much in common with the life that we are now leading together. Theatre, empathy and all that.

At Chickenshed, I was touched to find him chatting to Susan Jamson, Press and PR manager, whom I've known for a long time, when I came back from the loo before the show. Susan had been chatting to both of us and was now very gently trying to get Nick to talk – he's become very reticent because he's afraid of looking silly. At the point at which I returned to the table and stood away because I didn't want to interrupt, he was stumbling through a garbled account of having heard Sheku Kanneh-Mason's first performance of the Elgar *Cello Concerto* at Maidstone the week before. He couldn't remember Sheku's name but somehow there was communication, and it is very excellent for him to have something resembling a normal conversation with someone he doesn't know very well.

Shows are always tricky. I go to several, of various sorts, every week, but more often than not I now go alone. For a start – as last Thursday – I sometimes see two in a day without coming home in between, and I know that would now be far too tiring for Nick. Ms A ensures that he flags very quickly. In the past, he would have travelled to join me for the second one but that's no longer on. I'd be afraid he'd forget where to go or how to get there. He isn't reliable at locking the house securely behind him either. So it's a case of his coming out with me or staying at home.

At the weekend, I reviewed a classical music concert in Hastings on Saturday night and another in Brighton on Sunday afternoon. We stayed overnight with our younger son, Felix, and his family on Saturday and made a Sussex weekend of it. But my word, Nick got confused. Drinking tea in a Hastings teashop before the concert, he had no idea why we were there or what we were doing. "Is Felix joining us here?" he asked, vaguely. And an hour or two later, the tiredness caught up with him and he nodded off during *Winterreise*.

Then on Sunday morning he started packing his things until I told him to stop because he might want some of them later. "Aren't we going home in a minute?" he asked. At that point, I flipped (no, I don't have the patience of a saint and never did) and told him that I wasn't going to give him any more information. "I'll just tell you when the time comes and you need to know," I snapped crossly.

I later discovered that he then went to Felix and asked him what the plans were for the day. "You're going to a concert at the Dome. Then I'm cooking you dinner," said kind Felix, very patiently.

In short, Ms Alzheimer's clutches are gradually tightening. It's only ten months since diagnosis, but I don't have to look far for evidence of the inexorable downward tug.

So how do I stop her destroying me too? Well, I try to keep a sense of humour. It was quite funny, I suppose, in a grim sort of way, when I asked Nick to bring the concertina clothes airer downstairs and he got the cleaning lady to help him carry it erected because he didn't know how to collapse it. I'm not sure, incidentally, whether she didn't know either or was being tactful. Either way, it was a nice bit of sit com when they arrived in the dining room carrying it between them.

And a bit of respite is good occasionally. At the beginning of last week, I handed all my responsibilities to our elder son and escaped to Yorkshire for three days. There, a dear and lovely friend spoiled me rotten with tea in bed and gin by the fireside before delicious dinners in her beautiful home. And I came home feeling very refreshed. Being in sole charge of another human being – i.e., a baby or two – is one thing when you're in your twenties as I was. It's a bit different a few decades later.

21 February 2018

A young man needs a lover, a middle-aged man a housekeeper and an old man a nurse. Sexist but true. Well, to be fair, I didn't do much of the middle bit because we reversed roles, but I'm doing plenty of the latter now to make up for it.

Last week, chauffeur's hat on my head, I had to take Nick to the dentist for a filling and to see the hygienist. I took him into the waiting room and handed him over – the staff are very understanding – and repaired to the café over the road with my pencil and the book I was reading to review. Work never stops. When I returned to collect him, I was informed that the hygienist wanted to see me because she didn't think Nick had processed what she'd told him.

A flashback: When Nick was a young lad, he came off his bike, smashed his front teeth and in those bad old days of primitive dentistry lost the lot. He has worn a denture ever since. Is there a worse turn-off than false teeth? I am mildly phobic about them anyway. I find them utterly revolting to see or even think about. When he and I first became… er… intimate (and that was a jolly long time ago too), he promised me with ardent fervour that I would never need to see or have anything to do with the horrible denture.

And so it has proved. In half a century, I have almost never seen Nick without the repulsive thing. Even when a nasty ladder accident and foot reconstruction surgery put him out of action for months in 2002, and I had to do a lot of things for him, he still looked after his own teeth – thank goodness.

Until now. What the hygienist wanted to tell me was that, presumably thanks to Ms A, he is not cleaning any of his teeth – real ones or false ones – properly. He's heading, she says, for fungal infections, and there are already signs of problems. So we have to adopt a new procedure. And I have to supervise it. Ugh! I promised a lot of things in my marriage vows and I've kept them scrupulously, but I never agreed to be tooth monitor. In fact, I'd have probably bolted from the altar had I had any inkling that denture management would ever be on my job list. Surely 'in sickness and in health' carries a false teeth exemption?

Well, despite all that, you can't accuse me of not being conscientious. I bought a couple of tubes of Steradent (art come to this?), read the instructions and found a plastic pot. I dissolved one of the pesky things to make the blue solution, gave it to Nick and said, "Go into the downstairs loo. Put your teeth in this pot and leave them for five minutes. Don't come out until that time is up. Then rinse the pot, put your teeth in your mouth and carry on as normal."

It's meant to be a nightly routine and that was eight nights ago. Since then, I've had him several times wandering round the house with the pot in his hand. Once, I found it on the draining board. Another time, he wanted to bring it into the bedroom with the teeth floating in it. Five minutes seems an impossible concept. At other times, he'll say something vague about 'turning water blue', and no, I don't know what he means either. He has also several times left the denture downstairs and come up, toothless, to ask me what to do next – ghastly sight.

Left to himself, he does nothing except brush as usual for about fifteen seconds, which, of course, is woefully inadequate. He simply can't carry out a simple instruction and procedure anymore.

"Let me write it all down so I know what to do," he said. So we did that but he hasn't looked at the paper since. We've spiralled a long way downhill in recent months – even further than I realised. Damn Ms Alzheimer's and her intrusive awfulness.

I think I've been more stressed about his bloody teeth than about any other single thing since Alzheimer's was diagnosed. It's driving me potty and, a lifelong bruxism person, I'm probably grinding my own fragile teeth to stumps. I can't wear my mouthguard all day, after all. I cajole, explain, shout, fulminate, plead, cry and still he gets it wrong.

Normally, I try to be kind and empathetic. Sometimes, I even succeed. But false teeth (even typing those two words fills me with revulsion) are a step too far.

28 February 2018

In his prime, Nick used to run along the tops of beach breakwaters to show off to the kids and anyone else who was about. He was proud of his agility and balance and, to be honest, a bit boorish about it. Then came a ladder accident in 2002 which put him on crutches for months, and now Ms Alzheimer's has shoved in her pernicious oar.

Today, he has problems with walking down steps and stairs. Up isn't quite so bad, but the descent is tortuous. "I'm frightened of stairs because when I look down it's as if they're coming up to meet me," he says, explaining a not-much-discussed but, I suspect, quite common Alzheimer's symptom.

Ms A has, apparently, wormed her insidious way into the bit of his brain which manages balance – and scuppered it. I find this excruciatingly frustrating, for example, when I'm standing at the bottom of a flight of stairs on the Tube waiting for him and the train behind me – which of course I would have hopped on had I been alone – pulls out of the station. It must be even more frustrating for Nick himself, of course – and I do realise how selfish my plaints must sometimes sound.

The old house we moved out of in 2016 had fifty-two steps from attic to basement, and both Nick and I went up and down them easily all the time. I thought the new house, which has a single flight of fourteen stairs, would be even easier, but actually, step-wise, for Nick, it isn't.

It's to do with the relative space inside the two houses. All those steps in our former home were quite shallow and the staircases were a bit wider. Our fourteen 'new steps' are a good bit steeper and there's a tight turn (big metal hand grip on the bend for Nick now) at the top. In fact, our younger son, aged forty-two and as fit as a flea, managed to fall down the entire flight when, a few months ago, he tried to race down them in a hurry – fortunately sustaining only a couple of bruises. His three-year-old daughter still says solemnly whenever she sees us or our stairs, "Daddy fell down your stairs," and I expect she'll remember the drama of it for the rest of her life.

This potentially dangerous gradient means that Nick comes down our stairs very carefully, hanging on tightly to the banister rail – a new one put in for both cosmetic and safety reasons last year. The speed isn't even *andante*. It's *largo*. And it makes him look, alas, much older than his seventy-two years.

It's the same when we're out; I don't think I'd noticed until recently just how many flights of steps you walk down to get onto the Tube – or off many mainline stations. At Elephant and Castle, for example, there are two huge flights to get to ground level when you 'alight' (to borrow a bit of transport-speak) a Thameslink train, and it's so busy that it isn't always easy to get to the side of the staircase so that you can hold the rail. Nick has got into the habit of waiting until the crush has dispersed if necessary because he really must have access to that rail. Then, for the Underground, you go down in a lift and then down lots more steps, especially if you're heading for the Bakerloo line. It takes Nick quite a while, and I have to build in extra travelling time when he's with me.

Until recently, we were the sort of people who routinely walked up and down stairs from choice in hotels, big shops, and so on because it's healthier than the mechanical alternatives. And I still do. But if we're out together, it's now quite a relief to put him safely on an escalator, or even in a lift, and know that he doesn't have to do all that painful step by step, one foot looking anxiously down as he does so.

Those breakwaters seem a very long time ago.

7 March 2018

Last Saturday, I pushed, shoved and forced Nick a million miles out of his comfort zone. "Piss off, Ms Alzheimer's," I said to our horrible predatory resident and took her victim to a singing day in Folkestone.

Some background: I have been almost continually involved in some form of amateur music-making since I first warbled in the infants' school choir at age five. In contrast, Nick, although a lifelong music lover (mostly a 'classical' chap), hasn't been a participant since he confronted his hitherto suppressed atheistic misgivings and left the church choir at age sixteen. So it was fifty-five years since he last sang with others and, of course, he doesn't read music.

The singing day in question is an annual Gilbert and Sullivan (and we both love G&S) event run by someone I know through the huge and informal Kent music-making network. It's the usual deal – rehearse during the day with local soloists, then sing it all to an audience in the evening. Using the Tower Theatre in Folkestone, it routinely raises several hundred pounds for charity.

I'd asked the organiser/Musical Director in advance to seat Nick next to someone 'strong' in the basses. The upshot was that as soon as we arrived, we were introduced to a delightful father and son – the older man is an organist and retired clergyman. They looked after Nick all day with heart-warming kindness, helping him to keep his place in the score and to stick the Post-its I'd given him in useful places. The programme was *Trial by Jury* – which Nick knows well by ear – and extracts from *Utopia Limited*, which he doesn't, but neither did anyone else so it didn't matter.

Most important of all, Nick had to chat to people he'd only just met and that is vital. Reclusiveness is just an open invitation to Ms A to do her worst because it creates a vacuum for her to move into. And his new friends gently involved him in conversation in such a way that Nick was able to acquit himself with dignity.

He was, however, excruciatingly nervous. At lunchtime, he told me that he was going to opt out of the concert in the evening and sit in the audience. Then during the afternoon a little miracle happened. Suddenly Nick seemed to 'get it' and was able to start singing a bit and enjoying himself. From my place in the *altos*, further along the same row, I could actually see the change taking place. By 7pm, he was looking lovely in his DJ and ready for off. 'Lively' might be a bit of an exaggeration, but there was definitely a sense that I had got nine-tenths of my husband back – on temporary loan from Ms A, as it were.

The concert was fun. I haven't sung *Trial by Jury* for ages and *Utopia* was quite an adventure. At the end, Nick's eyes were shining – yes, shining. He'd taken part in an event with others and had a good time. He talked about it animatedly for most of the drive home to London too. He was on a high and Ms A was definitely absent, and I managed not to feel sad or angry for several hours.

That's what music-making does, of course. Those of us who do it regularly and often know that the satisfaction of having done whatever it is, is a very heady drug. Taking Nick to this event was an experiment. I couldn't, as it turned out, be more pleased with the result. He's already looking forward to *HMS Pinafore* at Folkestone next March, and I shall find other similar things for him (and me) between now and then. Apart from anything else, there's a lot to be said, at this stage in proceedings, for something we can enjoy together.

14 March 2018

When Nick was finally given his devastating, condemnatory diagnosis eleven months ago, I had great difficulty holding on for the rest of the consultation. Kind and helpful though the doctor was, the dreadful words, "My husband has Alzheimer's" kept rattling round my head, and my face wouldn't behave itself. It was only my trusty old friend 'Professional Mode' which kept me speaking articulately for a further twenty minutes or so, although I've no idea what I said.

When we finally got out of that room, we staggered over the road, literally holding each other up, to a coffee shop where I let go. I cried and cried and cried – which probably didn't help Nick very much. He, after all, had just been struck with a metaphorical sledgehammer and told that he must surrender his driving licence immediately. In that first hour, I think he was in such shock that he didn't really take in the whole truth, and it was a case of his comforting me rather than the other way round.

Well, somehow we numbly got through the rest of that day. I had the presence of mind to inform close family: our sons, my sister and my dearest friend, who's effectively another sister. All four of them came back immediately with supportive warmth – which, as I've said before, is immeasurably sustaining.

Then the next day my usual practical self began to surface and I found myself thinking: *Okay. Ms Alzheimer's is here to stay. Crying isn't going to get rid of her, so just how are we going to deal with this horror?* My automatic instinct, as a writer, was to get it into words. But of course you can't write about someone else's illness – even someone who's been as close to you as Nick has to me for half a century – without his permission.

"How would you feel about me writing a piece – and then maybe following it up with subsequent pieces – about all this?" I asked him tentatively. He's always been a pretty private person and I expected him to say no unequivocally. To my astonishment, he said, "Okay, why not? You'll do it very well and perhaps it will help other people. Can I read them as you post them?"

There's more to 'going public' than blogging, of course. It's a whole attitude of mind. Neither of us dissembles with anyone, ever. Nick has learned to say to people when he's in difficulties: "Can you help me, please? I have Alzheimer's and I can't find my way back to where my wife is." (That actually happened last week at the Coliseum where we saw *Iolanthe*. I shouldn't have let him go off to the loo alone in an unfamiliar building.) Then, inevitably, once the words are said, people are wonderfully helpful.

"Please could my husband have that seat? He has Alzheimer's and he's shaky on his feet," I say to people casually on the Tube. And I order for both of us in restaurants so that waiting staff can see what the problem is – he usually forgets what he's decided to order by the time he has to say it aloud.

"Sorry, that's how I am now," he will say to anyone we spend any time with when he loses his way in a sentence. And he's learned to be matter-of-fact about the things he can't do anymore, such as the paperwork relating to my business. "I used to be an administrator but now I can't work out what I have to do," I've heard him say several times to people who don't know him very well. And he's got used to the oddness of meeting strangers who know quite a lot about him because they've read the blogs.

Denial really doesn't help Ms A's victim or anyone else. "I think we've made a really sensible decision to be open about my problems," Nick remarked the other day, apropos of nothing in particular, in a rare, bright and positive moment. "Once people know, and realise that it's okay to talk about it, they can react honestly without having to pretend that they haven't noticed how I am. It's so much easier for everybody."

Meanwhile, I'm amused to note that for a man who's always tended to introversion, he seems actually to enjoy being the centre of attention. "Have you written anything about me this week?" he'll ask, childlike and hopeful. And of course when we're out, everyone we meet (and I know hundreds of people in the performing arts world) makes a point of asking him how he is and allowing him to answer with dignity. And that would have been much harder if we hadn't been truthful.

Everyone in our (unenviable) position has to find his/her own way of dealing with it. We've come a long way in eleven months.

21 March 2018

Luke Adamson's play *One Last Waltz* has just completed its run in the studio space at Greenwich Theatre. I hope he manages to get it out on tour as soon as possible because Ms Alzheimer's is the central – invisible but palpable – character, and the play needs to be seen by as many people as possible.

Luke invited me first because I am a seasoned (or something) theatre critic and second because I am – a role I never sought – becoming ever better known as an Alzheimer's commentator. *One Last Waltz* is a meeting of my two worlds.

When I mentioned, *en passant*, to Nick that I'd agreed to review a play about Alzheimer's, he said, quite brightly by his standards, "Well, I suppose I ought to see that too. Can I come with you?" So I contacted Luke to explain and, of course, we were both welcome.

To be honest, I wasn't at all sure it was a good idea for Nick to see it. Plays and films about Alzheimer's (remember *Iris* and *Still Alice*?) tend to be pretty devastating because they focus on an inexorable downward trajectory and can end only one way. I try to keep Nick as chirpy as possible and I don't encourage him to reflect on the possible (probable/inevitable) ghastliness of the future. In our situation, it's healthier to dwell in the moment and take each day as it comes.

I needn't have worried. *One Last Waltz* tells the story of Alice (played by Amanda Reed). She has memory problems and her daughter is beginning to feel anxious about her. The three-person play, written as a tribute to Luke's late grandfather, is about coming to terms with the illness and seeking help – which means admitting that there are problems. Oh yes, Nick and I have been there, done that and are collecting a whole drawerful of tee-shirts.

We grinned at each other in recognition several times during the eighty-minute piece because Luke's observations are uncannily truthful. Yes, it's difficult to be sure what day of the week it is when your world is steadily narrowing. And that means you have little idea whether the appointment you're fretting about is today, tomorrow or next week. Of course, you struggle to remember where you've put things, which makes you irritable even with yourself. Then there's the general getting annoyed with yourself and others because you're not as you were – and disbelief when someone else puts you straight.

And we empathised a lot with Alice's decision to go to Blackpool for a last waltz in the place she used to dance with her husband, who has recently died. Nick has recently mentioned several things he'd like to do again and places with happy memories that he'd like to revisit. That's why we're going on holiday to Northumberland next month. He wants to go back to Cragside, which has long been our favourite National Trust property. Fortunately, he's no dancer.

Of course, *One Last Waltz* is poignant. It has one of the most powerful final lines I've heard in the theatre in quite a while. I had to mop up tears several times. Seeing it was, however, more cathartic than upsetting.

I've said before that one of the best ways of fighting Ms Alzheimer's is to confront her openly, fearlessly and proactively rather than treating her as an unmentionable horror. Part of Luke's agenda is to help to get Alzheimer's freely discussed without stigma. "After all," he said to me before the show, "cancer used to frighten people so much that they couldn't talk about it. Now they do and it's much better. We have to do the same with Alzheimer's."

The most moving moment of all – for me at least – came after the play had ended. We stayed for the Q/A but listened rather than contributing. Then I popped off to the ladies', which is up a few steps at Greenwich Theatre, and told Nick to wait for me in the foyer at the lower level. When I emerged, I could see him down in the foyer, deep in conversation with Amanda Reed. I didn't want to interrupt or affect the dynamic, so I lurked behind a shelf of leaflets and watched quietly.

He was telling her, I think, how much he'd identified with her character in the play. Alice gets lost in Blackpool. Nick was describing the horror of getting lost in a large shopping centre on holiday last year. She was listening intently – an actor observing life, I suppose. And his dignity was intact because she was allowing him to communicate like a fully-fledged human being, despite the stumbles and hesitancies. What surprised and pleased me most about it was Nick finding the confidence spontaneously to share a few feelings with a stranger. That's how much the play had freed him up.

Of course, on the way home, I asked, "Well? Was that the right decision? Are you glad you saw that?"

"Definitely," he replied.

Never underestimate the power of drama. I've said/written that a few hundred times in other contexts, but it applies forcefully to Alzheimer's too.

28 March 2018

Just occasionally, Ms Alzheimer's presents me with a little bonus – something that's actually quite useful as opposed to destructive.

It's reasonably well documented that changing taste in food is a fairly common Alzheimer's symptom. And Nick is definitely an example of that. Quite an extreme one, in fact.

I married the fussiest, faddiest eater on the planet. (I blame his mother, naturally.) He wouldn't eat tomatoes, mushrooms, onions, cooked cheese, mayonnaise, anything with a sauce on it, casseroles and about a million other things.

And I mean, wouldn't eat. Being invited out was a nightmarish embarrassment. I really don't like pears but if a pear dish is put in front of me in someone's house – and it has happened – of course, I eat it out of politeness. Not Nick. If he was served something on his lengthy 'don't eat' list, well, then he just wouldn't. End of. And when we both became vegetarian in the late 1970s, in some ways it was even worse because when people obligingly, kindly try to cater for you, they tend to dish up all the things Nick refused to countenance. He was effectively a vegetarian who wouldn't eat (most) vegetables, and you really can't expect people to work round that. I seemed always to be apologising for him.

At home, I had decades of making quiches with cheese on one side only, mincing onion and mushroom to make it invisible, always doing stir fries in separate pans, lying about the provenance of redness in dishes and getting annoyed with him in restaurants when he said loftily: "There's nothing on this menu I can eat," even when there were three or four veggie options.

Then, about ten years ago, it all began to change. He realised he liked leeks, beetroot, parsnips and several other previously rejected things. He even started to eat macaroni cheese and lasagne with their dependence on lots of lovely cheese sauce. Most odd of all, a lifelong tea hater, he's decided that green tea is okay so we share a pot at breakfast time, which still seems hilarious, given how he used to be. With hindsight, I suppose that those changes were early Alzheimer's indicators, although at the time I just marvelled and rejoiced gratefully.

Today, I rough chop onions in the normal way and they go in casseroles and other dishes, along with dried tomatoes, tomato puree and anything else I fancy adding. He just chomps away at the result, usually has a second helping and says he's enjoyed it. For a long time, I said nothing because half the battle has always been keeping the truth about ingredients from him.

Then I stopped pretending. I just tease him, saying: "It's taken me nearly fifty years, but you've become a normal eater. There really isn't much you won't eat now. What a pity it took you so long!" He grins back.

"Just don't give me cauliflower!" Little does he know that I quite often chop up the loathed brassica and sneak it into burgers, pies and other things.

Last week, when I was going out on one of my frequent evening review jobs, I fried some onion and red pepper in a frying pan with some tofu, then added a pot of red (tomato) pesto. All he had to do was heat it through and eat it with pitta bread.

When I got home, Nick said: “Well, I don’t know what that sauce was but it was absolutely delicious!” Gotcha. Thanks, Ms A. I’m very rarely grateful to you, so you’d better make the most of it.

4 April 2018

As you get older, you need less sleep. Right? Well, I'm not at all sure that's true, although if you've suffered from decades of insomnia as I have, then it's what you tell yourself – to offset all those gloomy media stories unhelpfully informing you that lack of sleep is as harmful to health as smoking and junk food.

Nick didn't sleep well for a long time either. I suspect we're a pretty typical couple. You sleep like logs, often right round the clock, when you're young and first together. Then the children arrive. And, after the initial awfulness of night feeds and sleep deprivation, you both eventually learn to sleep with one ear cocked as you get on with life. Somehow, after a few years of that, one's relationship with sleep is never quite the same again.

Then Ms Alzheimer's turns up. Unlike the much-wanted children, she is, of course, a totally uninvited and unwelcome arrival. Odd, though, that just as children, like Macbeth, murder sleep, Ms A seems to enhance it – or at least that is Nick's current experience.

He is now sleeping better than he has done since his twenties. Like nearly all men his age, he usually needs to pop out to the bathroom once or twice in the night but falls straight back into deep sleep – almost as if he was twenty-three again, the age he was when we married.

There is an issue, though. His night vision is terrible and I think that's probably yet another Alzheimer's symptom because it's a fairly recent development. I can slip out of our bedroom across the landing and into the bathroom without turning on any lights at all – there's a streetlight in front of the house which beams in. Not so Nick, who seems to need floodlights. Similarly, if I'm awake in the night and decide to read for a while, I can turn on my bedside light and he is impervious. His tolerance of light is very high.

Now I loathe light in the bedroom. It makes it even harder for me to nod off. So, for quite a while now, we've had curtains with blackout linings – bought for our old house and altered for the one we moved to eighteen months ago. For Nick, that has recently become totally unsatisfactory. Every night – sometimes more than once – he would grope round the bed, muttering, usually waking me up (if he hadn't already done so) by cannoning into the corner and grabbing my feet to save himself. Sometimes, he would simply turn on his bedside light and wake me up anyway. Not good for bedroom compatibility. I thought about this for a few months before coming up with a solution – of sorts.

He now has a child's nightlight on his side of the room which is just enough to enable him to make his way round the bed. As far as I'm concerned, though, that light is so hideously bright that I could almost read a book by it and certainly wouldn't be able to rest properly. So I wear a sleep mask – which makes me look like Isobel Barnett on *What's My Line?* (now that dates me!) or a burglar in a child's comic. But it works. I'm away in my personal darkness – often not even noticing when he opens the bedroom door and turns on the landing light. He, meanwhile, can walk to where he needs to go in the night safely and often without disturbing me at all. It took me a while to get used to it, though. I woke up at least twice in the beginning thinking, *Oh blimey. I've gone blind – as if I don't have enough problems!*

Living with Ms Alzheimer's is like that. She bowls problems at you all the time. The skill is to find solutions and compromises so that you can more or less carry on as normal. It feels like outwitting an enemy in a minor skirmish. We both know we shall lose the war eventually but I, for one, shall go down fighting with every shred of initiative and ingenuity I can summon.

And do you know what? I'm beginning to sleep better than I have for a while too – presumably because I know my 'charge' is safely asleep and okay.

11 April 2018

There is a common assumption that Alzheimer's disease – and the dementia which characterises it – is mostly about loss of memory.

In Luke Adamson's fine play *One Last Waltz*, the central character, Alice, eventually admits: "I need to see someone about my memory."

Our consultant is attached to the 'Lewisham Memory Service' – as if they could serve us up some extra memory like a phone shop.

Everyone you speak to has some experience of Alzheimer's, and it's nearly always memory loss they want to tell you about.

Yes of course Nick has memory problems. I have to tell him simple things such as it's Tuesday and the cleaner will be here at 10am over and over again. He often struggles for words too, starting a sentence only to find the key word has gone AWOL before he gets to it. If we're seeing people we haven't seen for a while, I have to rehearse names with him carefully in advance.

But memory loss is only a tiny part of what life with Ms Alzheimer's actually means. Here, in no particular order, are ten other symptoms we're dealing with daily.

1. Nick is shaky on his feet and tends to shuffle because it feels safer. He walks at about half my speed. This, of course, has the effect of making him look quite elderly, and someone almost

always leaps to his or her feet to allow him to sit down on trains and buses – an indicator of physical frailty clearly visible to strangers.

2. Keys are a problem. If he tries to let himself in and out of the house, he can't put the key in the slot and turn it. He also has problems with the window locks. The other day, he noticed that I'd accidentally left a car window open and wanted to close it. I said, "It's an electronic window. You'll have to turn the engine on," but he couldn't do that either – and this, bear in mind, is a man who was regularly driving his own car less than a year ago.

3. Nick tires very quickly and is often sleepy. If we go, for example, to a museum or exhibition, he flags and needs to sit down for a break in less than an hour. And he nods off over his book after dinner almost every night – now, I know there are plenty of people who do this all their lives but in this case it's new.

4. He feels the cold in a way he used not to. Like his father, who died in 2014, Nick now wears thick pullovers almost all the time, sports a thick coat and woolly hat to go out and we argue about the window in the bedroom, which I want open and he doesn't.

5. He is very insecure when going down stairs. At home, he clings tightly to the banister rail and we have a grab rail at the turn of the staircase. When out, he is very slow, ponderous and careful – especially in busy railway stations where there tends to be loads of steps unnoticed by the rest of us who are untroubled by them.

6. Sense of direction has gone. If, for example, standing outside Victoria station I tell Nick we're heading north for Buckingham Place towards St James's Park, a route we've walked hundreds

of times, I see a blank look because he has no idea what I'm talking about. It's the same if I come in from somewhere and tell him where I've been. Until recently, he'd be able to meet me in pre-arranged places – unthinkable now.

7. Spatial awareness is dwindling fast too. That's partly why he can't put things away accurately in the kitchen cupboards – he can't visualise the space inside. It's also why he says with a shudder, "I wouldn't want to do that now," when, for example, I back into a tight parking space.

8. Food tastes have changed – as I described recently. He now eats, with enjoyment, lots of foods he used to dislike with passion.

9. Nick's personality is different. Thank goodness there is no aggression. Instead, we've all (sons and I) noticed a new compliance. Most of the time, this formerly stubborn man simply does what we tell him to without argument or protest. And that makes us a bit sad.

10. He can't do paperwork. A professional administrator, he was wont to have every file orderly and up to date. For years, Nick did all the administration for my business Susan Elkin Ltd, for example. He was extremely efficient. Today, he is beaten by the simplest clerical task and we've had to take it almost all away from him – although he did manage to renew the National Trust membership recently. I try to delegate simple discrete tasks to him on the grounds that it's important that he does what he can.

Memory loss? Yes. And the rest.

18 April 2018

Last week, we – Nick, Ms Alzheimer's and I – went on holiday. I hired a cottage, a converted stable attached to a multi-use farm on the outskirts of Hexham, and drove 300 miles north to get us there.

I'm nervous about holidays these days, not least because it's pretty tricky to find something which will work for our present situation. In the fairly recent past, we've driven round America, South Africa, Australia and Malaysia and loved it. We also like city breaks and rural retreats in the UK. Neither of us likes groups or organised tours of any sort.

Now, suddenly none of the things we've previously enjoyed is quite right. I was prepared, however, to try the UK self-catering break once more because I'm trying to accede to any wish Nick expresses. Loss of interest in activities and hobbies is part of the disease and it's increasingly evident, so I was delighted when he said firmly that he'd like to revisit Cragside, which has long been our favourite National Trust property. Pity, then, that it's in Northumberland and we live in south London, but I decided it was doable and booked the accommodation near Hexham.

The journey up was a nightmare. Including a very welcome two-hour break with a dear friend near Northallerton who provided lunch, respite and a bit of sanity, it took eleven hours –

traffic hold-up after hold-up. Moreover, taking Nick anywhere is exactly like taking a rather tiresome child out. He needs frequent loo stops, and lavatories in service stations are never situated for the convenience of customers. I reckon – and I've timed it – that by the time you leave the motorway, drive round a roundabout or two, get parked and traipse across the car park and through the building, it's a minimum of twenty minutes. I try not to get exasperated (and yes, since I bet you're wondering, we do keep an emergency receptacle in the car) but I frequently fail. Fortunately, the drive home a week later was free of hold-ups, much easier and quicker.

The accommodation – nicely done up with splendid views down the valley – was all on one level, but because this is hilly Northumberland it was on a quasi-terrace with steps up to the door, and the new Nick makes very heavy weather of steps. This is, I've learned, a recognised Alzheimer's symptom called 'visuospatial difficulty' on one website I consulted. It meant I had to do all the loading of cases, boxes, and so on, in and out of the car (I used to have a bit of back trouble but it seems to have gone away – a case of finding strength when you need it?) as well as leading him up and down the steps every time we went in or out.

The Cragside day was great. For a start, and I think this was my fifth visit, it was the first time either of us had been there in sunshine. We both gasped at the house and its contents in delight as usual and marvelled at the astonishing views down the slope from the windows. Then we tried to walk round the nearer grounds. The place lives up to its name and the descent to Debbon Burn, the river hundreds of feet below the house, is via rough steps formed of big flat boulders. Nick took one look and decided, wisely, that he could no longer manage those. In the end – well done, National Trust – we found a cindered path intended for wheelchairs (new, I think, since our last visit), which enabled us to get down the iron bridge across the burn. We also walked through the pinetum, which has conifers as tall as the redwoods we've seen in the US – they grow from the burn-side almost to level with the top of the house above. Yes, it really is quite a place and Nick was smiling quite cheerfully for most of the time we were there.

Often, though, on other days, he looked fed up and uninterested. And it's quite impossible to get him to think about or discuss plans for what we might do. So I say things like: "I thought, tomorrow, if you're agreeable, we might go south to the Bowes museum?" or "I think we'll go into Newcastle by train for the day. Okay?" He always agrees because, like an obedient child, he wants to please me, but I know jolly well his heart isn't in it. So we do whatever I've decided, which usually ends up as little more than quite a lot of slow trudging, although occasionally something nice happens such as my spotting a pretty vase in a Corbridge craft shop and his saying (relatively) brightly, "I could get that for your birthday." Said *anniversaire* isn't for another six weeks, but he's clearly fretting about it already, which means that the date has yet to fall off his brain's hard drive. His bank card was produced and I have the vase.

Then there's the tiredness. By early afternoon, whatever we do – and it isn't often a lot more than having coffee, a stroll and eating lunch – he's flagging. Back at base, my routine was to settle down in the late afternoon to do a couple of hours' work. Try as I might, I hadn't succeeded in clearing the decks completely before the holiday and I had five features to write while we were away. In times gone by, Nick would have objected to that and grumbled at me. Now, I think he's quite grateful because if I'm busy writing, I'm not making any demands on him. I'd work at the dining table on my tablet with keyboard while he settled on the sofa with *The Times* on the other side of the room. Within minutes, he'd be fast asleep and Ms A would be leering at me gleefully over his shoulder.

It was a pleasant break and generally I'm glad we went, although I was relieved to get him home safely because it's feels like a lot of responsibility to shoulder on my own. He was glad to be home too – and managed to redeem a bit of self-esteem by unloading the car single-handedly because it's all on the flat and I can back right up to the front door.

So what next? Is there anything else Nick would especially like to do? He has mentioned Vienna and a concert in the Musikverein. He has also talked about going back to Washington DC and staying in Georgetown, which we both liked. I'm not at all sure about either, although I suppose I could book assistance at airports and on flights. Or we could just stay at home. But I worry that if he spends too much time there, he will lose even more interest even faster. Decisions, decisions.

25 April 2018

Barn dancing as Alzheimer's therapy? Well, why not? It's probably a marginally better bet than some of the fragile straws you are led to clutch when you live with Ms Alzheimer's.

Last weekend, we went to a ceilidh/barn dance in a village hall in Romney Marsh in Kent. Run by the two-year-old Romney Marsh Morris side (yes, it's okay, thanks, I know all the jokes about buggery and morris dancing), it was a charity event to support the child of one of their number, and others like him, suffering from a rare and life-threatening disease.

Because our parents were heavily involved in the 1960s folk revival, my sister and I grew up steeped in this sort of thing. And our father, Ken Hillyer, led a fine and very respected ceilidh band, The Southerners, for decades. Later in life, when rheumatism made three hours with his fiddle under his chin a bit difficult, he successfully reinvented himself as a barn dance caller for hire.

My sister has now returned to her roots and recently taken up fiddling for Romney Marsh Morris (as well as playing classical music with me in other contexts). When she invited us to the barn dance, I was very curious to see how Nick would cope with it. It isn't as though it was new to him. In the early years of our marriage, we did a great deal of square, folk, country and other vaguely traditional forms of dance – through the clubs, events and venues I'd known most of my life. And when we moved to the Midlands for a few years, we joined a group in order to meet like-minded people. It's been a while, though.

So there we were, feeling as if we were in a time warp, at this wonderfully English – amateurish but efficient – hop. How would Nick fare? I first got him on his feet to do a simple longways set dance. 'Bemused' is a polite word for how he looked but somehow we coped. Apart from anything else, it was a good example of how kind other people are. Barn dances are friendly, family-orientated events, and the man next to Nick could see the problem instantly. Every time (we did the dance eight times through) Nick had to cast away from me with the other men, our new friend steered him until I could grab him again at the other end of the set. Not once did he remember what he had to do which, objectively, I thought was interesting. A combination of short-term memory loss and diminishing spatial awareness doesn't help much in a folk dance.

He did it, though, which pleased me. Sadly, he said afterwards that he felt stupid and didn't want to spoil things for others. Of course, he hadn't spoiled anything for anybody. There were plenty of people there who hadn't got a clue and it didn't matter at all – but I didn't manage to get him up again until the very end of the evening. "Come on," I said, "you'll be okay with Circassian Circle because – you remember? – it's a couple dance and I'll be there all the time." And so it proved. I think he actually remembered the dance from years ago and even managed to feel the rhythm – more or less. At the end, he was smiling and laughing as you're meant to at the end of a cheerful dance and a rather uplifting evening.

Will we make a habit of it? I wouldn't rule it out if the opportunity arose. Nick raises his game when he's in a social space with other people and that's got to be a good thing. As for the dance itself, I think there probably is some mileage in it because it exercises the memory and encourages you to move independently.

Decades ago, my mother used to teach folk dancing to a group of adults with learning difficulties (as we'd now describe them) at Leybourne Grange near Maidstone. She was always impressed with, and moved by, what a lot they seemed to get out of it, and I suppose this is the same sort of thing. I also remember that one of the groups the parents were tied up with went regularly to Dorton House, a school for the blind, near Sevenoaks to help with an early-evening folk dance club and I often went too. Formation dancing – because that's effectively what most of it is – did wonders for the confidence of children who couldn't see where they were going. They had great fun too.

I reckon, therefore, that many Alzheimer's folk could probably benefit. Most are elderly, of course, but most of this sort of dancing requires only a rhythmic walk. No arabesques or somersaults are required. And the gentle exercise gained is a bonus.

2 May 2018

My Mad Dad, published earlier this month, is the antithesis of 'yet another Alzheimer's book'. It's raw, visceral, poignant, and I cried for so long at the end that I didn't dare go downstairs for a while in case Nick noticed. As it is, I don't think this is one I'm going to be downloading to his Kindle (normally, we share download titles), because I suspect it would tear him to shreds, and what would be the point?

When she was twenty-five, Robyn Hollingsworth went home to Pontypool, where she grew up, to help her mother with her Alzheimer's-smitten father. She stayed for eight months, at the end of which time both her parents were dead.

Yes, Robyn's parents, who were only in their sixties, suffered the much-feared fate that hovers nightmarishly over all couples living with Alzheimer's. Her mother, always very fit, active, still working and never ill, quite suddenly succumbed to cancer and died very quickly, leaving the titular 'Mad Dad' a widower.

Cue for this reader's blood to run cold. Suppose that happened to me. What would become of Nick, who is increasingly dependent on me for everything, from telling him what day of the week it is to administering his pills and reminding him to sterilise his denture? Best not go there. One day at a time and all that.

Robyn kept a searingly honest diary during those eight months. Now, ten years later, she has dug it out and *My Mad Dad* is the result. Sometimes, in the early months, she is wryly amused. She is often angry and exasperated, saying furious things to her dad that she regrets afterwards – and goodness knows, I identify with that. She is also, by implication, dealing with a few demons of her own. She hints that her London life as a fashion buyer, whose main leisure activity was heavy drinking with 'friends', was going wrong and that she wasn't all that sorry to leave it. Yet she misses the buzz and is witty about the contrast of small-town life in Wales.

Her dad – she never tells us his name – had been a talented and successful engineer who worked all over the world. Robyn was born in Dubai and her rather wonderful brother, Gareth, who's five years her senior, in Kenya. He's been a loving and adored father and a very competent man. Now he struggles to make a cup of coffee, on one occasion serving it to his wife in a large soup bowl. He also cusses aggressively much of the time (thank goodness I don't – yet? – have to deal with that). Later, he frequently forgets that Robyn has come home to stay and thinks, for example, that she's popped home from university. But it gets worse, and there's a horrifying incident in which he fails to recognise her altogether, mistakes her for a burglar and grabs the carving knife. The pain and grief of watching your lovely daddy succumb to this is almost unimaginable.

Losing your parents is a terrible experience, irrespective of your age and whatever the circumstances, for which nothing can prepare you. My parents died in 1997 and 2001. Neither had Alzheimer's. They were a crucial part of my life for half a century and they leave a gaping hole which nothing will ever fill. I still think of them every day and often chat to them, especially my mother, in my head. I agree with Robyn that it's nonsense to suggest that time heals. It doesn't. It simply gives you the space to learn to live with the loss. You grow up knowing, vaguely, that one day your parents will die and that it's part of the generational pattern of life, but I'm not sure most of us accept that fact until it's staring us in the face.

So I sympathise deeply with Robyn, who went through these horrors at quite a young age. On the other hand, because of her relative youth, she has a future – and it's a bright one. She admits it took her a long time to sort herself out, but she is now happily married (to someone she originally met in primary school – how wonderful!), and she and Andy are expecting their first child in a few weeks. She has also just published a book which has enjoyed a huge amount of publicity with big features in several national newspapers. I expect sales are good and I'm delighted for her.

It's very different for someone in my position. When you're more or less the same age (I'm younger than Nick but not by much) as the person you're caring for, there is no future. Only bleakness and decline await. You somehow have to get your head round the peculiar idea that most of your 'future' is behind you. You try to enjoy happy memories of how things used to be but, however much you work at it, that's never going to be quite as good as looking forward to things.

In short, Alzheimer's is horrendous but maybe, just maybe, marginally less so when it's a parent than a for-life spouse.

9 May 2018

I've decided – big gulp – to apply for attendance allowance for Nick. That should be 'we've decided', of course, but the constant presence of Ms Alzheimer's means that 'our' decisions these days consist mostly of my explaining what we're going to do. He then says "Okay," and half an hour later, he's forgotten the conversation. I tell myself that we've conferred, but it's not exactly collaborative.

I have downloaded and printed the form – the version you can fill in with a pen and then send off. It is, I'm horrified to note, forty-five pages long. (Good job I had a new packet of A4 paper handy – alas, poor trees.) When I look at it closely, I see that the first sixteen pages are notes. The form itself is a 'mere' twenty-nine sides.

Well, I presume people who don't have someone like me on hand get some sort of official help with filling it in. Otherwise, it would be so daunting that I can't see how most people who are ill and in need would ever manage it. There is no way that Nick – formerly very competent with pens and words – would, as he is now, be able to fill in this form, for instance.

Even the ballot paper at elections is a struggle, and you can't get a simpler form than that. In the past, we've been pretty independent (of each other) about voting, and I know we've sometimes voted differently. Last week, before we went to the polling station, we sat down at home together with the list of candidates on my computer screen and I suggested who we would both vote for.

"Okay?" I asked.

"Okay," he said. I then wrote the names on a piece of paper for him. He was a long time in the booth. Goodness knows who actually got his vote. Proof – as if I needed it – that the complex attendance allowance form is definitely down to me.

Why do we need attendance allowance? Well, of course, an additional £57 a week (the lowest level) would be useful but that's not critical. More important is that being awarded this allowance seems to be a gateway to other things. Several times recently I've been asked by organisations and individuals whether we have it. Then, when I say we don't, it shuts down the conversation.

Watch this space, then. I'm reasonably confident that I can present the information in such a way that the application will succeed and I shall brandish the power of attorney that I've had lined up for some time.

Meanwhile, some of the things I shall mention on the form are opening and closing doors and locks and descending steps. I've written about both in these blogs before but inevitably it's getting worse.

When we got home from the press night of *Present Laughter* at Chichester a couple of weeks back, it was nearly midnight and raining hard. I was a bit weary after the seventy-mile drive and in a hurry to get the house open so that Nick could get to the loo. I then locked the car remotely – or thought I did. It simply didn't occur to me that he had left the passenger door and nearside rear door wide open, and I couldn't see them from the porch because I'd parked the car next to the side wall. In the morning, the car was soaked and we were very lucky that no one had been in it. Perhaps even opportunist thieves are put off by heavy rain. It took a lot of ingenuity (hot water bottles on the seats, for example) to get the car dry. And I was so horrified that I forgot to be cross.

And as for the steps problem, bugger you, Ms A. Why did you have to turn my lovely, fit, active man into a shambling geriatric? I try not to dwell too much on how things once were because it's destructively upsetting but sometimes…

To my surprise, Nick decided to come out with me at the weekend when I set off to do the 5.4 mile, Section 11 of south east London's Green Chain Walk. I'm trying to cover the whole length during 2018. Sydenham Hill Wood (new to me) is an absolutely glorious nature reserve, but there are a lot of steps down to the former railway line and Nick was very wary. I had to help him every time and if I forgot, he'd stand helplessly and say, "Can you help me, please," and these are, I'm afraid, very well-spaced, shallow steps – the sort an able person would hardly notice.

I use the technique I perfected for my elderly infirm mother who died in 2001. I take his left hand firmly in my left hand across my body and tuck our joined hands under my right arm. That way, I'm braced to catch him if he slips. It feels hideously familiar. I never thought I'd have to do it for Nick. I always assumed we'd grow gently old together. We had to abort the walk halfway and get the bus home, by the way. It was, of course, too far for Nick and Ms A.

Now, where's my pen and that bloody form?

16 May 2018

Despite my hollow, personifying quips about the loathsome, invasive Ms Alzheimer's – and the combative language widely used in the media – dealing with illness is not a fight. It isn't something you battle against. You simply have to find ways of living with and through it.

I suppose 'journey' is a better metaphor and one lots of quite wise people use along the lines of 'Thinking of you both and your journey'. *Pilgrim's Progress* maybe? Well, there is certainly plenty of bumpy terrain along the way as well as smoother bits, although neither Nick nor I harbour any religious delusions about ultimate arrival at the Celestial City.

On Saturday, I reached Bunyan's Slough of Despond. Not for long but just for a few self-pitying minutes, I could feel its miserable muddiness churning beneath me.

For me, it was a two-show day. I had to review *Stories on a String* (jolly and charming) at Little Angel Theatre in Islington in the afternoon and *Così fan tutte* (variety, spice of life and all that) at Opera Holland Park in Kensington in the evening. As usual, I'd intended to write the first review, and on this occasion also an overdue feature, in a coffee shop and get something to eat in the gap.

The problem was that I'd planned to take Nick to the evening opera because that's very much his thing. As I'd first organised it, that would have been fine. But then – foolishly – I promised to review the children's show as well and that meant he'd have to come with me to both.

In a previous life, I would simply have asked him to meet me in Kensington at say, 6pm, for a pre-show bite. That is no longer an option, for two reasons.

First, he wouldn't be able to manage the journey. Although he can still do simple one-bus A to B journeys on his own, the thought of his arriving at a mainline station, finding his way onto the right Underground line, remembering his destination and finding the agreed rendezvous is unthinkable.

Second, his inability to do doors, keys, locks and the intruder alarm means that he is unable to secure the house in order to leave it safely. Someone else has to be there when he leaves home to make sure everything is done properly.

So, knowing that I shouldn't, I took him with me to both shows. By the end of the Little Angel piece, it was 3pm, and to say he was 'wilting' would be a gross understatement. He looked drained and exhausted. He also, as usual, needed the lavatory. I steered him into Caffè Nero in Upper Street where I know there are decent loos, although in the event, one of them was out of order. Cue for more weary hassle while I investigated, explained, told him to wait, etc. – with the kind, smiling acquiescence of one of the staff who took in the problem with one glance.

Meanwhile, I bought tea, sat down – and hit the buffers. We can't carry on like this, I thought. It was an absurd triumph of hope over experience to think he could cope with a day like this, especially after a show at Chichester the night before. I reluctantly decided I'd take him straight home – which would just about give me enough time to get back to Kensington on my own, although I wouldn't get anything to eat and the overdue copy wouldn't get written.

I shed a few tears of self-pity. Did I really sign up for this bloody nightmare? No, of course I didn't, but you have to get on with whatever life throws at you and normally I remind myself that there are many people far worse off than we are. We have each other. We've had a good life. Money is not a problem. We have two wonderfully supportive sons, and so on. But for a while in Caffè Nero, none of that worked and I felt utterly bereft and miserable.

When he eventually came back from the loo, I told him what I'd decided – and that upset him too. In the end, it was him comforting me, which isn't the usual pattern. He also declared – quite assertively compared with how he usually is these days – that he definitely didn't want me to scupper my day by my taking him home, although we both knew that would really have been his preferred option.

In the end, we both went to Kensington, trudging at a snail's pace, as usual, through the Tube stations. I wrote my stuff and he had a bit of a rest in a cool, quietish place with his Kindle while I worked. And *Così fan tutte* was delightful. He got through it all – just. I'd learned a lesson, though. That will be the last time I take him out for a long 'demanding' day. One show at a time in future, and I'll avoid two consecutive days.

Or perhaps I should work less? Not an option. Family and close friends rarely suggest it because they know, as I do, that it's working which keeps me sane. It's a sort of escape. If I couldn't get out and about to work, meet people in the real ongoing world and write about it then I really would topple headfirst into the Slough of Despond, and then where would we be? It has to be business as usual – for as long as possible.

23 May 2018

So it's Alzheimer's Awareness Week. Well, yes please, we need plenty of that.

I've also just spotted, in newspapers and on the Tube, adverts for the 'Alzheimer's Show' at Olympia next month, as if the hapless victims of Ms Alzheimer's were like Ideal Homes, yachts or fancy cars. An Alzheimer's joke? We don't get many of those. In all seriousness, there's not a lot that's 'showy' about this horrible illness, but I suppose it all helps with awareness.

Meanwhile, back at the sharp end, I find myself worrying increasingly about balance. All the advice from experts is that you should keep your Alzheimer's person doing as many normal things as possible for as long as you/he/she can – even if it means that tasks aren't done properly. Well, it makes sense, but I suspect the advice comes, in general, from people who, well meaning as they are, don't actually have to live this illness twenty-four seven.

Twenty months after moving in, I'm trying to get our 'new' garden into shape. Among other things, I bought a bottle of bug spray and a bottle of weed killer. "Here you are," I said to Nick, handing him the latter. "This is a present for you. Now you can sweep the brick paving and spray between the cracks on the driveway." He'd mentioned several times that it needed doing, and it was always his job to keep the brick paving tidy in our old house.

On Sunday afternoon, I put my old clothes on and went out to do some serious weeding. Ten minutes later, Nick was hovering nearby. This is the usual pattern these days when I start any domestic job. He stands and watches me. I can never decide whether it's because he's critical of the way I'm doing something (emptying the dishwasher, for example) which he used to do and no longer can, merely curious or suffering from some sort of anguished envy.

Anyway, there we were in the back garden. The next time I looked up from the dandelions, he was trying (and failing, fortunately) to open the weed killer spray. Opening almost anything is a problem these days. "I'll just spray those aphids on the roses," he said. "NO!" I shrieked, which led to a quite cross rejoinder: "Why do you always shout at me when I try to help?"

Well, I know I'm supposed to let him do things but that certainly isn't going to include passively allowing him to spray weed killer onto the plants I'm trying to nurture. In the end, I opened both sprays and got them working and sent him firmly round to the front with weed killer, where he made an adequate job of the tidying-up. It took him all afternoon; he was exhausted at the end of it and I later found two little piles of leaves and bits which he'd forgotten to sweep up… but never mind. I haven't bothered to try and explain that we have two sorts of pest – weeds and bugs aka flora and fauna – and they need treating differently. In the old days, of course, he would have known that as well as I do.

He still manages a bit of shopping with one of those geriatric four-wheeled trolleys. I get all the groceries delivered and just send him to choose fresh fruit and vegetables, which is genuinely useful and I feel virtuous for facilitating it. The walk – about a mile each way – is doubtless good for him too. It takes him well over two hours, but he's not exactly time-poor. He does other single-task errands too such as walking to the post office with a packet or collecting one from the sorting office – as long as I'm there to let him in when he gets back, because he can't operate keys in locks.

And he's obsessed with going to banks for statements. I've told him repeatedly that I now have everything online and he has only to ask and I will tell him or show him the balance and transactions on any of our accounts. But I suppose getting a statement for himself makes him feel independently grown up and, I frequently have to remind myself, that's very important.

It's still jolly difficult, though, to strike a loving balance between enabling that independence and getting everything done when you're very busy – as I am, coping with all this at home as well as working full time.

It's not unlike looking after a small child – the one who says brightly "Can I help?" when you're in the middle of something and you say "Yes" to humour the child but it would be much quicker to do it solo. When I change the sheets on our very large bed, for instance – a Sunday morning routine – he invariably appears and starts 'helping'. I then have to issue a continuous flow of instructions such as "Can you pull that hem straight, please" and "Now tuck it in your side." I could finish it in half the time if I were just allowed to get on with it. But there's Nick's self-esteem to manage too.

And, incidentally, I really never dreamed I'd be comparing him to a pre-school child when he's still only seventy-two.

I continue to do what I can to raise awareness of Alzheimer's – this week in particular. I think I'll give that show at Olympia a miss, though. Shows such as *A Midsummer Night's Dream* at Watermill, Newbury – booked for Nick to come with me next month – look like a lot more fun. Music and drama are probably a better way of keeping an ailing brain active than constantly thinking about your own illness.

30 May 2018

Oh, Shakespeare. You knew a thing or two about human life, didn't you? You (and Claudius) are spot-on about sorrows, single spies and battalions.

As if it isn't enough to be confronting bloody Ms Alzheimer's with her fangs and wily ways, Nick now has skin cancer. It's a non-aggressive type and, as I keep telling him, this is a pretty minor blip in the scheme of things. It's not in the least like getting, say, cancer of the bowel or lung. It's fixable – and will be dealt with very soon – although I expect it will be pretty sore and uncomfortable after surgery and we've been told he'll probably need a skin graft, so it isn't exactly something pleasant to look forward to.

One way and another, he seems to be running out of luck. If this lesion (I gather that's the technical term for the rapidly growing cherry-sized growth on the bridge of his nose) had been elsewhere on his face, the dermatology department would have been able to sort it more or less instantly. As it is, he's been referred on to Ear, Nose and Throat, which means waiting a bit longer and he's lower in spirits than I've seen him at any point since the Alzheimer's diagnosis.

So how can I cheer him up? I took him straight down to the surprisingly nice café at Lewisham Hospital and bought him a double espresso and big chocolate cookie after we'd seen the dermatologist. I think I've bought and handed out more chocolate biscuits in the last twelve months than in my entire life but, of course, that isn't really the answer. It just creates other problems. He is now beginning to say that some of his trousers no longer fit.

It is, however, becoming ever more difficult to find things which give him any pleasure. For many years, we've been frequent theatregoers because of my work. Well, for the last year or so, I haven't included him in some of the more way-out 'fringe' excursions because I'm pretty sure he wouldn't like them. He's a pretty conventional sort of chap. Besides, he no longer has the stamina for too many outings and gets very tired.

Last week, we saw (and I reviewed) *Peter Pan* at the Open Air Theatre, Regent's Park. Well, the OAT is pretty easy to get to from our new base in south London. It's a venue we're both very fond of. We saw the show when it first aired in 2014 and I was pretty sure it would be good, so I thought I was on to a winner with Nick. Not a bit of it.

'Good' is an understatement. Predicating *Peter Pan* on the fact that the lost boys would have been cannon fodder ten years later and set in a field hospital, it is theatrically astonishing and almost unbearably moving. Most of the critics writing for publications with star systems gave it five, as I would have done. Yet, Nick sat impassive next to me and I could sense that the show wasn't working for him.

Afterwards, I said, "You didn't enjoy that, did you?" to which he replied, "No, not much." Once I'd had time to digest the baldness of that and we were on the train home, I pursued it. He couldn't, however, articulate why he hadn't liked it. And the same thing has happened on the last two or three occasions he has accompanied me to the theatre.

"You don't seem to enjoy going to the theatre much anymore. What do you REALLY like doing?" I asked, in the end.

"I don't know. And that's the trouble," he replied.

So where do you go from there? In fairness, classical music concerts still seem to work. We heard a magnificent performance of Haydn's *The Creation* at Temple Church London last week, and his eyes did shine for a bit. Sort of.

He tells me, when I push, that he's worried about the squamous cell carcinoma (except that with his usual lack of scientific understanding, he doesn't know that's what it's called) and the outcomes. I've told him over and over that it will almost certainly be okay and it's very, very common. But he doesn't hear me.

Part of the problem, I think, is the newfound bluntness of the medical profession. I'm a spade-is-a-spade person and usually all for frankness, but Nick grew up in a family where people whispered behind their hands of 'growths' and 'losing it'.

When we got the Alzheimer's diagnosis, all he heard was the word 'Alzheimer's'. It was the same this time. The dermatologist simply checked the rest of his body, then measured and inspected the lesion before saying, "That is a skin cancer and it will have to be removed." Nick heard one word and has been panicking ever since.

So how do I distract him since chocolate biscuits and theatre (for different reasons) no longer work? "Let's book a holiday for late September," I said brightly. "That will be something for you to look forward to once this thing on your face has gone and you've got over it."

I got a half-grin and a bit of low-level enthusiasm, so organising that is my current project – once I've sorted arrangements for *Catus Domesticus*, the real ruler of this household.

13 June 2018

Chin up, Susan. It could be worse. Self-pity is deeply destructive. So I've been reflecting on some positive things about living with Alzheimer's. Watching Ms A nibble her way into your life and marriage is no bed of roses, but of course it isn't all bad all the time.

Here are ten pluses. Sort of.

1. I have some very supportive friends, most of whom have stood back and let me get on with it for years because I'm a pretty independent person. Now, in their different ways, and using a fabulous range of talents, they are surging forward with practical offers of help. And I'm gradually finding the humility to accept them. I feel quite spoilt and very loved.

2. I'm learning to prioritise and get things in proportion – probably for the first time ever. If Nick accidentally takes a second loaf out of the freezer which then gets wasted because we can't eat it fast enough and it's now thawed, does it really matter? Is it worth a major strop? No. A good lesson in forbearance.

3. Sometimes, Ms A makes me laugh aloud. Driving into Worthing recently, a town I don't know at all, I told Nick that

the railway line was my landmark. "Once we've crossed it, we're virtually at the venue and I'll look for somewhere to park," I said. Five minutes later, he was anxiously trying to direct me to one of Worthing's two railway stations. We were going to a concert. Why on earth did he think I wanted to go to a railway station? Smile with me.

4. I have 'met' hundreds of delightful people through writing these blogs. Some are simply kind and friendly. Many are, or have been, dealing with Alzheimer's. The empathy and the universality of the experience are heart-warming.

5. I have discovered a talent for form filling. I did the twenty-nine-page monstrosity masquerading as the Attendance Allowance form. It took me three hours. but the application was successful and we've recently been awarded the upper level. Then I did the Blue Badge one – and we've been approved. Perhaps I should set up as form-filling consultant. New sideline?

6. My driving has improved. I was always okay but now I have no one to share it with, I am more resilient and, I think, more aware of all the things you need to be aware of. I've driven 10,000 miles in the last twelve months. As with anything else, there's a lot to be said for plenty of practice – although the car is always filthy because Nick cannot take it to the lovely polishing Poles as he used to, and I never seem to have time.

7. We can still share the things – mostly classical music – that we've always enjoyed together. That means plenty of concerts, ballets, operas, and so on. Occasionally, he'll still look at me with his eyes shining in the middle of something good, and for a few moments, it's like old times.

8. I think I'm getting generally more capable, as I have to develop new skills to make up for the ones Nick is losing. I'm now a dab hand with the dishwasher, washing machine and dustbin routine, all of which he used to do. I can also lift and carry things that I didn't previously think I could. I deal with most of our admin too. I can even tell you how much our utility bills and council tax are (I won't, though, because it's very boring). Until recently, I wouldn't have had a clue. Life is one long learning curve.

9. We are closer than ever to our sons, who are astonishingly supportive. When I go off on a music course or a little break with one of my kind, generous friends, one of the 'boys' willingly downs tools (literally) and comes to take charge. They often house-sit if I take Nick on holiday too, which is a real bonus, especially for our cat, who then doesn't need to go to a cattery.

10. Nick's appetite, while still good, is less than it was. So my new project, rather than eating all the leftovers, is to cook less and adjust portion sizes. And that means I might lose some weight. Hurrah.

20 June 2018

John Steinbeck's heart-wrenching novella *Of Mice and Men* (1937) must, in recent years, have become one of the most widely read stories in English. For decades, it was a GCSE set text. I taught it to dozens of classes. That means millions of teenagers (and often their families) will have read it. There have also been some pretty impressive film and stage adaptations.

So we all remember how George and Lennie are migrant farm workers in 1930s California. Lennie has what would now carefully be called 'learning difficulties'. George, often exasperated but gruffly loving, is Lennie's self-appointed carer. The relationship is fraternal, complex and based on mutual dependence.

Well, I've thought a lot about *Of Mice and Men* lately because I often feel I'm living it (without the Californian sunshine, unfortunately). Lennie's problems – not understanding, willing to please and forever doing things he regrets because he doesn't want to upset George – are very similar to the dementia which characterises worsening Alzheimer's.

Lennie, unlike Nick, is on the one hand physically very powerful and on the other has a child-like love of stroking soft things. It is this combination that often leads him into serious trouble whereupon he often says to George, "I've done a bad thing."

Nick's strikingly similar new line is "I've done something silly" and when he says this, my heart, like the fictional George's, plummets. *OMG, now what?* I think. He's trying, like a child who knows he's in the wrong, to be open and honest with this mother figure I've reluctantly morphed into. The trouble is, he's usually so anxious about whatever it is that he can't explain what he's done.

Recent 'silly things' have included writing a cheque with an extra nought on it so that, for the first time ever, Nick's cheque bounced. Fortunately, it was only made payable to me and it's all sorted now. His banking habits are stuck in 1952 but not for much longer: I'm in the process of assuming control of his personal account. Then we shall fast forward to 2018 and it will all be online.

We had a classic 'silly thing' instance last week when I was out working. I phoned home between jobs, as is my wont, to check that Nick was okay and to have a chat. It was a warm sunny day and, before leaving the house. I'd installed the umbrella on the patio table and wound it half up – enough to give him a bit of shade if he wanted to sit at the table for a while. He's never liked strong sunlight and now – given the skin cancer on his face – I think it's sensible to be careful. The reason I hadn't wound the umbrella any further was because one of my carefully nurtured and rather beautiful hanging baskets was in the way – because we've extended the patio and I need to rethink where things go.

No prizes for guessing what happened. Yes, he tried to put the umbrella up fully and knocked down the hanging basket because he, his brain all twisted up by Ms Alzheimer's, can no longer work out that if I've done something in a particular way then there must have been a good reason for it – best, therefore, to leave it alone and not fiddle with it.

The conversation on the phone went something like this: Me: "Something silly? What's happened?" Him: "It's that pink thing outside." Me (cottoning on): "Do you mean the hanging basket? You didn't fiddle with the umbrella. did you?" Him: "It's in the middle of the table." Me: "Did you knock the hanging basket down?" Him: "I think so." Me: "Is it damaged?" Him (voice beginning to crack): "I'm not sure." Me: "Well, can't you hang it up again?" Him: "I thought of that but you know that round thing..?" Me: "You mean the hook?" And so it continued.

In the end, I took a deep breath, told myself (for the millionth time) that I have to keep things in proportion and said: "Okay. I'll look at it when I get home. And if you've damaged it badly, well, it's only a hanging basket. We'll buy another one." By then, the man at the next table in the coffee shop was giving me very sympathetic looks.

In the event, all I had to do was hang the basket up and remove a few trailing bits damaged by the whole thing falling to the ground. It's a rather worrying indication of how things are and where they're going that he couldn't work out what was needed.

At the end of *Of Mice and Men*, George has to shoot Lennie to save him from a much worse fate. I rather hope it doesn't come to that.

27 June 2018

I adapted surprisingly quickly to saying firmly, "My husband has Alzheimer's" to anyone who needs to know – and that's most people we come into contact with.

It's taken me much longer to get used to the predictable – actually quite funny in a rueful kind of way – reactions I get, particularly if Nick is not there.

To be clear and fair: everyone I've had such a conversation with has been kind and sympathetic. People are extraordinarily decent and I'm often deeply touched by just how caring almost everybody is, ranging from close friends and family to casual acquaintances and complete strangers.

It's just the way many of them go about it which makes me giggle. They mean so well and they have no idea that they are conforming to a well-worn pattern. First, they look me in the eye, squeeze my arm or hand and murmur something warm and heartfelt about how sorry they are. Then, after a pause, they say: "And I know what it's like. My granny/uncle/mother/grandfather/aunt/father (substitute as appropriate) had Alzheimer's."

"Yes, it's in every family. Just the shit life throws at you" is my stock response as I try to keep it light. But I know what's coming. My comment triggers an enthusiastic nod before the person I'm talking to launches headlong into a lengthy, often very detailed, account of just how ghastly it all was.

I then spend ten minutes or so hearing how Mum (or whoever) lived to be 102, not recognising anyone in her family for several years before she died. She became, moreover, hideously and uncharacteristically aggressive and had to go into a nursing home for her own protection and that of other people. Meanwhile, she was also doubly incontinent for ten years… and so on and on.

I must have heard dozens of these sad and appalling stories since we went public about our predicament and I started these blogs. I made that particular one up – it's a composite but you get the gist.

Well, I suppose it's beneficial for people to get such sadness off their chests even if it all happened a while ago. If, however, they think it helps me to hear about it then it doesn't. It's a bit like telling a young woman pregnant for the first time graphic scare stories about childbirth. You just don't do it (I hope). I have schooled myself simply to rise above it when someone tells me an Alzheimer's horror story. I just chuckle inwardly, look seriously at the speaker and think: *Here comes another one*. I find it funny because, obviously, not a single one of these lovely folk realises how stereotypically he or she is behaving.

The only way I can 'manage' (sounds like running a corporation) what I have to deal with is by taking every day as it comes and refusing to think (much) about the future. I'm not in denial. Of course, I know that once Ms Alzheimer's has her fangs in you, it's a downward trajectory. There will be better days and bad days, but the general trend is gradual deterioration. What good would it do me, Nick or anyone else to be getting stressed and worried because this time next year he might not be able to do some of the things he can do now – such as remain in the house alone for a few hours and prepare himself a simple meal, which is what he is doing as I draft this blog on my laptop in a coffee shop fifty miles from base?

I'm thankful too that Nick has never been a very imaginative man. I honestly don't think he can visualise what might lie ahead and nobody, thank goodness, is regaling him with their graphic Alzheimer's anecdotes. He's vaguely frightened about the future but his fairly prosaic brain – not the bit that Ms Alzheimer's is occupying – doesn't seem to be filling in the details. Naturally, he is anxious about the forthcoming surgery for the skin cancer on his face in a couple of weeks, but I don't think he dwells on the rest of it much, which can only be a good thing. The people he meets are gentle and tactful with him as well as admirably unpatronising – and I find that quite moving.

But I don't suppose anyone will stop bombarding me with the awful stories they dish up for me when Nick is absent. Good job I still have a healthy sense of humour really.

4 July 2018

Dealing with Nick's delusions is hardcore. It's yet another thing that people who haven't had close experience of it don't realise is, apparently, part of Alzheimer's.

It is both disconcerting and oddly isolating when someone you've known for over five-sixths of your life and lived with for nearly fifty years starts burbling nonsense.

I first noticed it last year on the way home from our holiday in Malaysia when, in the middle of the night, about seven hours into the twelve-hour flight, he refused to believe we were airborne. It took me a long time to convince him.

Does altitude, cabin pressure, and so on affect an Alzheimer's-polluted brain more than it impacts on the rest of us? Who knows! We're going to Washington DC in September on the grounds that Nick has said he'd like to go back there and I think, in that case, that we'd better do it while we can. I'm apprehensive about what effect the flight might have, though, and am planning to book airport and airline support in case I find myself dealing with a serious delusional problem.

But perhaps it's nothing to do with flying. A couple of weeks ago, he phoned me while I was out working to tell me, because he thought I should know straightaway, that "Someone has had a baby." He seemed to think that he had to take charge of said infant. Blimey! Dealing with something like that on the phone from a distance sent shivers through me. "No," I said, taking a silent, deep breath and speaking with the assertive clarity and simplicity I used to use for students with learning difficulties. "No one we know is having a baby. I think you're in one of your muddles. Did you nod off? Have you been dreaming?" After a lot of humming, hawing and broken-off sentences, he finally acknowledged that I was probably right.

If you or I have a dream, we surface, think *that was a bit weird* and get on with our day. It no longer seems to work like that once Ms Alzheimer's is towering over you. Nick sleeps, dreams, wakes and then can't separate the dream from real life. It's as if his fuddled brain is blurring the boundaries, although once he's fully awake, and I've talked to him, he will usually admit that he's 'being silly'. And in a way that's worse because the realisation is inclined to upset him, and goodness knows I can understand why. It must be a dreadful feeling.

At present, Nick, poor man, is desperately anxious about the forthcoming surgery to remove the now revoltingly prominent cancerous lesion on his face. He seems to be terrified both of the surgery itself – although he's been repeatedly reassured that it's a pretty straightforward minor procedure – and, understandably, of the possible outcome. 'Cancer' remains a very emotive word.

Because he's so worried, he seems to dream about it nightly, with the result that he wakes up almost every morning convinced that the surgery is happening that day. One morning last week, for example, he opened his eyes and said, "Now what?" I patiently suggested that we get dressed and have breakfast as usual. "Isn't it today I'm going to the hospital?" he asked. On the day that I'm drafting this blog, he actually got dressed very early. When I asked why, he said he had to be ready to go to the hospital. It now seems to be a daily delusion. It's like a very young child who hasn't quite sorted out time and keeps asking whether it's, say, Christmas yet, except that in this case it's driven by dread rather than eager anticipation. The surgery appointment is next week. Thank goodness this particular problem should ease then.

I expect some other dream or delusion will replace it, though. I suppose this is what people mean when they talk about patients with dementia being 'confused'. In a bygone, less euphemistic, age, they would have called it madness. *King Lear* suddenly seems very relevant.

11 July 2018

When someone can process only part of what is said, normal conversation becomes impossible. The sort of casual remarks which human beings make to each other all the time get misunderstood and/or distorted when you're involuntarily shacked up with Ms Alzheimer's.

For example, if I say, "I'll put the bins out in a bit but I need to empty the inside ones first," then a few minutes later I'm quite likely to find Nick toiling out to the front with the bins.

When I remonstrate, he'll say: "I'm sure you mentioned bins."

One day, recently, I had to take my passport to the sorting office (ridiculous but there you go) in order to collect a parcel. On my return, I removed the passport from my handbag and put it on the shelf on the upstairs landing to remind myself to put it away in its accustomed drawer when I next went downstairs.

"What's this passport doing here?" asked Nick.

"Oh, can you put it in the drawer in the dining room if you're going down?" I said, as if he were a normal person. Cue for Big Panic half an hour later when I checked and said passport was not in the drawer. I did find it in the end, but hiding things is beginning to be a problem.

I know exactly where everything is in this house. He doesn't. If he moves things, then neither of us will know where they are; we're really in a pickle. And as I keep telling him, all he has to do is to listen to instructions and not fiddle with things – but of course it's nothing like as simple as that.

Take the two big bags of bark chippings I brought home from the garden centre last week. I managed, with difficulty, to lever them both out of the car boot, rest them against the back of the car and then to drag one round to the back garden, but it was really too heavy for me. "Is there any way you could bring that second bag round?" I asked Nick, because he is still probably a little stronger than I am, a male body, etc. He tried but told me he couldn't shift it. "Okay, leave it where it is," I said. "I'll think of something." When I later went back to the front, the bag was missing. The silly twerp had, most unhelpfully, humped it back into the car boot.

We had a pretty graphic example of sequential failed understanding at Pease Pottage services on the way to Chichester this week – which ended up with me in tears of despair. I asked too much of him, thereby managing to upset us both. Well done, Susan.

The problem is that I routinely overestimate what's doable, and as the situation worsens, I suppose it will get ever harder to adjust. On this occasion, I shoved him into the Costa queue and told him to buy two bottles of water while I shot into next-door M&S to buy sandwiches. Five minutes later, Nick appeared beside me while I was paying for the sandwiches at a self-service till. "What are you doing here?" I demanded, rather too crossly. "GO INTO COSTA AND BUY TWO BOTTLES OF WATER – please."

Well, he wandered off but when I went to join him in Costa, sandwiches in hand, he had completely disappeared. A worrying five minutes later, I spotted him in the M&S queue trying to buy sandwiches.

Well, I'm afraid I don't have the patience of a saint... Furiously, I dragged him to a table, sat him down and forbade him to move while I went and bought two bottles of water. When I got back, he was anxiously examining the packets of sandwiches I'd bought because he was afraid he'd accidentally shoplifted them. That was the point at which I broke down and cried.

It is all very wearing as well as dispiriting, and I'm ashamed to admit that it's considerably easier to do jobs such as reviewing in Chichester or central London on my own. Then it's quite therapeutic to be out working like a grown-up and, at present (long may it last), he's okay at home by himself. If I take him out with me, the whole experience is, increasingly often, as stressful as it is upsetting.

I have 'coffee shop offices' all over London and quite a few in other towns and cities. I'm drafting this blog in one which is new to me – the quite nice coffee shop inside Lewisham Hospital, which has delightfully friendly, cheerful staff and they make a decent cup of tea. After a frustrating four-hour wait beyond our appointment time, Nick is – at last – upstairs in theatre having the carcinoma removed from his face. Fingers crossed that the anxiously anticipated surgery is going well.

18 July 2018

Sometimes, thing go according to plan. Good. Nick deserves a bit of luck occasionally. Hooking up with Ms Alzheimer's when he was still only seventy-one was definitely not part of his life plan, so anything which offsets the horror of that even a tiny bit is to be warmly welcomed.

Last week, a nice surgeon (who chatted to me about how much he'd enjoyed *War Horse* as soon as he sussed me) whipped Nick into an operating theatre at Lewisham Hospital and got rid of the filthy, very prominent, plum-sized purple lesion which was growing on the side of his nose. I expected him to return looking like Dick Bruna's illustration for *Miffy Goes to Hospital* and probably with 'two lovely black eyes'. I also thought he'd be pretty shaken up.

Not a bit of it. He emerged quite cheerfully with a very neat sticking plaster across his nose and as soon as we got home, he tucked into a large bowl of muesli washed down with peppermint tea. Despite the decision to go for a local anaesthetic, they insisted that he fast for six hours first and then kept us waiting for four hours when we got there, so it really was a very long time since he'd eaten.

Five days later, I removed the plaster as instructed, cleaned him up a bit and apart from a healing wound, more or less concealed by his glasses, Nick looks as good as new. It hasn't hurt at all. He hasn't needed so much as a single paracetamol. Let's hope the medics are as pleased with it as we are when he goes back for the follow-up appointment.

Then, as if that weren't enough, two days later came his seventy-third birthday. For obvious reasons, the family decided that we should celebrate and make a big fuss of him this year. It will be a long, uncertain twelve months to the next one.

The day started a bit oddly. After I'd given him my present and the cards that had arrived in the previous day or two, he rummaged about and then presented me with an envelope. It was a Golden Wedding anniversary card. Oh dear. He had clearly remembered that there was something to celebrate but couldn't quite remember what. Our Big Fifty is next March. I swallowed hard and said, "Oh, how lovely. Thank you. It isn't quite our anniversary yet but we're in our fiftieth year so it's spot-on."

He replied: "I tried to work it out but couldn't quite."

I took him to see David Haig's *Pressure* in the afternoon as a birthday treat. I'd reviewed it at Park Theatre earlier in the year and was very taken with it – so, of course, were lots of other people, which is why it has transferred to the West End. I was pretty sure Nick would like it too and I was right. Despite the time it now takes to walk him through Covent Garden – he has only one speed: trudge – he seemed to be engaged and pleased to be there. When the play was over, I bundled him into a taxi and whisked him off to Blackfriars as fast as possible for the train home.

He had some idea that our elder son, Lucas, was coming, although I'd been very vague, telling him that we were going out for curry when we got home, probably on our own, although Lucas and his wife might join us. In his now customary compliant mood, he didn't ask me why there was a hurry to get home.

In fact, I knew that sons, their warmly supportive partners and our younger two granddaughters, aged seven and three, were all at home busy festooning the house with streamers and balloons.

Nick arrived home to six people awaiting him, table laid, beer in the fridge and food pre-ordered by our younger son. All he had to do was to sit down and open his presents. It was all extremely jolly and a real pleasure to see the 'patient' being relatively with it as *pater familias* and clearly feeling cherished. And I'm really grateful for all the effort that went into that.

Let's hope Nick is still able to enjoy the planned celebrations when March 2019 finally arrives. We're all (sons, wives, GDs *et al.*) going to spend a weekend in a very big house in Kent so that we can mark the occasion all together. Other family members will join us on the Sunday. No doubt there will be balloons.

Meanwhile, an article in the *Daily Express* reports on an American study which finds that the best ways to fight Ms A are dancing, gardening and swimming. Hmm. I took him dancing earlier in the year and I have to say it was very hard work. His idea of gardening is to stand in the middle of the grass and watch me do it. And he's a non-swimmer. Next idea, please?

25 July 2018

The Alzheimer's Society logo is based on a forget-me-not, and how very apt that is. It's all too easy to shut Alzheimer's people away and forget them – so much easier than dragging them out to places, and I'm as guilty of that as anyone. And, although I often observe that this ghastly illness is much more than memory loss, forgetfulness is certainly a major symptom.

I see this increasingly in Nick's reading habits. I'm relieved he still reads a lot because neither of us has ever been a habitual TV viewer and, of course, he needs a default activity. Mostly, he reads on his Kindle. We share downloads. "What are you reading?" I ask brightly. He simply can't tell me. He doesn't seem to be able to remember a word of it. Not only can he not tell me the title or author but he can't even explain what it's about. Whether he's able to pick up the thread of a book when he returns to it, I have no idea – and frankly don't want to know because if he really can't follow a plot and is just 'reading' mechanically out of habit then that's almost too sad to bear. To think this is a man with whom I used to discuss books. What a long time ago that begins to seem.

Then there are dates and commitments. He has no idea what day of the week it is and will say, for example, "This must be school traffic," if I'm driving him to the garden centre on a

Saturday afternoon. I keep a big calendar on the kitchen notice board and cross off the days, but old habits die hard and he still likes to write things (handwriting now quite shaky) in his diary. Quite often, he notes things down on the wrong date and then gets anxious about it. I tell him over and over again that he's made a mistake and usually end up correcting it in his diary myself. Every morning, I tell him what day of the week it is and what's going on today, but it doesn't stick for long – information is now for Nick what one of the educationists I studied at college called 'plasters on the mind'.

Sometimes, I suppose forgetfulness is a mercy. What you can't remember can't upset you. I even hanker for a bit of it myself. Instead, I'm blessed (cursed?) with a razor-sharp memory. If you want to know the name of the dog who lived next door to my grandparents in 1960, I'm your woman. Ask me what I was reading on 9/11 or what grades most of my students got and I'll tell you. Journalistically, it's useful. I write most reviews and interviews without looking much at the copious notes I've made. But when it comes to reflecting on Nick and life with Ms A, it's distressing territory because the decline is so clear.

Two years ago, we were preparing to move from our big house in Sittingbourne to a much smaller one in Catford – which we eventually did at the end of September. In July that year, Nick was routinely driving up and down the M2 to see estate agents, sort out temporary accommodation for the cat and lots more. He also went more than once to Ramsgate to deliver paperwork to our solicitor. At home, he competently joined me in packing/wrapping sessions – by the time we actually left, we had filled many boxes with our most precious things ourselves because I didn't fancy the removal men doing it. Saucepans are one thing. My collection of Wedgwood is another. He was perfectly able to talk to estate agents, solicitors and the like on the phone too.

And if I went to London for work, he would routinely lock the house and come up on the train to meet me for an evening show – we'd agree a convenient meeting place. We did that hundreds of times and it never failed, until one occasion the week we moved when he couldn't find the rendezvous and at the time (probably wrongly with hindsight), I put that down mostly to stress.

Well, thank goodness we moved when we did, because he wouldn't be able to do a single one of those things now. If I take him into town as I did last week for a show at the Old Vic (a review job for me), I have to lead him by the hand so I know where he is. I also help him on and off trains and down steps.

Much of the time, he seems very vague about where we are and where we're going. "We'll go to Waterloo East because that's handy for the Old Vic," I said several times, seeing off repeated enquiries about London Bridge and Charing Cross. On the Tube – especially if he's across the carriage – I keep mouthing the name of the destination station or counting them off on my fingers for him as you would for a child.

When we came out of the Albert Hall at the end of the evening on Saturday after a Prom, he said he was very tired (too tired to walk the ten minutes to South Kensington Tube station?) and I had to get a taxi to take us back to Charing Cross. Where has my lively, energetic, healthy husband gone? Forget him not.

1 August 2018

Last week, I interviewed an exceptionally lovely theatre director. At the end of our discussion, he turned the tables and began to ask me warm, genuinely interested questions about my own life and work.

Very few interviewees do that. It's as if journalists are a special breed of automata who don't have mortgages and dogs like everyone else. And, anyway, they're usually not interested. In fact, it's quite common to spend two hours in close conversation with someone and then be completely ignored when you see him/her at an event the following week.

So it was rather uplifting to tell this nice man a few things about myself and what I do in real life. And, of course, I ended up mentioning the presence of Ms Alzheimer's in my marriage and home – it simmers near the top of my mind almost all the time, even when I'm working.

Most people, as I've said before, immediately launch into an account of someone close to them who has died horrendously of the illness. Not this charming man, who clearly had no experience of Alzheimer's at all. "Oh dear," he said. "I've heard that's a ghastly disease. What causes it? Is there a cure?"

What refreshing questions. I hadn't meant to go into details but of course I found myself trying to explain Alzheimer's, which was useful because – as every teacher knows – the best possible way of straightening something out in your own mind is communicating it to someone else.

It's easy to say that nobody knows what causes Alzheimer's. Actually, we do. Amyloid proteins in the brain clump together to form amyloid plaques. And those are very bad news. What we don't know is why this clumping business happens in some people and not in others.

I've read dozens and dozens of theories since Nick was diagnosed, many of them based on very serious, reputable scientific studies. Is it linked to diet? Or lifestyle? Or smoking? Or alcohol? Or whether or not you do mind puzzles? Is there a correlation with depression? Could it be hereditary? Is it triggered by drugs taken for a different health problem?

None of those fits Nick's profile. What about regular migraines, which he used to suffer from quite badly in his twenties and thirties? As far as I know, that possibility has not been explored, but perhaps it should be.

On and on it goes. Scientists are doing their best (although there's still too little money spent on Alzheimer's research), but we're not really much further forward. Even the drugs prescribed to hold back symptoms for a few months have been around for decades.

Then a day or two after my chat with Mr Theatre Director came a study reported at the Alzheimer's Association International Conference in Chicago which could – just possibly – be a turning point.

Throughout the US, Europe and Japan, 856 patients, all showing early signs of cognitive decline, were given fortnightly injections of BAN 2401 (no, I don't know what that is, either). Cautiously described by commentators in the know as 'encouraging', the results show that this drug improves BOTH the physical changes in the brain tissue and the symptoms of the illness. And that's a first.

Of course, even if the research is corroborated via much larger studies and the drug, or something similar to it, is eventually licensed, it will come far too late to help Nick. But I cling to hope for future generations.

Meanwhile, Nick isn't getting any better, as I say in my understated, double negative English way to all the kind people who routinely ask.

On Sunday, I wrote a birthday card, put a stamp on it and said: "Could you pop over the road and post this for me, do you think?" I do this on the grounds that it's vital to keep him involved and feeling useful, although it's a job I could do myself in about three minutes.

He disappeared upstairs for ten minutes, having apparently decided that he couldn't walk the 150 yards to the post box in his sandals and needed to put on a pair of lace-up shoes. Then he asked whether I'd be here to let him in when he got back because he struggles with locks. "Yes, I'll be here, but please do take the keys from the hook because it's feeble not even to try," I said. He trudged off.

Fifteen minutes later (he really does walk very slowly now), the doorbell rang. I found him outside failing to open the outer porch door with the car key, which was on the same ring. Heavy, heavy weather. That's life with Ms A as she tightens her grip.

8 August 2018

I don't think it would have occurred to me until recently that being diagnosed with a serious, degenerative, ultimately terminal condition would generate a load of paperwork, but believe me, it does.

Take applying for Attendance Allowance. I decided that I could and would tackle the twenty-nine-page monster by myself to which end, earlier this year, I sat down with pen and plenty of tea one Sunday afternoon and got going. Surely it couldn't be that difficult? It wasn't but it did take me three hours. Nick wanted to sign it himself, so we did everything according to the instructions (me writing as if I were him, for example) and sent it off.

A week later, to my astonishment, we were informed that we'd been awarded the higher level of allowance. It felt like winning Wimbledon. Something had gone right for a change. Hurrah. It was the principle I was most pleased about but, obviously, it also means that there's some spare money if we need anything extra – I'm beginning to think about an additional rail on the staircase, for example, and Nick quite often needs a taxi these days. I might, at some point, have to pay someone to come in and help if I'm out working too. Worryingly, only this week, he burnt out a saucepan because I left him some potatoes to cook to go with his salad – for instance.

Having got the attendance allowance, I thought we'd do the Blue Badge for parking next. One of the eligibility criteria is receipt of attendance allowance. I filled in the forms, photocopied things like the consultant's diagnosis letter, and sent it all off to Lewisham Borough Council.

I was a bit irritated that they summoned him for an assessment by a physiotherapist as if they didn't believe either me or the consultant, although she was very courteous when we got there. Having watched him on stairs, taken him for a walk round the car park and asked lots of questions, she was evidently convinced, because a week later we had a letter telling us we could collect the Blue Badge after a specific date.

I was annoyed with LBC about that too. In this borough, Blue Badges can only be collected IN PERSON (imagine the complications if someone were really badly incapacitated because of course, ironically, there's no parking anywhere near the office) at set hours on Tuesdays and Thursdays. Even if the badge is for a child, he or she has to be with you so presumably you're expected to take him or her out of school, which I think is outrageous. When we collected ours, the administrator told me firmly – it's obviously a script – that if I abused the badge then I'd be fined £1,000 if I were caught, which I thought was both insulting and rude. That information was included in the pack anyway and I'm literate.

For the record, my brother-in-law in south Kent was recently sent his Blue Badge through the post, as was a friend with a disabled child in Hertfordshire, so this is obviously LBC being unnecessarily hostile and obstructive.

Finally, I thought it was time I applied for council tax exemption for Nick, which several people had advised me to do. More forms which I got endorsed by some unknown (to us) signatory at our GP practice. Silence. I only knew that LBC had done it when I received a council tax statement on which the reduction showed.

He is now deemed a 'disregarded person', which seems unpleasantly Orwellian to me. You'd think someone could come up with a more tactful term. Or perhaps I'm being oversensitive.

It's been a lot of tedious work but it's oddly satisfying when it achieves its purpose. Of course, I wish desperately that we weren't entitled to any of these things but given the situation, it feels as if I've done the right thing, although none of it should be the post code lottery it appears to be, with so much depending on the whims and prejudices of remote decision-makers.

15 August 2018

Twice a year, a friend stays with us for a fortnight or so. Temporarily, we become a four-person (sort of) household: Nick, Resident Friend, Ms Alzheimer's and me.

RF and I were at school together (lovely leafy – back then – Sydenham High School), and Nick has known her nearly as long as I have. She likes to spend regular time in her native London because she is mostly based somewhere else – and ours has, over the years, become her London home. She's currently here for her summer residency.

It makes a big difference to me to have someone else in the house to chat to on a casual daily basis. It reminds me just how much of the ordinary companionship Ms A has leeched out of my marriage. Nick used to be my best friend. He was also my business partner. We could and would chat all the time about everything and anything. Now it's like living with a dependent child who has, maybe, low-level special needs and has to be told everything very slowly several times. I have to be careful what I tell him and how I put it. Ordinary chance remarks are off limits. There's no longer anything equal about any of it.

I dare not, for example, mention anything which is not happening today or he's liable to get confused. My own head is full of arrangements and plans for tomorrow, next week, next month, and so on, but I have to be very controlled about sharing any of it. If you can't speak spontaneously, naturally and normally then communication is strained. Suddenly the relationship morphs into something quite different.

It's also, I'm ashamed to admit, a pleasure to go to the theatre to review with someone who can walk up and down steps unaided and doesn't need to visit the loo every ten minutes. It's almost as if RF, on holiday herself, is also giving me a bit of one just by being there. And, fortunately, Nick can still cope at home on his own for a few hours provided no one makes any demands on him and I leave him something very simple and pre-prepared to eat.

The other great benefit of having RF here is that she is admirably patient with Ms A's victim. She'll gently help him fold the tablecloth after a meal, for example, even if it takes several attempts, whereas I'm inclined to snatch it out of his hand and snap: "I'll do that." She's very willingly agreed to take him to a hospital appointment this weekend too, so that I can whizz off to an all-day, escapist string orchestra workshop in Folkestone. She makes him hot drinks, helps him kindly when she can see he needs it and tries to include him in activities such as collaborative crossword solving – at which he sometimes surprises us both. RF and I know nothing about cricket but Nick produced the name 'Shane Warne' without missing a beat the other day. Alzheimer's is such an unpredictable, patchy illness.

On the other hand, I am well aware that when she arrived at the beginning of the month, she hadn't seen Nick since 1 January. Although RF and I are in touch all the time and she knows in some detail what's going on, when she gets here I'm suddenly conscious of how things have deteriorated and what changes she will notice. Seven months is a long time when Ms A has her fangs buried in you. The deterioration is relentless.

For himself, Nick sometimes forgets she's in the house. He'll put cutlery on the table for the two of us and I have to remind him that RF's upstairs and will be down for breakfast shortly. She is gloriously unfazed if she meets him wandering naked on the upstairs landing because he's forgotten a) when it's his turn for the bathroom and b) that there's anyone in the house apart from me.

When I was out reviewing at the Proms last week and, unusually, both sons were staying over because they were working locally, I was told afterwards about a high-comedy moment when Nick turned to RF and said very politely: "Would you like to stay and have dinner with us?"

If you couldn't laugh, you'd weep. A lot.

22 August 2018

When Nick was first diagnosed with Alzheimer's, one of my first questions to the consultant was "Is it hereditary?"

She assured me very firmly that it isn't. Later on that nightmarish day, it was a priority to pass that fragment of good news on to both our sons because I know that it had been worrying them.

The consultant then went on to tell me that her youngest patient is thirty-seven with a young family – which promptly put our problems into some sort of perspective. "Early onset Alzheimer's like that does tend to run in families, but age-related Alzheimer's, such as your husband has, does not," she said.

I have read this in other reputable places too. Received, informed wisdom seems to concur. It isn't genetic – although no one knows what the cause is, of course, which is why there's so much groping about for a way forward.

Then an odd thing happened. At the end of last year, we were asked to take part in some research being conducted by Cardiff University. Two researchers came to our home and interviewed us at length, and in detail, in separate rooms.

When the pleasant young woman who wanted to come phoned me to make an appointment, she told me that twenty-nine genes associated with Alzheimer's had been identified. What? Did I hear that right? Bit of a volte-face surely?

Before they came, I did a bit of family research in anticipation of some of the questions I thought (rightly) we'd be asked.

Neither of Nick's parents, who died of physical illnesses at age eighty-two and eighty-nine, showed any sign of dementia. His paternal grandmother, however, died in a nursing home in her early seventies, having completely 'lost it'. I checked the death certificate. Putting two and two together from the vague terminology often used back in 1970, I've concluded that hers was almost certainly vascular dementia, which is a different illness. And none of Nick's cousins, all around the same age as him, have Alzheimer's.

Then there was Nick's mother's younger brother who died in 2010. In that case, we know it was definitely vascular dementia following strokes and other incidents.

In short, I found no familial links whatever with 'ordinary' Alzheimer's, although it's hard to research back far because a) people died younger b) death certificates were a lot less reliable by modern standards and c) family folklore often gets it wrong.

So I decided to stop worrying about genetic links. After all, even if they exist, I can't do anything about it. And I'm not convinced they're there anyway in Nick's case. I don't understand the science of genetics other than at the most basic level, but I suspect twenty-nine genes is probably a miniscule part of the human genome.

But, this month, I've had cause to think again. The Alzheimer's Disease Sequencing Project (ADSP) at Boston University School of Medicine has just announced the results of an investigation which worked with 6,000 Alzheimer's patients and 5,000 'cognitively healthy' (nice turn of phrase) people and found various genetic risk factors which predispose people to Alzheimer's.

Cue for a lot of muted excitement from all sorts of people and organisations about the possibility of some form of therapy linked to this which could eventually make a difference. The word 'breakthrough' was cautiously bandied about.

What we need – and need pretty desperately, given the ageing population – is something that will work on the root cause or prevent the disease altogether. At present, we only have medication which might (and often it doesn't) alleviate symptoms in the very short term. And those drugs have been around for quite a while. No real progress has been made for a long time.

None of it will help us. We just have to keep buggering on as Churchill advised, taking each day as it comes, with Nick able to do ever fewer things competently and my getting ever more frustrated.

Irrationally, it's the trivia which get me crossest. I sent him to the pharmacy to collect his medication this week. They wouldn't give it to him, presumably, because he told them some garbled rubbish. So I shall have to go myself. He keeps getting out his holiday wash bag, putting additional items in it and then telling me he's run out of deodorant or aftershave and – having used tablecloths all my life – I think I'm going to have to give them up because they now cause so much aggravation. And so it goes on. And on. Polish up your sense of humour, Susan, smile and keep telling the boys that It Is Definitely Not Hereditary.

29 August 2018

If the brain is the conductor of the orchestral body (sorry – I've probably reviewed too many Proms lately) then of course it controls/directs/manages every section of it. So once Alzheimer's gets into the works, then any body function can diminish or fail in consequence – even eyes.

Nick has been slightly short-sighted for most of his adult life and like almost everyone else has needed glasses for long sight since age forty-five or so. For some while now, he has, like me, opted for varifocals and worn them all the time, simply because it's easier than constantly taking them on and off and then tediously hunting for them. He's had his current pair for about a year.

Recently, he has complained several times that he can no longer see the 'small' (i.e., normal) print in the newspaper. "Okay, that, unlike many of your problems, ought to be fixable," said I, reaching for the phone to book him an eye test. And in the interim I dug out the fancy illuminated magnifying glass that Father-in-Law used to use, to make life a bit easier between now and new glasses

Golly, what a tiresome business it was at the optician's. We were there for two and a quarter hours and I take this opportunity publicly to thank the very kind staff at Boots Opticians, Beckenham who treated him with cheerful, unpatronising patience throughout. And of course a queue of late-running appointments was building up behind us but no one grumbled. People can be heart-warmingly considerate sometimes.

The test itself with the optometrist took twice as long as it should because of his indecisiveness and forgetfulness. He then 'failed' the field vision test twice and they had difficulty getting him to sit naturally and look in the right direction so that the technicians could get the measurements right for the new glasses. It throws him ever more and he gets increasingly flustered if people keep asking him questions or issuing instructions, however gently. He tries hard to co-operate, obviously, but I could see him floundering and, thank goodness, so could the staff. The highlight of the otherwise tedious morning, though, was when Nick suddenly caught my eye and grinned naturally at the absurdity of it all. The technician saw it too and we all laughed.

The upshot of that long session is that we collect new glasses this week and repeat the field vision test – "when he's fresh" – at the same time. And we have to go back next month for the dilation test with eye drops. They ran out of time to do this latter procedure last week, besides which I think they could see that he wasn't going to be able to cope with much more.

Within hours of this lengthy episode at the optician's, I read about a new study in Washington, reported in *JAMA Opthalmology*. Researchers using a non-invasive technique, somewhat unsnappily called optical coherence tomography angiography (do they call it OCTA for short?), have collected some evidence which suggests that there are detectable changes in the eyes of pre-clinical Alzheimer's patients.

There is, in these people, significant thinning in the centre of the retina, many years before memory loss and cognitive decline begins to show. Or as one scientist working on the study put it,

'*Changes in brain cells can be detected in the retina.*' I rest my case: there IS a link between Alzheimer's and eyes just as with every other organ and function in the body.

Well, if this test had been available twenty years ago, it wouldn't have helped us much to know that once Nick was a septuagenarian, Alzheimer's would set in fast. But think about it. In time, it could make a difference to others now much younger than us.

At present, there is no way of warding off Alzheimer's other than by making sensible lifestyle choices – and that's by no means reliable. It's not like lung cancer or type 2 diabetes, which can be (but are not always) directly associated with smoking and diet. The only available Alzheimer's drugs just alleviate worsening symptoms in the very short term. The disease is incurable.

If, however, very early-detection technology can be developed, then maybe – just maybe – drug therapies that can zap or control the disease before it takes hold could follow. And that's a glimmer of hope for future generations.

Meanwhile, I strongly suspect that Nick's worsening sight problems are Alzheimer's-related. Fortunately, he can just go on having ever-stronger glasses if he needs them, and if I think very hard and apply myself, I might remember how to enlarge the font on his elderly Kindle.

5 September 2018

Sixteen months on from diagnosis and Ms Alzheimer's is unstoppably tightening her grip. Or to put that another way, I can almost see those sinister, devastating, toxic amyloid clumps in Nick's brain growing bigger and more numerous every day.

He has forgotten how to operate the microwave. All my attempts to re-teach a very simple procedure have failed, so I have now given up. He can't turn on either level of our double oven either. It confuses him that there are two. He can't work out which switches control which and is thrown by the fact that there are two switches (on/off/mode and temperature) for each.

One evening a few weeks ago, I went out about 5pm and left the oven on for him. "Just put this pie in when you're ready and give it about twenty-five minutes," I said. When I spoke to him before my show started a couple of hours later, he reported that: "The pie wasn't very nice. Cold in the middle." I suppose he didn't time it properly or put it in the wrong oven. So that's another strategy which clearly doesn't work.

Until recently, he could warm, say, a casserole through in a saucepan on the hob. Then, a couple of weeks ago, I left some potatoes, all prepped and in water in the pan, for him to cook and eat with a cold meal. When I got home, the saucepan was a burned-out, charred object – although I did, eventually, manage to save it with a lot of bicarbonate of soda and elbow grease. Fortunately, he had noticed and turned off the hob. It was cold when I found it. If he hadn't done that? Oh dear. At that point, I decided against leaving him anything which requires heating or cooking.

So choices are now pretty limited when I am out working in the evening. Fortunately, he's always liked salad (barring tomatoes and cucumber). Just as well because he now has to eat a lot of it, and I'm rapidly morphing into Catford's most creative salad maker so that he doesn't have to eat the same thing two days running.

I arrange it prettily on a plate, cover it with cling film and put it in the fridge. We've both been vegetarian since the late 1970s so I have to find non-meat/fish protein to add to it. I'm a dab hand with all sorts of lettuce, shoots, peppers, chicory, cress, carrot fruit, nuts, marinated fried tofu or Quorn, hard-boiled eggs, pulses, cubes of cheese, herbs, seeds, and so on and on. Infinite variety, like Cleopatra.

At present, it works – with instructions to eat it with bread and butter, which he still seems to know how to assemble.

One of the questions professional assessors (nurses, occupational therapists *et al.*) routinely ask is about ability to prepare food independently. The answer to that would now have to be: "Not really."

Part of the problem is that we're both rather inflexibly locked into a lifelong habit of eating our main meal in the evening, although I have started sometimes giving him an eggs-on-toast type hot snack at lunchtime so that he doesn't feel he lives on an exclusive diet of cold food. Actually, come to think of it, he probably wouldn't notice, but I'd feel I was selling him short. And of course when I get an evening at home, I cook nice hot things for us.

The bottom line is that the time is coming – and it's coming frighteningly fast – when I shan't be able to go out and leave him alone in the evenings at all. And I really find the prospect of not being able to work very alarming indeed – it's my mainstay. It's real life. It's what keeps me sane and (reasonably!) sensible.

I phone Nick a lot while I'm out. I also write a schedule for each day telling him what I'm doing, what he's doing, what's happening, where I shall be and what sort of time I expect to be home. I have to print it in large letters as you would for a child. It usually keeps him calm, although there was one occasion recently when he rang me in a panic to tell me that there was a lot of traffic in our street (accident on parallel main road, although he hadn't worked that out) and he was worried about me. My car was on our drive. I'd gone out by train. Heaven knows what jumbled thoughts were alarming him.

If, Ms Alzheimer's, you were a real person rather than a metaphorical construct of my imagination, I'd tear your bloody eyes out.

12 September 2018

Last Saturday, our younger son, Felix, married his lovely, tolerant, kind, long-term partner, Liz, at Lewes Register Office (a very pretty venue). In effect, the weekend was one long joyous party, continuously redolent with more glowing happiness than I can possibly describe here.

Of course, Ms Alzheimer's, who tagged along with Nick and me, was the least welcome guest, but she's not, unfortunately, a presence you can simply strike off the list of invitees.

I drove us both (or should that be the three of us?) to nearby Alfriston on Friday where we stayed overnight in a hotel with my sister and brother-in-law. Logistics were complicated and I tried to tell Nick only what he needed to know from hour to hour. I feared that otherwise he'd get very confused. And I was right. He kept asking me on Friday whether lots of people were coming (including when we stopped – just the two of us) for a pub lunch in Burwash. He ricocheted all day between thinking we were going somewhere to celebrate our Golden Wedding Anniversary (coming up next spring) and it being a birthday party for our son, who was actually born in March but, thanks to Ms A, calendar awareness is slipping away rapidly.

For the first time ever, I had to supervise his packing closely, ensuring that he had the right shirt, cufflinks, tie, decent socks, etc., as well as the suit, which I carefully laid on the back seat of the car. Unfortunately, I missed the fact that there was no razor in his washbag so he had to make do (grumpily) with my little plastic one. Packing a male razor has never, until now, been on my radar – but I'm learning.

On Saturday morning, he found he'd forgotten how to tie a tie. Absurdly (considering I did it every day at school for seven years), so had I. Later, my very efficient nephew tied the most perfect Windsor knot for Nick and made him look suitably respectable.

The arrangement was that I would leave Nick in my sister's charge early Saturday morning while I drove my car into Brighton so that it would be in the right place at the end of the day. I then met Nick and co at the register office, having trained it into Lewes with other family members after brunch in Brighton.

It all worked out but I have to say that Nick looked bemused and puzzled for most of the day. He was okay during the really rather lovely ceremony (poem read by Rosie, aged eight, and her bridegroom dad – tears all round) but of course for the rest of the day there were a lot of people all thoughtfully trying to talk to him but actually fazing him even more. Great, of course – and a sort of break for me, incidentally – to have every single member of the immediate family on hand to watch out for him.

I'd been asked by the best man (whom I've known for forty years since he and Felix were in nursery school together) to make a mother-of-the-groom speech. There wasn't, of course, a person in the room who didn't know why they were getting me rather than the bridegroom's father. I quipped – I'm fairly used to addressing crowds one way and another – that it was a blow for feminism. In fact, it wasn't that at all.

A sit-down meal, chosen/collected from the cooking area isn't ideal for Nick either. He is shaky on his feet, clumsy and no good at squeezing through tight spaces. So I told him to sit still while I fetched him some food. Another problem is dizzy spells, which are, apparently, a recognised Alzheimer's symptom in some sufferers. It's just one more example of Alzheimer's being much, much more than memory loss, and that's rarely understood by people who haven't lived with it. In Nick's case, it means he really can't stand about – which is exactly what you do at weddings often for quite lengthy stretches of time. Wherever we go, I seem to be continually looking for places he can sit down, and the wedding was no exception, although being in the presence of so many understanding people helped.

He has never liked loud music and the evening's entertainment was a live seven-piece soul band for dancing – and very good they were too. Predictably, Nick found the volume stressful and he spent quite a while sitting outside with our other son, who fielded his dad with unobtrusive care. Hurrah for a brilliant family.

We were booked on the earlier hired bus back to Brighton with the two youngest grandchildren and our elder son and daughter-in-law. By then – 10pm – I'm not sure who was more tired and disorientated: Nick or Libby, aged three, who'd had a wonderful day wowing people as a very engaging bridesmaid to her mum.

On Sunday, and since then, Nick was/has been able to remember and talk quite coherently about the wedding and some of the people who were there. And he seemed relatively focused on Sunday when the new Mr and Mrs E returned to their home, which was still full of unwinding overnighters, and we handed back the children. I doubt that it will be long, though, before it all falls off his brain's hard drive.

Ms Alzheimer's is a ruthless companion. She makes no exceptions for weddings, however special and memorable they are for everyone else.

19 September 2018

This Friday (21 September) is World Alzheimer's Day. September is, in fact, World Alzheimer's Month, with this one day as the focus. Driven in the UK by the Alzheimer's Society and other charities, the idea is that everyone – organisations and individuals around the world – work together to '*raise awareness, highlight issues faced by people affected by dementia and demonstrate how we can overcome them to help people live well with dementia*'. That last bit is a quote from the Alzheimer's Society website.

It is, of course, exactly what I aim to do with these blogs. Every week, more and more people tell me that they find them enlightening and helpful. Sometimes, I'm even told that I've 'moved' someone, which is humbling. And the feedback often comes from complete strangers. The other day, I was in John Lewis in Ashford, Kent, applying for one of their rather good credit cards. Of course, I was asked what I do for a living and after a bit I mentioned these blogs. "I bet that's helping many other people," said the warm, tactful woman who was processing my application.

As a journalist, I get sent information about 'awareness' days of one sort or another all the time. There's one almost every day of the year, arguably far too many to be effective. It's different for Alzheimer's, though. Globally, dementia is one of the biggest challenges we face, with nearly fifty million people living with dementia worldwide, and we are told all the time that there are 850,000 people in the UK with dementia, 650,000 of them with Alzheimer's. Of course, Nick never planned or wanted to be a statistic but there it is.

So if you get the chance this week to attend a fundraising event or to contribute to an Alzheimer's charity, then I urge you to do it. Or maybe you might think about a little monthly direct debit, which is what I've done. As the Alzheimer's Society puts it: '*To tackle this global dementia challenge we need to work together, and to collaborate and share best practice with one another*'. But, of course, like everything else, it costs money.

I've been thinking about Christmas cards too (sorry, yes, I know it's only September, but I'm an organised sort). For many years, I've bought and sent cards in aid of Kidney Care UK and the Donkey Sanctuary. The former was in memory of my father, who died of kidney disease in 1997 and the latter because I like, really like, donkeys. This year, under the circumstances, I've decided it has to be something different, and I've ordered cards from the Alzheimer's Society, which declares that one hundred per cent of their profits are spent on their work. Every little helps, as a certain supermarket likes to remind us.

Meanwhile, back on the home front, I seem to find myself increasingly fielding semi-verbal non-sequiturs. "I can't find the thing with the spout," Nick said recently.

"Do you mean the teapot? If so, it's in the dishwasher. Why do you want it?" said I.

"No [fumbling for words], I meant a green thing." I eventually ascertained that he was looking for the small watering can for the hanging baskets. If you live with Alzheimer's, you need to be psychic – especially when, as often happens – the question and answer bear no relation to each other.

You need to maintain a sense of humour too. A couple of weeks ago, we had a problem with the controls on heating, hot water, radiators, etc. I emailed our younger son, Felix (the family pro plumber who'd set it all up), asked for advice and went off to the theatre for work. I hadn't expected our heroic offspring to drive up from Brighton and be on the doorstep by 7.15 – but he'd forgotten the keys he has to our house so he rang the bell.

Now, living with Alzheimer's is, in many ways, like caring for a child again. I have 'forbidden' Nick as forcefully as I can from opening the front door to anyone he doesn't know when I'm not in the house. He's supposed to peep through the porch door to see who it is. On this occasion, he partially remembered what he'd been told and didn't open either door. Result? A frustrated but ultimately amused son, who had to phone me and then call his dad up on the landline to say he was outside. But when I came out of the theatre, there was a very welcome text from Felix telling me laconically: '*Heating fixed*'.

Yes, we need to keep raising awareness of, and funding research into, this hideous illness. Do what you can this week.

26 September 2018

Readers of these blogs, who don't know me in person, often kindly tell me what a patient, kind, loving person I am. Well, I suppose I've created an online persona – if only I could live up to it. The stark truth is that most of the time I'm a brusque, crosspatch sort of individual. And I don't, on the whole, 'do' slowly and never have done. I was absent when sweetness was given out – racing about trying to get some job done, I expect. Former pupils, with retrospective affection, have often said that I scared them silly. I never meant to but…

When I was a child, tiresome grown-ups would intone preachily at me: "Patience is a virtue which can be acquired." (It was the 1950s, not the 1850s, by the way.) Well, they were all wrong – about me anyway – because I've never acquired it. And that's one of the main reasons that I find Ms Alzheimer's such a very difficult presence. As Nick gets slower and less comprehending, I get crosser and more impatient – as if we were the painted couple on the weather forecast ornament my grandparents had: always moving in opposite directions. Then, of course, I feel terrible and beat myself up for my own shortcomings. He can't help the state he's in, and I know that, so I ought to be able to control my irritation.

An impatient person like me, for example, is driven spare by Nick's habit (and it's only come with the illness) of constantly interfering with things. I load the dishwasher and set it running only to find that he's opened the door half an hour later and interrupted the programme because he wasn't sure 'what was going on'. He's constantly fiddling with the day's newspapers, too often throwing into the (wrong, invariably) bin the bits he doesn't want to read before I've had a chance to look at them. Worst of all is his 'hiding' things. He thinks he's put away, say, the outdoor short-handled brush (currently missing), the tin opener or (twice in the last few months) a quite large and important cheque. He then can't remember where he put it and I of course have no idea, so the item is effectively lost. I can buy a new brush or tin opener, but getting a cheque re-issued is a tedious business.

Then there's his inability to hold information even for a few seconds. "What can I do to help?" he'll ask.

"Can you empty the airing cupboard? Just take everything upstairs, put in on our bed and I'll sort it from there," I answer. Ten minutes later, I find him scrabbling about in a food cupboard.

"You wanted me to do something in a cupboard…?" Grrr.

Standing at our local station awaiting a Blackfriars train en route to a concert at Cadogan Hall last week, we narrowly missed a through train to Luton while I was, as usual, laboriously helping him down the steps on the footbridge. I said chattily, "It's okay, that train's going all the way to Luton. Our train will be here in five minutes." A few moments later, I asked him: "Do you remember where we're going?" Pause for a long think.

Then, brightly: "Are we going to Luton?" Oh, for a bit of that saintly patience that has eluded me all my life.

By the time you read this, Nick and I will be enjoying (or something) a ten-day holiday in Georgetown, Washington DC while our elder son, Lucas (now he really IS saintly – not sure where he got it from), moves in to look after house, cat and supervise the repainting of our kitchen and dining room. I have misgivings but Nick has long wanted to revisit Georgetown. *Carpe diem*. Time is not on our side. I'll report on how it all works out next time. Perhaps the rest (if that's what it turns out to be) will help me to be a bit calmer and less cross.

3 October 2018

As Ms Alzheimer's slowly but ruthlessly tightens her stranglehold, it's unfathomably difficult to recognise and accept the truth about where you're heading. And holidays are a particularly challenging time because, sadly and stressfully, they force you to confront that reality. It's partly, I think, because if I'm not racing about working manically, I have time to think and reflect. It's also because it's impossible not to compare the current holiday with earlier remembered ones.

Not so many years ago, Nick could drive a powerful hire car on confusing (to me, at any rate) eight-lane motorways in the US. Today, he cannot descend a flight of steps unaided. In the recent past, he would have booked flights, accommodation, ordered currency and arranged insurance. He doesn't have a clue about any of that now and all the admin falls to me. Until two years or so ago, on holiday, we'd spend whole days out and about seeing or doing several things each day. The new Nick can sometimes manage an hour or two before he flags, but not always.

We've just spent eight nights on holiday in Washington DC. By the time this is posted, we shall be home, although I'm writing it on our last day in the US. Why Washington? Well, we both had fond memories of visiting Georgetown on a trip a few years ago when we then picked up a hire car and headed south to Baltimore, Maryland and Virginia, and Nick had said several times he'd like to revisit. So I fixed it. I had misgivings, of course, but I carefully ignored them.

I booked special assistance at the airports and it worked very well. Of course, he doesn't normally need a wheelchair but unsteadiness and inability to stand in, for example, queues for more than a minute or two meant that it was really useful. It also meant I had a helper to look after him while I dealt with hand luggage paperwork, overcoats, etc. – I only have two hands and two arms, after all.

Once airborne, there was continual confusion about where we were going and why. Halfway across the Atlantic on the outward journey, he thought we were heading for Heathrow, for example. I must have reminded him a dozen times that we were going to Washington. I think cabin pressure or altitude (or something) must worsen the effects of Alzheimer's. I noticed this twice last year when we flew to and from Malaysia and Greece.

Making decent use of the time while away is another problem because I have to deal with his often feeling unwell and not wanting to do anything. It's easy to delude oneself that this is apathy or lethargy, but it's really just the illness. Fortunately, I'd booked one of those American 'suites' which gives you a sitting/kitchen area attached to the bedroom, so 'staying in' was reasonably comfortable. And sometimes I left him resting and went out on my own – bliss to be able to walk at my own natural speed and be temporarily 'free', although I'm ashamed of the thought.

We did, however, manage to take in Arlington Cemetery, the Smithsonian Museum of American History, Dumbarton Oaks and Oak Hill Cemetery as well as exploring Georgetown pretty thoroughly. We also walked through the White House and Lincoln Memorial area and on the last day went to Newseum, a powerful and moving history of news/journalism which seemed to have my name firmly on it. At each of these, though, time had to be limited, and I had to make sure that Nick could sit down as often as possible. The jury is out, though, on whether we really got value for money overall in terms of sightseeing.

I was hoping I'd get a rest and I suppose I did to an extent. It's not very relaxing, though, to have to be alert for problems all the time and to assume full responsibility for another person. It often reminds me of having a small child again (I even have to oversee choice of clothes, collect his buffet breakfast and open the butter packets, etc., for him), especially during the night. I've learned to snap awake instantly if I hear him stumbling about doing anything other than just going to and from the bathroom. He has very powerful dreams these days and often gets very confused. It means I have to be able to reassure him calmly, irrespective of how deeply asleep I might have been. As a young parent, I did this and more, of course, but it was... well, never mind how long ago, but I was a little shorter in the tooth then.

The problem with holidays is that they are, by definition, a break with routine, and that's not good for someone with Alzheimer's, so I'm left wondering what, if anything, to do about holidays in the future. Maybe a cottage somewhere not too far away that I can drive to and then recreate home routines within it while we get a change of scenery? In all honesty, I think Washington was almost certainly our last long-haul holiday. Pity really, I love travelling far afield, especially in the US, and I'd dearly like to see my friend in Australia again. Trouble is that Ms A has her fangs buried in her husband too, so it looks as if neither of us can travel.

The chances are, therefore, that I shan't get to see the orangutans in Indonesia or the Taj Mahal after all. Not that I can possibly complain. We've travelled a lot in the last fifteen years or so and I'm lucky enough to have seen wild bears in Canada, rhinos in

S Africa, alligators in Louisiana and, marvellously, a platypus in Tasmania. There have been many other wonders too, both natural and man-made, from the Petronas Towers to Table Mountain and Sydney Opera House to the Grand Canyon.

It's just a struggle to accept that the best is probably behind you.

10 October 2018

We seem to be morphing into a box-ticking case study. Whenever an Alzheimer's patient is 'assessed' (like being back in the classroom), he or she and/or the carer is always asked about dressing, undressing and eating. Until recently, the answer to such questions has always been, "Fine. No problems."

But things are changing. '*Was the hope drunk wherein you dressed yourself?*' I often find myself thinking, although Lady Macbeth's context was different. I don't want Nick to commit regicide, but it would be good if he could find and put on his socks.

For the first time ever, I packed his case as well as mine for our recent trip to the US. I knew there was no chance whatever of his working out what he needed, finding it and putting it in a suitcase. So I put socks, pants, shirts, trousers, night things and his washbag into his trusty black suitcase, along with the vests, to which my now cold-blooded man has become inseparably attached irrespective of the temperature. I told him that it's meant to be warm and sunny in late September in Washington DC (and it was) but he wasn't having it. He has travelled the world with that case. Mine is brown and we keep his things and mine separate-ish, although sometimes it gets a bit fluid on the return journey when it's just a question of getting everything in somewhere.

On the first morning in Washington, I emerged from the bathroom to find him naked, in a flap and rummaging in my case. "I think I've come away without any pants and socks," he said anxiously.

"Nonsense, I packed them myself," I said, getting them out of his case and passing them to him. An incident like that makes me go chilly with horror – yet one more thing he can't do. I can almost see his brain fogging up. For the rest of the time we were away, I mostly had to supervise his choice of clothes and dressing.

And I have, come to think of it, been helping, with pullovers and coats for some time. Child-like, he can't seem to get his arms lined up with the sleeves. Sometimes, moreover, I find myself offering advice about appropriateness too. "There's a reception before this show. You might be more comfortable in a jacket" or "That pullover looks really tatty. Why don't you wear this nicer, newer one instead?"

Back home, since our September 2016 house move, all his clothes have lived in the big fitted wardrobe we had put into the next-door bedroom, which he uses as a quasi-dressing room. These days, I often find him, puzzled, opening the doors of the wardrobes in the smaller bedroom we sleep in, where my clothes live, because, thanks to Ms Alzheimer's, he can't remember where his own are.

Then there's eating. By his own admission – so it clearly worries him – he now struggles to use cutlery to get food to his mouth. Well, we comfortably abandoned rigid traditional British table manners in favour of common sense and convenience decades ago – all that silly business about eating everything with a knife and fork and never turning the latter that we grew up with, for example. If we're eating, say, curry, casserole or risotto, we lay a spoon and fork. If it's roast potatoes and some cut-able vegetarian nut thing or if we're having something like omelettes, we use knives and forks as our parents would have done. Sometimes (for instance, for a pasta dish with a side salad), we lay both. There's nothing remotely 'tricky' or formal about eating in our house, so it's a bit tragic to see Nick struggling. The food seems to fall off the spoon or fork and he gets bitterly frustrated. I think it must be a co-ordination problem that prevents him loading spoon or fork securely and then keeping it horizontal. I've offered to cut his food up and suggested that he stick to a spoon perhaps with a shallow dish rather than a flat plate, but he's, understandably, not keen on being served up food as if he were a toddler. One more nail in the coffin of normality.

Did you ever read Martin Amis's 1991 novel *Time's Arrow*? It is mainly a holocaust story, but the central conceit is that the main character is whizzing through his life in reverse so that eventually he gets reabsorbed into the womb. Well, of course, this is real life and that's not going to happen to Nick, but I can certainly see him moving inexorably back towards what Shakespeare called 'second childishness'. Our youngest granddaughter, Libby, approaching her fourth birthday, is now probably better – and improving all the time – at dressing and eating. Any day now, they'll shoot past each other like vehicles heading in opposite directions on a long road.

17 October 2018

Most people are understanding. I've written before about the kind consideration that Nick – Ms Alzheimer's glowering menacingly over his shoulder – routinely gets from total strangers, but it's so very striking that I make no apology for returning to the subject.

Seats are readily vacated on buses and trains and there's a lot of courteous standing back as soon as they spot that Nick is shaky on his pins – which, just to make sure, I routinely signal to all and sundry by saying clearly, "Mind this step" or "Hold on to me," which is as much for those around us as for Nick himself.

On one occasion, the other day, the Tube train was very crowded. I managed to lever Nick into a priority seat but stood, 'strap hanging' (as we used to call it), near the door myself. Inevitably, lots more people got on and stood between him and me, so I started to worry about how I was going to get him off when we reached our station. In the event, I managed to weave an arm through the bodies. Nick got the message and reached towards me. Then the crowd miraculously parted, like a mini-parting of the Red Sea, so that I could haul him out. All done in typically British silence, of course – apart from my saying thank you – but so thoughtful and decent. I suppose it's the same mentality as pulling over for an ambulance.

On our recent trip to the US, we explored Arlington Cemetery (both interesting and powerfully poignant) via a hop-on hop-off bus tour of the site. Nick is no longer proficient at hopping and had to take the three steps on and off the bus very carefully – usually with me standing at the bottom to proffer a steadying hand. When we reached the place where they do the changing of the guard at the tomb of the unknown soldier (the only bit of the whole holiday Nick now remembers with clarity, by the way), there was a big brawny twenty-something in front of us. He was covered in tattoos and wearing a baseball cap, which in another life might have made me leap to unreasonable stereotypical conclusions. In fact, he bounded down the steps before turning to support Nick with exquisite courtesy. I was almost as moved by that as by the changing of the guard which, for the record, I thought was a rather repetitive 3* piece of theatre. Good to see 'vets' in wheelchairs brought from all over the US by charities to witness it, though.

I am also impressed by the cheerful kindness of the people who provide 'special assistance' at airports. The pleasant, chatty, caring young woman who was awaiting us with a wheelchair at the aircraft door in Washington took us all the way through immigration, baggage reclaim, customs, on an airport 'train' and right out to a taxi outside. By then – maybe forty-five minutes in her company – I'd heard her entire life story (grandmother in California with Alzheimer's) and felt really welcome in her country. Yes, I know that's her job, but she clearly takes real pride in it and she earned every cent of the $5 I tipped her. The service is kind enough at Heathrow, too, but less efficient and with a lot more hanging about because, I gather, it's 'outsourced'.

Needing the loo frequently and urgently is an ongoing problem. In one coffee shop, recently, there were two unisex lavatories but one was out of order. I got the code number for the door from the counter and told Nick about six times what it was, but he still came back to me inarticulate with panic. So I went round to said door and punched the number in myself. Of course, it was occupied and there was, anyway, a woman waiting. "Well, it's a queue," I said. "You'll have to stand behind this lady and wait."

She spotted the problem instantly: "No, no, you go first," she said warmly. What a star. The vast majority of people are fabulous. I rest my case.

At our local Next this week, where Costa is on the first floor, we decided to go up for coffee or, in my case, tea. Well, I expect there's a lift but I really do believe I have to keep Nick moving for as long as possible. When we'd finished our drinks, we set off slowly down the steps with me, as usual, walking two steps in front, holding his free hand firmly. We were watched by the fascinated security guard at the foot of the staircase by the main door. "I wish I had a wife as kind as you," he said, going on to inform us that his wife had left him and taken most of his money. Life with Ms Alzheimer's certainly triggers some strange conversations.

When I was at school, we didn't have assembly. The whole-school morning gathering was unequivocally called 'Prayers'. And once we were there, our deeply Christian headmistress regularly addressed her Almighty in these simple supplicatory words: "Help us to be kind." Well, I have no truck with her God but by golly she was right with that thought. Kindness is probably the most important factor in human behaviour. If we are kind to each other, we can cope with almost anything.

24 October 2018

Much missed in my new hard-to-adjust-to, Alzheimer's-polluted marriage, are companionable walks.

We used to walk miles together. In the early 1990s, we did, in sections, both the North Downs Way (Medway to Dover) and the Stour Valley Walk (Ashford to Sandwich), and I wrote about them for *Kent Life*. Later, even after Nick fell off a ladder and smashed his foot in 2002 and could no longer manage a full 12-mile day, we had a whole battery of favourite Kent five/six-mile walks which we did, with great pleasure, over and over again.

When we moved 'home' to south London in 2016, I had lots of plans for our doing the Green Chain Walk and the Thames River Path in bits, along with casually and routinely walking a couple of miles to nearby places rather than taking the car or bus. Alas, Ms Alzheimer's moved in and none of that has happened.

Nick now walks very slowly indeed, dragging his feet in a sort of weary trudge. I reckon his new natural walking speed is about half the speed of mine which, of course, makes walking together impossible other than functionally – across a car park or through a station, for example. He gets awfully tired very quickly and shows no interest whatever in walking for pleasure. A grind to the (very near) railway station, to the doctor's (maybe half a mile) or from our son's house in Brighton to the Dome for a concert is one thing. Choosing to do it for no practical purpose is another.

When I walk with him over short distances, I usually hang on to him for his safety and so that (as you would with a child) I know where he is. It often reminds me of taking a very reluctant dog for a walk, because I'm constantly tugging while he resists because, however hard I try to adjust, his speed is slower and as soon as I stop thinking about it consciously, I accelerate automatically. Hard work for the puller and, I presume, a bit irritating for the pulled.

The advice from all the medics, websites and people in the know (except that no one really 'knows' this hideous and horrible disease) is that the sufferer should keep physically active. Well, in a sense he does because he will walk short distances to places he needs to get to if there's no alternative. If only I could persuade him to join me round the park occasionally. Alas, a combination of physical and mental blocks seems to get in the way. I'm never sure where or when 'can't' turns into 'won't'.

It's oddly divisive because, for myself, I try – and have done so for decades – to walk as much and as briskly as I can, usually by building it into daily life. If I have to go, for instance, to Little Angel Theatre, I generally go to St Pancras and walk down Pentonville Road rather than going direct to Angel Tube. If I'm heading for Covent Garden or the West End, I try to build in enough time to walk from Blackfriars Station rather than taking the District and Circle line – and so on and on. I also go out for walks from home whenever time permits, even if it's only forty minutes round nearby streets. And, yes, I have done several sections of the Green Chain on my own and discovered places and roads not far away from home but new to me. I'm afraid, moreover, that I'm also one of those irritating (smug?) people who chooses stairs rather than lifts or escalators if it's only a flight or two. These days, I sometimes put Nick in the lift and then pop up the stairs myself. I'm usually there first.

Time was when Nick would have done all this and more with me – willingly and naturally because it was what we did. Now, I wander (or stride more likely) lonely as a cloud.

I've been sorting out some clothes and other textiles for refugees in Syria because my daughter-in-law, Liz, is organising a collection. I think I might as well put Nick's walking boots on the pile. He isn't going to wear them again and some poor – but younger and fitter – soul might be glad of them. It's emotionally quite a hard thing to do, though. Another door clanging shut.

31 October 2018

Money, money, money... managing it gets ever more difficult when you have destructive, unhelpful Ms Alzheimer's as your new partner.

Like most people, we don't use much cash these days. But last week, by chance, we had to collect the cat from the cattery, pay the window cleaner and the garden odd-job man, who dug out a couple of small, ugly mini conifers – all within twenty-four hours. And they all expect cash.

On the day in question, I was rushed off my feet trying to meet deadlines with two features, get the ironing done, take in a supermarket delivery and loads of other things before setting off to do a late-afternoon magazine interview in north London. So when Nick said, "I could walk round to the cash machine and get what we need," I agreed to it.

Of course, that was a very stupid decision and I'm now jolly cross with myself. I really ought to know better by now, but he sounded sort of grown up when he offered. I had misgivings because I'm aware how frail he looks, and although it was broad daylight, south London is not exactly free of lawlessness. I was therefore pleased to see him home safely half an hour later.

Then he gave me the receipt and the money. He was £80 short.

I don't know what happened. There was some confusion about having to take it out in two lots. Perhaps he left it there. Returning to the machine – as you'd expect – was fruitless, and the crosser I got, the less coherent he became. Then, while I felt ever more remorseful, he spent most of the remainder of the afternoon sitting on the sofa gazing miserably into the distance. "I don't feel very well," he said, when I pressed him.

Well, infuriating as this is, the loss of £80 is not going to sink the ship, but I've learned an important lesson: Nick can no longer be 'trusted' with money, and I need to treat him as if he's a child of, say, seven. That's what Ms A does to people – saps away their adult status.

We have a personal account each and two joint accounts. I have been operating his personal account through power of attorney for several months and have now 'confiscated' (still a teacher at heart) all his other cards.

"I'll need that purple one, though, won't I?" he said in confusion.

"Yes," I replied. "You can keep your bus pass. It's MONEY I'm concerned about." Cue for vacant, blank look.

Then I went to a bank and withdrew the rest of the cash we needed to pay our dues. When I got home, I gave him £15 so that if we go into a coffee shop together and he wants to feel gallant, he can pay. Pocket money – literally. I'll replenish it when it's gone.

It's so difficult to safeguard the last vestiges of self-worth in all this. Nick is an adult, until recently perfectly able to manage money, and being treated like a child must be awful, although the worst complaint I ever get is: "Oh, you're so bossy."

And what on earth do I do about Christmas, now on the horizon? Since we first stopped being 'just friends' and became a 'proper item' in 1967, we have bought each other nice Christmas presents every year. There's nothing either of us needs, of course, but it's an enjoyable tradition. Of course, I have a present planned for him. But he won't be able to reciprocate and he'll fret – especially on Christmas day and Boxing Day when others are exchanging presents.

I expect I shall end up choosing and buying a present for myself using his personal account. I shall then hand it to him to give back to me (maybe wrapped after a fashion if Ms A lets up for an hour or two at some point) on Christmas morning. Seems absolutely daft. But it will allow him to feel like a proper participant – and that matters very much.

7 November 2018

I've been thinking a lot lately about my paternal grandparents, William and Dorothy Hillyer. She, universally known as Dolly and to me as Grandma, has been particularly in my thoughts because I've just realised I've morphed into her. History repeating itself, generational patterns and all that.

I was very close to Grandma, who lived on to her ninety-second year, by which time her cherished little granddaughter was over forty. We lived with them when I was very small because my war-generation parents had nowhere to live after my father was demobbed from the RAF. Grandma looked after me (and her cantankerous old mother-in-law) as well as shopping, cooking and cleaning for the entire household of seven. No wonder she always nodded off when we 'listened' to *Mrs Dale's Diary* after lunch. Meanwhile, my parents went out to work to try and amass enough money to get us a place of our own. When they eventually did, it was 200 yards up the road, so I saw my grandparents almost every day for the rest of my childhood and adolescence. The result of all this was that Grandma and I always had a special bond – helped, I suppose, by my being the first grandchild.

Scroll forward twenty years and she's around the same age that I am now – dealing with major illness in her beloved spouse just as I am today. In their case, it was throat cancer which finally killed my poor grandfather, aged seventy-three (Nick's current age), in 1969, a few months after we were married. She coped magnificently with his illness, finding solutions to the hideous problems the disease threw at them. For a long time before he died, he had a naso/pharangeal tube to bypass his tracheotomy so that he could 'eat'. She made nourishing soups from the home-grown vegetables in the garden and poured them cheerfully into him via the funnel. She was convinced that the good nourishment was helping him and, with hindsight, I suspect her care really did keep him going for a bit longer than might otherwise have been the case. She visited him in hospital daily when he was local and wrote him nice letters (a few of which I still have because he kept them and his papers eventually came to me) when he was in the Royal Marsden but home at weekends.

I just hope that I'm doing even a tenth as well as she did. My grandparents swore they'd never rowed in their forty-eight-year marriage, and I certainly never heard either of them utter a cross word – not even the mildest expression of irritation. I'm not remotely like her in that. I get really cross when I've said the same thing four (or six or ten) times and Nick still hasn't retained it. Then I get loud and snappy and say lots of things I regret very soon afterwards. I get ratty when he doesn't feel well enough to do what I think he should do too. Grandma would tell me off roundly if she were around to hear it. I often have her voice in my head saying, "Don't talk like that, dear" or quoting one of her aphorisms, often biblical or *Book of Common Prayer*. "In sickness and in health, dear," she would probably say to me now.

I think I've got some of her practicality, though. Suddenly, after sleeping on a single pillow for fifty years, Nick has started sleeping propped up like a Victorian gent and says that he'd like a second pillow. So I 'borrowed' one temporarily from the spare bed and have now been out and bought a couple of additional ones. I've taken to writing down for him very clearly where I'm going and when I'll be back when I have to go out too. I've sorted out his glasses and insist that he puts them in a particular place to try and minimise the number of times they get 'lost'. And, like Grandma, I do my utmost to provide really healthy, nutritious food because that's one of the few things that's actually within my control.

I am, of course, better educated than she was. Grandma left a Dorset village school aged fourteen, although she was a whizz at word puzzles and she could add a column of figures faster than I've ever been able to. She was blessed with a lack of imagination too, but it meant that she failed to face the inevitability of where she and my grandfather were headed. That denial meant that she fell apart totally when he died, although she picked up again in time and went back to work in my uncle's business for a further fifteen years. She didn't 'do' retirement any more than I do. I am, however, much more of a spade-is-a-spade realist, and more knowledgeable about illness than she was. And I have Google. Perhaps it helps, bleak as the information is.

Meanwhile, I look at myself and see Grandma every day. Some of Nick's peripheral health problems now create an awful lot of washing. I seem to put big loads out daily. The neighbours probably think I'm taking it in as a sideline. Bit sad really because Nick used to be family laundry monitor. I remember fondly how good he was at ironing and how we used to joke about it. Now he sits and watches me ironing his shirts.

But Grandma would have loved it. Washing was her passion in life. To her dying day, when I rang once or twice a week for my regular chat with her, she'd say almost before she'd said hello: "It's a lovely day. Have you got your washing out, dear?" or "What shocking weather! What have you done about your washing, dear?" When she stayed with us, as she often did, she'd be trotting into the garden every five minutes to feel the clothes on the line. Then there'd be much folding – without my ever asking her to do it – ready for ironing. I do all that and more now and smile as I remember her.

If she were alive (she'd have been 122 this month!), we could compare notes about sick husbands.

14 November 2018

Vivid dreams – effectively nightmares – seem to be one of Ms Alzheimer's less welcome bestowals. And I hope the people who think this dreadful disease is just memory loss and cognitive decline are listening.

Whenever Nick falls asleep, he disappears into a weird alternative world. And he sleeps a lot: most of the night and increasingly often for a couple of hours in the morning, afternoon or sometimes both. He's perpetually tired and now often also complains of feeling dizzy or says he has 'the shakes'. When he surfaces, he's lost to me, sometimes for several hours, and the last ten days or so have shown a sharp decline.

Take the night last week when I drove to Canterbury to review Glyndebourne's touring production of *La Traviata*. Nick should have been with me but decided on the day (like the Duke of Edinburgh, except that HRH is ninety-seven, not seventy-three) that he didn't feel up to it. I rang him on the hands-free as I left the Canterbury car park after the show. "I've had a terrible evening," he said agitatedly and in considerable distress. "People are coming and I'm really worried. I've phoned the NHS mental health people and they'll be here soon to take me away." I knew immediately he'd been dreaming and that he couldn't possibly have phoned anyone

– he's no longer capable of looking up a number and dialling it independently. So I went into teacher/professional mode and simply kept him talking, reassuring him until he seemed calmer. It took to the Medway Bridge to achieve that, by which time I was only forty minutes from home.

Since that night, I've been repeatedly told that a crime has been committed and that we shall both end up in prison and that he can hear voices in the house and that he has to get to the bank for George (referring to his father, who died four years ago).

Sometimes, it can be quite funny. When I pressed him about the aforementioned crime at a less confused time when he'd been awake for a while and wasn't quite so distant and distrait, he told me it was bigamy. "Gosh! How exciting," I said. "Perhaps we should write a novel because it's all fiction. Neither of us is a bigamist. Trust me!"

One morning, also last week, he woke up very puzzled – he often thinks we're in a hotel or holiday let and that he can hear other guests. I said firmly, "No. There's nothing to worry about. Nobody lives here except you, me and a big tabby and white cat."

Pause while he processed the information and then: "Well, it would have been frowned upon even thirty years ago."

My turn to be bemused: "What would?"

Him: "Living together like this."

Well, that did make me laugh. I held up my left hand and said as cheerfully as I could: "Darling, we've been MARRIED for nearly FIFTY YEARS. Wedding rings and all that. We're having a family celebration in the spring."

It was his reaction that chilled me. "Oh really?" he said, clearly surprised and unconvinced.

It's both hilarious and utterly tragic because in his more lucid moments (and even that is relative), he knows that sometimes (often) he talks nonsense. "I have a different narrative running in my head for much of the time," he said recently and, on another occasion, "It's as if I'm two people, isn't it?" Yes, dead right it is, but I'm seeing the 'normal' one less and less often. My least favourite thing is when he wakes me in the small hours stumbling round the bedroom in a panic because he can't remember where the bathroom is, or anxious and alarmed by something in his alternative world that he can't explain to me, so I have to talk him back to calmness. A couple of nights ago, I was out of bed with him half a dozen times between midnight and 3.30am – it reminds me of having a fractious baby again, but I was twenty-four and twenty-eight when I dealt with that. I knew it would only be for a few weeks. It's not quite like that now.

So, we have to do things differently from here on. I shall obviously have to rethink some of my work habits. I am frequently out all day and all evening and that's too long to leave a man with worsening dementia alone in the house. It was all right for a while but it isn't now.

I am also looking into what is euphemistically called 'help'. I need to hire a very reliable person who will 'man-sit' while I'm out in the evenings. Various avenues to explore. I certainly don't want the standard 'carer' who drops in for ten minutes, mutters some hearty platitudes and races off to the next client.

Sometimes, I dream too – of how things once were – as an escape from the nightmarish reality. The other day, I was just walking out of the door and realised I hadn't made sure Nick was wearing one of the just-in-case pads I prefer him to wear when I'm out. "Have you got a pad on?" I asked.

"I think so," he said uncertainly. Hmm. Without thinking, I undid his fly to check. It felt vaguely familiar. What did it remind me of? Oh yes (blushing, but not much), I remember... a very long time ago (or so it seems)... and in a completely different life...

Who was it who said that a young man needs a lover and an old man a nurse? Been there. Done that. All of it. From romantic frisson to incontinence pads.

21 November 2018

It's now nineteen months since the official arrival of Ms Alzheimers's in our household, although of course, with hindsight, I now realise she'd been hovering at the gate for quite a while before Diagnosis Day. And I marvel at what a lot I've learned – the practical stuff, the theory, the trivial and the serious and, above all, there's the acquisition of new and often quite surprising self-knowledge.

And I've been more aware of all this than ever in the last three weeks, during which Ms A has suddenly tightened her grip and we've seen marked deterioration. At the time of writing, it's nine days since Nick has left the house.

I have, for example, learned that:

1. I can talk about death in a calm, matter-of-fact way, which I would never until now have imagined that I could. Of course, I've thought quite a lot in the last year or two about widowhood and how I might/will cope with it. Several times recently, Nick has raised the subject of his own death, so I know that he is beginning to think about the inevitable too. Gently, but truthfully, I have astonished myself with how straightforwardly we can talk about it when he raises the subject. No tears. Just honesty.

2. I have morphed into the kind of person who can march into Sainsburys (where, I've discovered, they're twenty-five per cent cheaper than in Boots), pick up three huge packets of incontinence pants and saunter out via the checkout with them without batting an eyelid.

3. Yes, I can survive and still work reasonably efficiently in the daytime even if I'm woken and have to get out of bed to help Nick half a dozen times during the night. I seem to be adjusting to getting my sleep – up to seven or eight hours maybe – in one-hour bursts. Moreover, I can now go back to sleep instantly (just like I did when I had babies), which I haven't been able to do for a very long time.

4. I (we) have some fabulous friends and an amazing family all ready to drop everything and do everything they possibly can to help me when I need it. They astonish me continually. I've said this several times before but it can't actually, in my view, be said too often.

5. If you're catering for someone who needs as much fibre as you can cram in then you can make variations on an Elkin-beans-on-toast theme. Nick doesn't actually like Heinz beans but he does like hummus. I've discovered that you can mash any sort of tinned bean with any sort of nut butter seasoned with a few herbs and a dash of, say, balsamic vinegar or soy sauce and pile it onto toast. Infinite variety. Borlotti beans with almond butter, anyone?

6. I now know how to turn the TV on. I'm with Cilla Black on this one. Remember when her beloved husband Bobby died and she couldn't get the news on because he'd always 'driven' the TV set? Everyone derided her but it was the same with us.

We've never been in the habit of much TV and I didn't operate it often enough to remember. Well, it took several texts to and from long-suffering sons, but I have now got the hang of it. I'm trying to persuade Nick to watch gardening and antiques programmes which won't disturb or distress him because he no longer reads much and I need entertainment for him which won't fuel his Alzheimer's-driven, frightened imaginings about crime and violence.

7. I'm much more patient than I often give myself credit for. I find I can usually repeat the same thing several times without getting cross. I do all this crawling out in the night, usually without grumbling. I generally manage not to rush him – although he's painfully slow at everything he does now. I probably blow about one time in twenty. Not bad really?

8. A trivial (but tiresome) health problem of my own worsens if I allow myself to get angry or stressed. I have only recently worked out the connection. It's a good reason for taking a deep breath and smiling rather than flipping my lid.

9. I can now write features, reviews and articles despite being repeatedly interrupted and called away. I used to be quite precious about needing, say, two hours entirely to myself to get a piece of work finished. These days, Nick appears frequently: hovering in my office looking troubled, anxious or vacant. "Can you help me, please?" or "Is it nearly time for 'them' [usually an imaginary visitation] to arrive?" or "I just wondered what you were doing." So I have to stop, deal with him and recover my train of thought ten minutes later. And it's okay. Usually I can.

10. It really doesn't matter if he forgets I'm his wife and thinks I'm a carer. I know exactly who I am and who he is so that will

do for both of us. I just chuckle at him when he says things like, "Do you help many people like me?" because I know – at present anyway – that I shall probably get him back at some point later. Today, for example, he pointed to the pendant I'm wearing and beamed. "I bought you that, didn't I?" It was only a few weeks back too, in a jeweller's in Chichester, so that was a good moment.

Stop learning, stop living?

28 November 2018

Finding, hiring and working with carers is a whole new ball game and one which – until recently – I never imagined I'd ever have to play. Nick and I were supposed to grow old together – the sort of couple people marvel at because they're still striding about busily in their nineties, indestructible on their vegetarian diet. Alas, fate and Ms Alzheimer's have decided otherwise. And I can, it seems, now add 'carer management' to my growing CV.

Most people in our position just want a bit of respite care so that the retired carer-partner can pop out for an escapist lunch with friends. Me, I've always been a stereotype defier. What I need is a man-sitting service while I go out to work, and that means a wide range of erratic hours, including a lot of evenings, especially in the busy run-up to Christmas. Nick was more or less okay left at home by himself in the warm with food put ready until this last month, during which his health has, I'm afraid, plummeted quite dramatically.

He is now very uneasy if he's on his own for long. Cue for panic calls to me, which I can't answer, of course, if I'm in the theatre, so he often starts anxiously phoning round the family to tell them he doesn't know where I am or 'what's going on'. I ring him all the time but it's an increasingly stressful situation. Time for carers. Definitely.

I found a website that operates like Checkatrade or Right Trader – but for carers. I was irritated that they really wanted me to pay a thumping annual membership in order to get information but signed up for the basic – free – service. Having explained what I need, I got over thirty responses over the course of a week or two. Well, we live in inner London's deep south east, and carers who live in Enfield, Kingston or Erith were clearly never going to be able to provide the service I need, whatever they said. So using location as the lead criterion, I picked two very local ones and invited them to come (separately) to meet us. They're very different types but I liked them both, and Nick – while not fully grasping what I was trying to do – seemed fairly relaxed about it.

In the last week, both have been here and done shifts for me. I was determined from the outset that I didn't want the sort of standard carer 'package' which involves someone from an agency who would dash in for ten minutes, make sure Nick was alive and shove a sandwich at him. I've seen too much of that with friends, relations and neighbours. I wanted people who would spend substantial blocks of quality time with Nick, and that's what I've got. He needs time and calm reassurance.

I've also met and 'hired' an impressively competent student from a local drama school who, for family reasons, is very used to looking after people. I've always argued that drama-trained people are some of the most capable you could meet, and she is a case in point. She's going to bring *Carry On* films to watch with Nick – the two of them were chuckling about it even before she left. One of the others wants to know where I keep our board games so that she can play them with the patient. Hurrah. I would no more think of sitting down and playing a board (bored) game with him than running naked along the South Circular, but I bet he'll enjoy a round or two of Sorry or Scrabble.

That gives me a list of three carers to call on, and I'm actively searching for a couple more so that I can get cover for any sort of work commitment. All quite encouraging.

On the three occasions so far that I've had one of them in, all seems to have been well. "She has a very full and interesting life," Nick told me later about one of them, so he'd clearly listened and retained some of what had been said – which is a nice change from him telling me continually for eight hours on Sunday that he was frightened of the water and was afraid he wouldn't see me again. He'd been dreaming and thought, unshakeably, that he was a refugee on an escape boat starting at 4am.

Having carers in, though, is not for the financially faint-hearted. I've worked hard all my life and am not short of money. We also have Attendance Allowance because of Nick's illness. Nonetheless, if I have to pay a minimum of £9/10, and sometimes it's double that, per hour every time I go out, it's soon going to clock up to hundreds of pounds every week just for the 'privilege' of working. And I don't think most of my editors would wear my charging the care fee as expenses either. They would simply – as would I in their position – get an unencumbered reviewer instead of me.

In short, I'm in the position that many mothers find themselves when they return to work after maternity leave. The cost of childcare – or carers – is so high that the work ceases to be economic. The point is, that like many a newish mother, for me, working is about a great deal more than money. It is actually what is going to stop me going completely dotty, and that's really rather important under the circumstances.

Terra nova.

5 December 2018

It seems that Ms Alzheimer's was a bit lonely in our house. So she's brought a few friends along to jolly us all up. Or to put it another way, Nick doesn't, apparently, have plain old Alzheimer's disease. It's more complex than that.

For some time, I've been puzzled by the range of symptoms he now has. Things like shuffling gait, dizziness, tremor, unsteadiness on stairs and bladder and bowel problems are not standard Alzheimer's fare in most cases. Well, of course, I'm a journalist and a compulsive researcher so naturally I went in search of information. It's what I'm programmed to do.

I concluded that he might – just might – have a different form of dementia such as Dementia with Lewy Bodies (DLB) which affects 100,000 people in the UK as opposed to 650,000 with Alzheimer's. I agonised long and hard about what to do with the information because, if I'm right, then maybe a different sort of medication might ease some of the symptoms. A bit. For a while. Perhaps. On the other hand, who am I to challenge an NHS diagnosis?

In the end, encouraged by our sons, who said that if I didn't do it I might always regret it, I cut through all the red tape and emailed our consultant as tactfully and politely as I know how. Of course, you're not supposed to do that. You're meant to go through your GP into whose care we were discharged last year. But Dr V, the consultant, for whom I have enormous respect, treats me like a fellow professional and – I think it was in connection with these blogs and the circulation of information – gave me her email address.

Within two hours of my hitting 'send', I had her secretary on the phone to make us an appointment. See why I like and respect Dr V so much? Said appointment took place last week.

We were there for a long time and she said several times that she, like everyone who knows Nick, can see a marked deterioration. We discussed the symptoms at length. Her opinion is that he probably has 'mixed dementia'. That means that instead of confining himself to Alzheimer's, he also has the symptoms of other dementia-related conditions such as vascular dementia, Parkinson's dementia and DLB. We don't do things by halves in this family, do we?

This is, by the way, simply her informed opinion. Medics can't be absolutely sure about different sorts of dementia until they can do a post-mortem – which might eventually be of interest to medical science but doesn't help us much in the here and now.

Meanwhile, is there anything at all that can be done about the worsening symptoms, some of which are becoming really very difficult? Well, it's clutching at straws but we have to consider anything which might improve quality of life, however marginally. At Dr V's suggestion, we are going to see a neurologist who may want more scans and tests and who may then prescribe Parkinson's medication to ease some of the motor problems.

All of that, obviously, is hedged about with ifs, buts and maybes. And naturally we have to go through the clumsy juggernaut NHS system, which means Dr V writes to the GP who contacts the neurologist whose department then sends an appointment (almost certainly at a time when we're away or I'm working) via snail mail. I will never understand why you can't phone and book an appointment with the person you need to see as you would the vet, hairdresser or dentist. It probably means it will be well into the new year before we get anywhere but we'll see.

[Note: that appointment didn't arrive for eight months, by which time it was irrelevant.]

And while all this is happening – life's rich tapestry – cognitive decline continues at helter-skelter speed. In the last week, I've variously been told we're on a refugee boat, that we're firefighters and that, mysteriously, I must deal with the benchmarks. One of the carers tried to play Scrabble with him and found that he couldn't do it at all – which didn't surprise me because I've noticed that his writing and spelling is rapidly going AWOL. I've suggested she try Sorry! next time, but I'm not holding my breath that he'll be able to manage that either. He's reading much less, too, as retention goes.

By the time you read this, I shall be away for a four-day residential music course learning to play (or something) the Schubert *Quintet in C Major*. Our elder son – what a hero! – is on man-sitting duties during my absence, so it will be a respite for me, which I'm beginning to feel I need pretty urgently. Apart from anything else, it will be the height of luxury to be able to rest all night undisturbed. And I don't feel remotely guilty about that because I am, after all, returning to the helm at the end of the week. And I love that Schubert!

19 December 2018

Anyone remember John Christopher's 1964 novel *The Possessors*? Not actually one of Christopher's best novels, but it scared the pants off me when I first read it, and I've thought a lot about it recently.

In short: An avalanche cuts off an Alpine hotel-chalet from the outside world. Unbeknown to the trapped families, who are quite comfortably riding out their temporary incarceration, the avalanche also releases some form of malevolent extra-terrestrial life which has lain dormant, waiting there for a very long time. It needs a dead human body to inhabit in order to work its evil. When a child dies (can't remember how), the parents grieve, obviously, and the body has to be put out in the snow. Then, of course, the child appears to come back to life, so the parents accept him in wonderment – but it isn't really their child. It's a predatory invader which has borrowed and now possesses the child's body, and from the inside of the chalet, he/it can admit others.

It was, I don't mind admitting, a very long time before I could open the back door in the dark without thinking about all this. I'm not good at horror and not even very keen on sci-fi, but we were, at the time, promoting John Christopher in a school I was teaching in during the late 1970s so I felt obliged to read it.

Alzheimer's is, I'm coming to realise, also a form of real-life possession. The fastidious, orderly, funny, intelligent, feisty man I married back in 1969 has gone – dead to me, in effect. In a sense, I am already widowed. Yet, his leaky, trembling body is still very much present, and the person who inhabits it often feels like a stranger. It is exactly as if that body were possessed by someone or something, and I suppose that's what I mean by the Ms Alzheimer's personification. The man who has forgotten geography, how to tell the time, elementary hygiene, how to make a cup of coffee, what month we're in, needs help to get down steps and much more is someone I barely recognise at all and yet I live with, and look after, him twenty-four seven.

Of course – and that's where the analogy with the John Christopher novel ends – there's nothing wilfully malevolent about this. It's an illness, it's random and it's part of nature. And, thank goodness, Nick has become meek (not an adjective anyone would ever have applied to him for most of his life) and compliant rather than awkward or, worse, aggressive. He just messes things up – table laying, laundry sorting, etc. – all the time because he can't retain what I've asked him to do even for five minutes. In practice, I 'allow' him to do less and less around the house because – probably a fault in me but I can't help it – it's easier for me to do everything myself in the first place than to let him get involved, which means I have to sort it out afterwards. And he gets desperately, and increasingly, confused and anxious if his lifeline – that's me – is out of sight for long.

The idea of 'possession' has been around a long time. They've found trepanned skulls in prehistoric sites all over the world probably because ancient healers thought they could release whatever was causing the problem via a drilled hole. In the *New Testament*, we read of the Jesus figure curing a man '*possessed by devils*' by directing said demons into a hapless nearby herd (collective noun for pigs?) of Gaderene swine. All a load of superstitious nonsense, of course, but when you live with someone whose personality is unravelling daily, as if there is a take-over in his brain, you can understand how such stories evolved.

And if you are sharing your life with a 'possessed' person, you have to keep adjusting, and that's one of the hardest things. I frequently forget briefly and try to speak to the real person I married in the normal way. Typically, he hasn't got a clue what I'm talking about if I chatter away about, for example, someone I met while I was out or something funny I saw. His concentration span is very short and I really need to keep communication very terse and tight and not attempt to burden him with things he doesn't need to know.

Whatever this situation is, it's certainly no longer the marriage of true minds.

28 December 2018

Well, Christmas Eve didn't start too well. At 4.30am, Nick was stumbling round the bedroom mumbling something about East Germany and the need to escape. I took him to the bathroom and got him back to bed. By 7am, when I next surfaced, he was fully dressed with his bag over his shoulder, something I didn't think he could still manage without help. "I have to get over the wall," he said earnestly.

"No," I replied with what I hope was firm kindness. "You've been dreaming again. It's just you and me here in Catford today, along with the lifelong friend who's spending Christmas with us and our nice cat. It's Christmas Eve. Carols on the radio and all that."

"Is she really?" said Nick, showing something approaching wakeful interest for the first time. "What's she talking about?" Carole is my sister's name. Oh dear, dear. It went on for a while. When I got him into the shower, he asked me who owned the building and repeatedly if I was really sure that we didn't need to get away urgently.

I still can't get used to the man with whom I have shared my life, and until recently almost every thought, talking nonsense like Lear in the storm or Hamlet during his antic disposition.

Christmas Day, which started with buckets and mops in the bathroom well before dawn (I'll spare you the grisly details), was marginally better. Once I'd got him up and dressed, we spent most of the morning unwrapping presents – a task he now finds physically difficult – with Resident Friend. Then she and I went for a brisk walk before I cooked a huge lunch, and we spent much of the rest of the day eating it. Nick seemed a bit bemused but reasonably cheerful. He enjoyed the *Call the Midwife* Christmas special too.

Boxing Day was our main family day and I had to get the three of us to Cambridge. I wanted to start early to avoid the traffic and that worked well, although when I dragged Nick into the shower at 6.30am, he said, sounding exactly like our youngest, almost-four-year-old granddaughter, "but I don't want to get up yet!" He'd forgotten, of course, where we were going.

It was a very jolly day with two sons, two daughters-in-law, two grandchildren and Resident Friend, and we could all stay overnight (games with Ms Alzheimer's in someone else's bathroom – heigh ho) because our son had negotiated the use of his absent neighbour's house.

The drink flowed and glowed; we ate a lot and wore daft hats. Nick sat impassive and often sleepy for much of the day while the rest of us played silly games, told jokes and ate lots, etc. around him and tried to jolly him along. It's always a treat for me to have other people around because it means that for a few hours the responsibility is shared. And I think he still likes being with the family, although small children are disruptive of his routines and I suspect he sometimes longs for the orderly peace of his own space at home. He finds conversation difficult because he often struggles to reach his end-of-sentence target, and awareness of that means that he often doesn't bother to try. Everyone is patient and encouraging, but it isn't any sort of proper discourse.

It's the presents season and he got lots. I shall remember it as the Biscuit Christmas. Given his state of health, clearly no one could think of anything else to buy their father, grandfather, etc. There are now eleven packets/boxes in our cupboard. I shan't need to buy another biscuit until Easter.

My parents died of physical illnesses – no dementia – in their mid-seventies, four years apart. Twice at Christmas, in 1997 and then again in 2001, I found myself looking first at my father and then my mother and thinking: *Twelve months is a very long time when you're as ill as this. I really don't think 'we' can go on like this for another whole year. Next Christmas? I doubt it somehow.* In both cases, my intuition was spot-on, although I didn't expect my father, who seemed in quite good (relatively) form on Christmas Day, to die on 30 December that year. I won't labour the point.

Part Three

2019

2 January 2019

"Never put off 'til tomorrow what you can do today," my grandmother used to say. Or, if she was feeling pithier: "Procrastination is the thief of time." Well, thanks for that, Grandma. Like you, I've always been a doer, not given to hanging about, and pretty good at time management. That's how I could do an enjoyable but demanding full-time job, my share of home stuff (mostly cooking while Nick did the rest) and still have some to spend with friends and family as well as practising and playing the violin, choral singing and doing a lot of reading.

Not anymore. Ms Bloody Alzheimer's has sapped much of that away, and I now seem to spend most of every day (and often the night as well) just skivvying from one mundane task to the next – sorry, I mean caring, mopping up, running errands, taking Nick to medical appointments and doing enough laundry every day for a family of twelve. It's as if life as I knew it has simply gone – and gone at breathtaking speed too.

I try – I really try – not to sound bitter or self-pitying but I feel obliged to tell it how it is. Typically, I start the day around 7am, usually having been up to help Nick several times in the night, if only to steer him out of some restless fantasy and back to bed. Then I tend to him in the shower, and assist with drying and dressing. It's very hands-on and takes a while. Nothing, but nothing, happens quickly these days. Then I pull a few clothes on myself and belt downstairs to organise breakfast, which eventually Nick will trudge down to eat. By the time I've tidied the bathroom, kitchen and bedroom, sorted/pegged out, etc., the inevitable washing and a few other, usually unanticipated, chores, I'm lucky if I get to my desk by 10am. For years, I reckoned to get my head down at 8.30am and forge on until 1pm. How else did I produce over fifty books and thousands of articles? I used to be able to return to work for several hours in the afternoon and/or get out to an evening review job, perhaps via a face-to-face interview too. Those were the days. Sadly, I failed to appreciate how perfectly the teamwork operated until it no longer did.

The truth is that I now struggle to find the time for two or three hours of Real Work a day, and I find that intensely frustrating. I've never wanted to retire. Working is my thing and it's what I want to do more than anything. I'm fortunate in having several very caring and patient editors who understand the problems and, even as things are, I don't miss deadlines. But, by golly, I resent not even having the time to pitch for more work or develop new projects. I'm a creative hard worker and still in my Jean Brodie-esque prime.

But now, as the chilly, uncertain light of 2019 dawns, I know that I have to accept that I shall be able to do even less work this year. Nick's health is heading southwards every day. Getting out to review, for example, is becoming problematic. Hiring a carer in to cover a couple of hours in the middle of the time I'm out of the house already seems to be too little. He often phones me (yes, he can still just about manage that on the landline) within minutes of the carer leaving. Usually, he's panicking about where I am, having dreamed or imagined that I'm in some kind of serious danger – generally, I'm in a theatre and can't answer, so that compounds the problem. I've lost count of the number of times in the last few months that I've seen a missed call and charged out in the interval to call him. And all this is despite my carefully writing down for him exactly where I'm going and why, with all the times. Unfortunately, Ms Alzheimer's is busy destroying his sense of time and ability to tell it, just as she is ruthlessly confiscating most of mine.

I am, therefore, now thinking very carefully before I agree to review a show, and that inevitably means I shall get to fewer this year. In the past, Nick would have come with me as my 'plus one' to some review commitments, but he now gets very tired and isn't actually interested in much, so I take him ever less often. He did come first to the English National Ballet's *Nutcracker* at the Coliseum and to *Messiah* at the Barbican just before Christmas and seemed to enjoy them, but those evenings were a gargantuan effort for him as well as for me, and I wonder how many more times that can/will happen.

I am far from wealthy but we have enough money to pay the bills and buy what we want without having to worry too much and, obviously, my continuing to work helps with that. But when it comes to time, I am rapidly becoming very poor indeed. I read only fifty books last year, for example. In the past, I've gobbled up twice as many. Some formal exercise would be good too, but when am I supposed to fit it in? I shall simply have to continue charging up and down stairs at every opportunity, marching along railway platforms if a train's late and doing lunges in the kitchen while I wait for the kettle to boil. And as for the Arriaga string quartet I'm trying to learn the first violin part of for a session later this month… practice in five-minute stints on a good day and often nothing at all. I know my fellow quartet-ers will understand, but that isn't the point.

There's a great deal written about almost every conceivable aspect of Alzheimer's, but nobody seems to talk about how time-consuming it is and how it steals your life – carer's as well as patient's. I find it one of the worst aspects.

9 January 2019

Fatigue, tiredness, weariness, bloody exhaustion – yes, it's all part of Ms Alzheimers's merry-go-round. And, with her usual lack of discrimination, she gets the whole household, not just her target victim.

Nick is perpetually tired – and it's getting worse and worse. That is, I presume, a symptom of the mixed dementias, which seems to be felling him alongside common-or-garden Alzheimer's. The fatigue is supposed to be at least partly related to his low Vitamin B12 levels for which he has twelve weekly top-up injections, but I can't say I've noticed them making much difference. So we have to live with it.

The effort of getting up, dressing and eating breakfast usually tires him so much that he (often accompanied by our delighted feline monster who adores sleepy, sedentary people) sits on the sofa to look at the newspaper but nods off within a few minutes. Sometimes, he's so tired that he will wander upstairs and lie on the bed for a daytime snooze, especially in the afternoons. From choice, if nothing else is happening, he likes to head for bed by about 9pm. He's also developing a habit of narcoleptic disappearance whatever he happens to be doing – I've seen his sleepy head almost drop into his dinner plate, for instance, and he rarely stays fully awake in a theatre or concert hall. The only place he doesn't fall asleep is in the car. Perhaps that's a comment on my driving.

The tiredness is also related to broken nights. Nick wakes up frequently, needing to go to the bathroom. This was so for some years before the Alzheimer's diagnosis actually, but back then he used to manage it solo and quietly. Today, it's much more often – sometimes every twenty minutes or so in the early part of the night and he needs help to avoid – ahem – 'accidents', so I'm in and out of bed all night too.

Yes, before you ask the obvious question (and I'm beyond delicacy), we've got all the protectors, pads and special pants, etc., to deal with leakage. I loathe the implications of the word 'nappy', but that's what we're reduced to. Nick, however, is a sensitive grown-up, and if he feels a call of nature, he, understandably, wants to heed it – in the bathroom. Dignity and all that. So there's a lot of laborious lumbering out of bed with me propelling him by the shoulders because he's often forgotten where the bathroom actually is.

It's odd too. This whole bathroom business brings out the worst in him. In general, Nick is compliant and sweet-natured (more so than in the past when he was well, for the record) and usually takes my bossy instructions about every aspect of life on the chin without making a fuss. He's grateful, I suppose, at some level, that I tell him what's going on and what he has to do, because he often hasn't got a clue. The only time he really snaps at me is when I say, perhaps, at 1.30am, "No, you don't need to get out of bed. You really don't. You went ten minutes ago. Trust me. You really did." I never win. And out we trudge in tandem. Again.

So broken nights simply have to be contended with. And it means, obviously, that I'm nearly as tired as he is. It is months now since I got more than two hours' sleep at a stretch, and often I have to be content with much shorter serial mini-sleeps, but I can't rest during the day to compensate because I have work – domestic and professional – which has to be done and commitments in my diary. Onwards and upwards is what it has to be. You do, as every new parent knows, gradually adjust and adapt to sleeping in short bursts. You become an accomplished opportunist sleeper, but that doesn't mean you don't feel tired. In fact, it's like permanent jet lag.

Even a healthy body like mine will try to claw back sleep deficit too. I rarely complete the twenty-five-minute train journey into central London without 'losing myself', for example, and I often find I can't read more than a page or two of a book before I'm gone. It's like a plug falling out.

There have, moreover, been a couple of occasions in recent months when I have sensibly, but very crossly, cancelled jobs involving longish drives because I have slept so little the previous night that I'm terrified of nodding off at the wheel. That's the tiresome Ms A compromising my work opportunities again. She really is pernicious.

It is often said that people with dementia become increasingly like babies. It's a lousy analogy. There's something wonderfully, powerfully hopeful in a new baby so that, in the scheme of things, you don't actually mind how many times he or she demands attention in the night. You know it won't be for ever either. Infant and parent have a future to strive for. It's a completely different kettle of fish when, fuzzy with tiredness, you know that this is a reverse journey.

16 January 2019

Time is one of the last abstract concepts to develop in children. It's why a three-year-old cannot conceive of ten more days until Christmas and many a nine– or ten-year-old struggles with the notion that Julius Caesar invaded these shores a thousand years – or ten centuries – before William of Normandy did. It was one of the very few useful observations I recall from my generally poor three-year teaching training at Bishop Otter College, Chichester in the 1960s.

It presumably then follows that when a brain is heading in the opposite direction, at the other end of life, time is likely to be one of the first things to slip off the mental hard drive. That is certainly our experience.

I used to joke (perish the thought) about people 'who don't know what day of the week it is'. Nick hasn't had a clue whether it's Monday, Thursday or Sunday for over a year now. I'm drafting this piece on 14 January. Before I disappeared off to my PC, I asked him what month we're in. After a bit of thought, he said brightly, like an approval-seeking child: "Is it September?" Asking him what the year is produces some unlikely answers too. Maybe because he lived the first fifty-five years of his life in the 20th century, he readily slips back there.

None of that matters much because he can simply take each day as it comes and I'll tell him what's going on – careful to avoid information overload, which always exacerbates confusion.

More disconcerting (for me, anyway) is his increasing inability to sort out what time of day it is or to be able to tell the time reliably on his watch or a clock. Several times in recent weeks I have told him, 6pm-ish, that I'll start cooking dinner next job only to discover that he's gone upstairs and started to undress because he thinks it's bedtime. More than once, he's tried to get dressed in the middle of the night because "It's time to get up." I've sometimes found him coated and scarfed by the front door too because "We're going to… wherever, aren't we?" when actually that planned excursion was the next day.

One night last week, I came in from a work job about an hour after the carer had finished her stint. Nick had painstakingly (although very badly – strange items in the wrong places) laid the table for a meal. "Oh," I said, a bit taken aback. "What's this for?" He said it was for breakfast. He wasn't sure how many people were coming so he'd laid it for three. He thought it was early morning. It's quite surprising really that I don't weep or tear my hair out more often.

Even odder – delusional, in effect – is his conviction that 'they' have in some way altered the time. "I don't understand it," he'll say. "Why did they have to change something which worked perfectly well?" I've patiently explained about a hundred times that nothing has changed. In the UK, we shift the time forward one hour in March and back one hour in October and have done so all his life, I point out. I get blank looks of disbelief as if I'm the one talking nonsense. It's an idea very firmly lodged in his dementia-afflicted mind and a conversation we have on repeat loop.

Of course, we've travelled a lot in recent years and have often had to deal with different time zones. Could that be why when I'm out working and ring him to touch base, he sometimes asks me,

"What time is it where you are?" I tell him it's nine o'clock at night, or whatever, just as it is for him.

"No. I don't think so," he'll say. "I simply don't understand this new system," and off we go again. It's a circular route.

One day last week, he was utterly convinced that if we go to Cambridge or Brighton where our sons and their families live, the time would be different when we got there. Patience, patience, Susan. I explain. Again. "There are no time zones within the UK and never have been. If it's midday in south London then it's also midday in Aberdeen and Penzance. Trust me!"

You are supposed, I gather, not to argue with someone who has dementia. The professional advice is that you simply agree with everything they say. Hmm. I try but I really can't have him getting dressed and wandering off at 2am or trying to go to bed when he hasn't had any supper.

When it's things that really don't matter, I'm trying to cultivate casual granddaughter-speak and that usefully impartial word "Whatever..." although I can't get it out without a note of irony. In a way, it's rather nice because such an expression is so absurdly far from my normal speech mode that even Nick recognises the incongruity and we smile together. Sometimes.

23 January 2019

Alzheimer's is not a bundle of laughs. But it isn't without humour, most of which, in my view comes from the wacky (straw-clutching?) suggestions made by research projects and the journalists who report on them. Comic relief disguised as research?

On 17 January, the *Daily Telegraph*, for example, ran a short piece headed '*Housework may protect elderly against dementia*'. There, I knew it. I should have made Nick, when he was well, work far harder at vacuuming, mopping and scrubbing. Why did I waste all that money employing cleaners? When I'd stopped giggling and actually read the piece, I learned that this was a twenty-year US study which found that physical activity – even housework – can, for some people, keep Ms Alzheimer's at bay. Not the same thing at all. It's hardly an original observation either.

The Times (18 January) reported the same research with a different spin. What you mustn't do, apparently, is to allow yourself to get frail. 'Ageing badly' (whatever that means) makes people more susceptible to Alzheimer's and other forms of dementia. Researchers measured their studied individuals against a 'frailty index' (who knew?) and then brain scanned them when they were dead, which is a bit... er... final.

Frailty thy name is dementia? I have to say that Nick is now frail by any standards, but I'm not at all sure what he or I was supposed to do to prevent that. He was always active, ate healthily, drank only modestly and has never smoked.

Earlier this month, a study in Rio de Janeiro was published. It identified a hormone produced by exercise which can, it seems, benefit mice with neurodegenerative disease. Its production is linked to a gene that can be faulty. Having genetically engineered their hapless rodents to be susceptible to Alzheimer's (which *The Times* cheerfully informs us leads to 'brain atrophy and memory loss leading to dementia, disability and death') by suppressing said gene, they then restored it – and bingo. Of course, this sort of thing is never going to benefit Nick, and it will be many years, I presume, before it might help anyone else. It's a long road from mice to people. But it supports my contention that there's an entertaining Alzheimer's research story almost every day.

Meanwhile, a Chinese research group has identified a gene variant that plays a key role in the development of Alzheimer's in Han Chinese, the largest ethnic group in China. Apparently, until now, none of the genes linked with Alzheimer's in European populations could be 'validated' in Chinese equivalents. Golly, what a lot you learn when you get involved with this horrible illness.

Only this week, British research has suggested that blood tests – snappily known as 'serum neurofilament dynamics' – can now spot Alzheimer's and other forms of dementia, etc., before symptoms arrive but only, at present, in those tragic 'early onset' cases where the disease kicks in, say, during the patient's thirties or forties. I struggle to understand why it's an advantage to know that, yes, you're going to get a neurodegenerative disease before you do so since every medic or support worker you speak to stresses bluntly that "there is no cure." It isn't like cancer when early diagnosis can often get the thing zapped before it spreads. But I suppose they know what they're doing.

One day, maybe, there will be a real breakthrough, although realistically it's more likely that lots of different studies and approaches will come together to chip away at the illness and gradually reduce its effects. Miracle cures are the stuff of science fiction.

And, anyway, it's too late for any of it to make any difference to Nick, who's firmly on a downward trajectory whichever way you look at it. So, thanks, research guys, anything that makes me chortle – however ironically – helps in a tiny, unintended way. A little laughter is a bonus.

30 January 2019

I know how Alice felt. Conversations between Nick, Ms Alzheimer's and me become 'curiouser and curiouser' by the day. I now get so many surreal non sequiturs in response to casual remarks, along with strange comments and questions, that I can almost feel the walls racing past as we fall together further and further down the most famous rabbit hole in fiction. Sometimes, as in Wonderland or beyond that crazy Looking Glass, it's quite entertaining. More often, it's pitifully puzzling.

Here are ten examples from the last week or two:

1. I'm trying to explain (and I've also written it down) that I'm off to review a show and that a carer will arrive in an hour's time to spend two hours with Nick. Him: "Well, I don't think it's on any sort of syllabus."

2. I say I'll make us a mid-morning hot drink. Him: "Good idea, because I can hear a dog barking." (Shades of Sherlock Holmes, curious incidents and the like?)

3. Me, dizzy with tiredness in the middle of the night and getting a bit fraught when he's laboriously trying to get up for about the fourth time in an hour: "PLEASE stay in bed."

Him: "Well, are you doing all the proper things?" When I press him about what these duties might be, he replies seriously: "Well, like mending the potholes." I can't resist observing tartly that I'm a very busy woman trying to spin a whole cupboard full of plates but that, thank goodness, pothole repairs aren't on my job sheet. I just drive round them. And now, for goodness' sake, let's go to sleep.

4. I've just helped Nick to shower and into his underwear. I say: "Now go into the bedroom and put your trousers on while I fetch a clean shirt," whereupon he asks me anxiously: "We're not expected to bow to anyone, are we?"

5. I tell him a decorator is coming to give me a price for painting the ramps our elder son recently built for his father's safety round the house. "But are you sure that's okay?" Nick asks, worried. "Have you checked with the management of this place?" This is an ongoing problem. He often thinks we're in some kind of holiday let. So I painstakingly explain for about the thirty-fifth time that we own the south London house which we bought in 2016. I am – effectively – the 'management'. I need no permission from anyone else to make changes. "Oh, I see..." he says mildly.

6. It's 2am and we're in bed but Nick is fidgety. I say for the fifth time that it's the middle of the night and therefore time to go to sleep. "But what about the benchmarks?" he says anxiously.
   Me (weakly): "Benchmarks?"
   He fires back witheringly: "Yes. Surely you know what benchmarks are?"

7. I make him a nice cheese sandwich for lunch, all cut up neatly. Eventually, he sits down to eat it but something is clearly

bothering him? "What's the matter?" I ask, so patiently that I'm quite impressed with myself.
"I think it's about nine and a half per cent," he says earnestly. Have we reached the Mad Hatter's tea party, do you think?

8. Nick is havering and hovering, aka 'faffing about'. I tell him, several times, to sit down and eat his breakfast. "Yes, we've had the message, haven't we?" he mutters mysteriously.

9. I'm in my office, trying (with great difficulty) to get a bit of Real Work done. I hear Nick come out of the dining room downstairs and laboriously start to climb the stairs. My heart sinks. When he arrives – and it takes several minutes – beside my desk, it's to ask me if there's a WC in 'this place'.

10. A folded piece of paper has arrived on my bedside table. On it – in Nick's now very spidery hand – is written: *2+ chile whilrst.* No. I haven't got a clue either. Perhaps Humpty Dumpty is right when he tells Alice that words mean what you want them to mean.

I've thought a lot about Charles Dodgson – Lewis Carroll – lately. I reckon, tucked away in that Oxford college (Christ Church) of his, he would have known all sorts of eccentric reclusives, some of them quite elderly and perhaps afflicted with what we now know as dementia and a symptom of Alzheimer's. Now that I have to live, partly anyway, in a sort of parallel Wonderland universe, I can hear the echoes quite clearly.

6 February 2019

When you get an Alzheimer's diagnosis, the medics quickly and brightly tell you that it's an unpredictable disease and that some people stay in much the same place without getting worse for twenty years. It's called trying to put a valiantly cheerful spin on a hideously unpalatable situation.

Well, of course, I Googled it. Within hours of Nick being diagnosed on 29 April, 2017 – just twenty-one months ago – I knew that the average time an Alzheimer's patient survives after diagnosis is four to eight years.

And averages, as every sensible person knows, can be very misleading. For everyone who falls within the parameters of the given average, there are others at both ends. That's how averages work.

Nick, sadly, is declining far faster than that average suggests. We haven't even reached the second anniversary of the diagnosis and there are things he can't cope with now which would have been okay just a few weeks or months ago.

Did I really, for example, take him to Washington DC as recently as September 2018? Well, thank goodness I did, because it would be unthinkable now. I have no idea how I'd manage his incontinence on a seven/eight-hour flight, and he'd find the travel unbearably tiring. He'd also have very little idea of where we were and why, and I certainly don't think that it would now be safe to leave him resting in a hotel room while I pottered off on my own as I did several times last autumn.

Until last summer, he would walk, alone, with one of those four-wheeled shopping trolleys, a mile to Sainsbury's each Sunday morning to get the fruit and vegetables which I preferred not to have delivered. Now he goes out only if there's someone (usually me) with him.

We could still share a joke, even a feeble one, until recently, but that now seems to have gone too. The other day, I was on all fours on the floor in front of him putting on his socks. "There!" I said, brightly. "I'm kneeling at your feet just as you've always wanted." He just looked at me with that awful blank stare – increasingly, his default expression.

I now do all the talking, ordering, bill paying, and so on in restaurants (usually pre-show, although he comes out with me less and less often) because he and I both know he'll get lost in his sentence long before he can get out what he's trying to say. It seems to be a mixture of memory loss and articulation failure.

Not that he has any day-to-day money anymore. It's one of the many things I have to tell him he's 'retired from'. And I'm grateful to Lucas, our elder son, for nailing that kind way of putting it. Lucas was with us the other day when Nick started fretting about keys and locks. I told him not to worry because he doesn't really do keys anymore. "You've retired from keys," chipped in Lucas with a cheerful twinkle, managing, as he usually does, to keep things light and good-humoured. In fact, Nick has 'retired from' most things in the last few months.

The 1-mile-per-hour trudging gait has worsened noticeably too. So has the painfully slow speed at which Nick does any tiny task. He makes the slow loris look like a boy racer. A ten-minute struggle to get himself into a pair of pull-on jogging trousers before eventually giving up and asking me to help him is the new norm. He still shaves himself (thank heaven) when directed to by me. It takes around forty minutes. Then there's all the help he needs with what the professionals tactfully call 'personal hygiene' (a nightly bath and a morning shower in this case). And so it goes on. Twenty-four seven.

Presumably – gloomy thought alert – in a few weeks' time, I shall be reflecting how easy things were back in early February compared with how they are in the future/ present time of writing, whenever that might be. It's all relative.

By the time you read this, we shall be in a holiday-let cottage in Dorset with my sister and her husband. She and I are hoping that Nick and my very elderly but reasonably 'with it' brother-in-law will be able to look out for each other while we escape for walks in Hardy country. There's another family member joining us who might help too.

I'm not holding my breath about any of this, though, because I suspect that Nick will find being in a strange house very disorientating – although it was reasonably okay when we did this on our own in Northumberland nine months ago. That's relentless deterioration for you.

More on the Dorset adventure next week.

13 February 2019

So was a week in a very rural holiday-let house on the Dorset/Wiltshire border a good idea for a man into whom Ms Alzheimer's fangs are now deeply embedded? Well, yes and no. Curate's eggs and the like.

We were away all last week, with my (younger) sister, C, and her nonagenarian husband. For most of the time, we were also joined by his elder daughter, M, whom I've now known for years. What this boiled down to was three chatty, lively, healthy sixty+ women and two elderly chaps with very little energy, often confused/irritable or both and in need of a lot of help with things like negotiating steps in an unfamiliar environment. Interesting dynamic, and it meant that much of the caring could be shared. Partial respite. Never let its importance be underestimated and grab it when you can.

One of the downsides – maybe – was that we did very little. Nick and I have always done a fair bit of travelling about to see or do things when we're on holiday, but perhaps I have to accept that those days are over. C and I went for a few good walks and sometimes she strode out with M while I stayed at base. We tootled about locally a bit, making forays in different combinations – coffee in Tisbury, the very pretty nearest village, or a light lunch in nearby Shaftesbury, for example. Nick looked mostly pretty bemused.

We spent a lot of time inside the (very comfortable) house we'd rented, however, not least because of some pretty wet and blustery weather. Thank goodness for newspapers and Wi-Fi. C did a big jigsaw. M, who is self-employed, found time for some work. I read three novels and also did a bit of writing. We listened to a lot of music; the others watched TV most evenings and it was fun to play violin duets with C, something we don't get enough opportunity to do. It all meant, of course, that I actually got a bit of a rest, which I sorely needed, although, as regular readers may have gathered, I am not very good at idling.

Nick, meanwhile, takes ever longer to do the most elementary task. I would, while we were away, as at home, shower him (literally – like hosing down, say, a car), dress him and then go off downstairs leaving him to put his pullover on. Twenty minutes later, I'd go back up to make sure he was okay, only to find him just wriggling into the sleeves or wandering puzzled round the bedroom and no sight of the pullover.

The nights were very disturbed. Typically, both at home and away, I have to get up three or four times in the night to help him in the bathroom. He's usually lost in some dream which won't lift and hasn't got a clue where he is or what he's meant to be doing. Again and again last week I'd say to him, in our en-suite bathroom, "Okay, job done – back to bed now, please," only for him to stand in the middle of the bathroom unable even to find his way through the bathroom door and into the bedroom. Sometimes, he would point questioningly at the bath or the towel rail. I see a bit of this in our own house, where the bathroom is across the landing, but it was much worse in an unfamiliar environment.

The most heart-sinkingly chilling moment in the whole week came when I was helping Nick to sit down at the breakfast table one morning. He looked me straight in the eye and asked: "Has Susan gone out? Will she be back soon?" That's a first. And, I suppose, the beginning of a new stage in this horrible, hideous, hateful illness.

On the other hand, it was very touching (and supportive) to see both C and M being heart-warmingly kind to Nick, taking him by the hand, helping him up from chairs, doing up his seatbelt, making him drinks and a lot more – especially as my brother-in-law really needed to be their top priority. Even Nick commented on how gentle and tender C was with him. "How old was she when I first met her?" I was asked at one point.

"Eight," I reminded him.

Communication was even worse than usual during the week, though. Nick seems to be losing oral volume so I often can't hear him, and my very deaf brother-in-law rarely can, so it's hard for the two of them to communicate with each other. Add to that the fact that Nick's sentences often make no sense anyway and – try as everyone did to be inclusive – conversation tended to be mostly the three of us women discussing our own interests, concerns and preoccupations with each other rather than with either man.

And as for food, well, we kept it casual and low-key, more or less taking it in turns to sort dinner. Lots of options seemed to be the way forward, especially as Nick and I have been vegetarian for forty years, but Brother-in-Law, while enjoying eggs on toast and jacket potatoes, is noticeably suspicious of anything relating to the V-word.

So was it a success and would I do it again? Yes and yes. I suspect it's about the best I'm going to get on the holiday front for the foreseeable future, and the opportunity to relax was very welcome. So was all that chat, because I'm somewhat short, these days, of ordinary conversation at home. Wish I'd been able to spend more time out in lovely Dorset, but I've seen most of it many times before and in my situation you have to make the best of compromises.

20 February 2019

Classical music has always been part of the glue which binds our marriage. When we met, I was fourteen and he was sixteen. We became good friends for several years before we morphed into an 'item'.

And music was key to all of that, although we came at it from different angles. I was discovering *Messiah*, *The Creation*, *Noye's Fludde*, Brahms's *Requiem*, Schubert's *Unfinished* and a lot more through singing and playing them at school. I also came from a home that rattled with music. My father was a semi-pro Ceilidh band leader and a lover of mainstream opera. And I'd heard it all like wallpaper for years.

The boy I'd recently met at a local youth club (who turned out to come from a family my father and uncle had known well before the war) was just a geeky teenager who'd turned his back on popular culture, thought he knew rather more than he did, and was busily building a vinyl library, including the entire *Ring Cycle* conducted by Herbert von Karajan.

So we went to lots of concerts together, mostly at the Royal Festival Hall (affordable for teenagers back then) and the Proms. We listened to music together too. He was very keen on several second-hand record exchange places in central

London. Eventually, I started going to some of those with him. On one occasion, we popped into a Soho shop where he knew the enthusiastic man quite well – or maybe not. Said man took one look at me, became very distant and, I was told later, cooled from then on. The truth was, of course, that the shop owner was gay and thought Nick was too. I'd been taken there that day as a covert message. Hmm.

But I digress. The point I am making is that we've been sharing a love of music since 1962: concerts, CDs, radio programmes and lots more. For years, he read *The Gramophone* regularly and rarely missed Saturday morning's *Building a Library* on Radio 3 (to which all our radios have always been set). On our travels in the last twenty years or so, we've also attended concerts in exciting overseas concert halls such as Sydney Opera House, Musikverein in Vienna, Berliner Philharmonie and big halls in, for example, Chicago, Boston and Hobart.

It seems, alas, that all that is now over. Ms Alzheimer's, who lives with us these days, is not keen on classical music. Nick is often restless. He often wanders aimlessly round the house fiddling with things in search of something to do. So, trying to settle him, I say something like: "Why don't you go and sit in the sitting room and put some music on?"

He has forgotten how to switch it on, so I generally go and set it up for him, either via our new TV, which does all sorts of wonderful things, or sometimes I leave him with my iPad on which I have a fair amount of music downloaded. "What would you like?" I ask, usually trying to encourage him towards something very familiar, such as a Beethoven symphony. So far so good, but ten minutes later he'll be drifting round the house again, clearly uncaptivated by the music. "What's the matter?" I ask. "You used to spend hours listening to music. Why have you left that symphony?"

The chilling answer last week was a casual "Oh, I don't seem to be interested in anything like that anymore." WHAT?

You bloody swine, Ms A. Did you really have to take that from him (us) as well?

It's a fairly recent development. Last summer, when I reviewed a number of proms I had only a single ticket for most of them so Nick would listen to the live broadcast on the radio at home. I could ring him in the interval and say "How about that, then? Wasn't it fabulous?" and he'd be able to have a sensible conversation with me about it. It's going to be very different this summer.

Of course, I still take him to concerts when I can, and he sits there conventionally but doesn't seem to engage with the music. He certainly can't discuss it afterwards. I suppose I just have to be thankful that he enjoys it in his own way in the moment, although how long will even that last?

This musical closing-down comes and goes, in and out of focus, like every other aspect of the cognitive decline which characterises this appalling illness. At the weekend, I heard, by chance, on Radio 3, the Gulda cello concerto, which was new to me. I've moved Nick's precious BOSE into the kitchen because he never now listens to it and it means that I can – and sometimes he's there too. Now, that concerto includes some virtuoso cello work which is so sparky and flamboyant that it literally stopped me in my tracks. I caught Nick's eye and, briefly, we shared the 'wow!' moment, as we always would have done. Be thankful for the occasional small things, Susan.

Shakespeare has Portia refer, in completely different context, to '*a swanlike end, fading in music*'. Yes, that's as good a summary as any.

27 February 2019

I'm truthful by nature. I can't help telling it how it is. And I suspect these days that other people sometimes find my unrestrained honesty a bit disconcerting. "How are things?" they ask kindly. Then when I reply bluntly that it's pretty awful, very difficult and getting worse every day, they look uneasy, because where does the conversation go from there? Sorry, folks.

Many people with Alzheimer's – or caring for someone with it – go into denial. I hear all the time, often from those same well-meaning enquirers, about their grannies, aunts, parents *et al.*, who simply refuse, or refused when they were alive, to acknowledge the truth of what is/was happening to them. Well, yes, I can understand that very well. If you ignore something determinedly enough, you can, in a sense, convince yourself that it's not real. In a way, it might be easier. But I'm cursed, not only with Ms Alzheimer's in my home, marriage and life, but also with a lifelong attachment to facing facts head-on.

When I was eleven and in my first term at a pettily rule-bound old-fashioned grammar school, I made a mistake with signing in on the dinner list so that the class numbers didn't add up. Not going into lunch and getting a tick was regarded as a heinous sin. When our form teacher told the form, very seriously, about this appalling crime the next day as a warning to the unidentified perpetrator, I immediately leapt to my feet and said, "Oh, Mrs Grant, it's all right. That was me. I'm really sorry. I made a mistake. I had to go into the other sitting because of my violin lesson." Problem solved. Now, I don't actually remember this incident but decades later at a reunion, Mrs Grant told me about it and said she had never met a child as straightforward and honest as me. I had, it seems, completely knocked the wind out of her sails with my open inability to dissemble. Well, I haven't changed much.

Nick is seriously ill. Alzheimer's is a terminal disease and that means that sooner or later it will kill him and I can't – absolutely can't – pretend otherwise. I don't spell it out to him, obviously, although occasionally he is both lucid and realistic and we have sometimes talked a bit about the future and the inevitability of where his illness is taking him. In general, though, I just jolly him along. I can't lie – never could – but I do my best to keep it light and casual.

I'm open with everyone else though to such an extent that I sometimes forget appropriateness. I found myself providing a graphic account – far too much information – of our frequent nocturnal bathroom trips to a sympathetic friend over lunch the other day, for example. She managed not to wince, bless her.

And I really should not have asked our elder son whether you can hire a church for a secular funeral. No wonder he looked askance, gulped, paused and finally said faintly: "Don't you think you're being a bit premature?" The trouble is that my very active brain is perpetually beavering away and coming up with a detailed plan of action for every eventuality. It's my way of coping.

These blogs are, I suppose, another aspect of that. What you get here is the bald, bleak unvarnished truth. When I started them almost two years ago, I asked Nick's permission to write about his condition and he gave it readily. At the time, he said, quite sensibly, that it's easier all round if there are no secrets about what's happening to him and that my writing about his illness might help others. He used to ask quite often: "Have you been writing about me?" Then he'd potter off and look at my website on his PC quite cheerfully. I think he rather enjoyed being the centre of my authorial attention for once.

Things have moved on since then. It is many months now since he has read one of these posts. He no longer knows how to turn his computer on (and I've semi-commandeered his unused office as a music room), and he shows no interest if I offer to show them to him on my PC or iPad. So I am now, effectively, communicating with the world without his knowledge, and there's no need to fudge anything, even here.

So I shall carry on describing the situation in all its awfulness, which, as a few wise people have recognised, does actually help me a bit. There is something therapeutic about truthfully writing down your experiences and feelings – it doesn't dispel them, of course, but it somehow feels as if the horror is managed and put to one side once it's openly committed to words.

6 March 2019

Not long after Nick and I 'came out' as an item in 1967 (not that anyone was surprised), he arrived one day at my family home to find me in the kitchen busy with the Tuxan and a couple of bushes, energetically cleaning my shoes.

"I'll do that," he said, taking them gently from me and picking up the brush. "And I'll go on cleaning your shoes until we have a son who can do it for you."

Sexist? Well, yes, I suppose so by 2019 standards. Back in 1967, I thought it was one of the nicest, most romantic things I'd ever heard. And I've always been a pragmatic feminist. If smiling sweetly and exploiting femininity can get a dirty job (changing a wheel on the car is another case in point) done by someone other than me, then I'll go for it, thanks very much.

The incident reminded me of Gommy, my lovely grandfather, too. He was an enthusiastic shoe cleaner and regarded it as every inch a male job, although he failed to pass that ethos on to his son, my father, which is why I was cleaning my own shoes that day. Throughout my childhood and teens when I arrived at the grandparental home, my grandmother would say, in her usual veiled, mildly critical way: "Oh, look at your shoes, dear. Pop them off and Gommy will clean them for you."

Nick kept his promise. Once married and sharing a home, it was a very long time before I ever had to get out the shoe polish. And he always made my shoes (and his own) look lovely, happily attacking them in the traditional old-fashioned way until they gleamed. For the record, though, we went on to have two marvellous sons, both of them caring, supportive and practical, especially these days when we need it most. I don't, however, remember either of them ever cleaning my shoes – or their own very often for that matter. Their father must have neglected to educate them in this specific form of gallantry/chauvinism. Delete as applicable. I must remember to ask them whether they clean their wives' shoes today. Somehow, I doubt it.

I'm sure you can see where this is going. Ms Alzheimer's knocks out the ability to do simple tasks at the rate of at least one a week. Shoe cleaning went long ago, along with bed making, loading the dishwasher, making toast, writing messages and getting washed in the shower – among many other things.

So shoe cleaning rather neatly symbolises our marriage and where we are now. I keep the shoe-cleaning box in the coat cupboard in the hall. Nick has no idea even where to find it. If I go for a walk in the park and my shoes get muddy then cleaning them is entirely down to me. I clean his occasionally too – unthinkable until a couple of years ago. And he sits in a different kitchen, in a sort of quiet vacancy, and watches me applying polish and buffing if off exactly as if the clock were wound back fifty-two years and we were back in my family home, except that he can't now offer to take over. Back then, we were eagerly looking forward to the future we were planning together. Now, we're unravelling. There is no future. Just a great deal of past – and many pairs of fondly remembered shiny shoes.

13 March 2019

Some organisations clearly don't understand dementia. They are so bound up in their own red tape, procedures, rules and lording it over their customers that they have completely forgotten (if they ever knew) what life with Ms Alzheimer's forever at your shoulder is actually like.

But first the positive. Most people and organisations are, thank goodness, wonderfully empathetic and helpful. Take the staff at Pret a Manger in St Martin's Lane last week, who were brilliant when Nick needed the loo but both the gents' and the disabled facility were out of action. An absolutely splendid male Pret employee helped Nick all the way down the steep stairs and temporarily closed the ladies' so that he could access it – and then fetched me when there was a problem. Or what about Thomas Sultana of All Gleaming Clean (who has done jobs for me before)? He recently came to clean our ailing, much-scrubbed landing carpet and said without a fuss: "You need Scotchgard. I'll come back and do it next week." Then there was an extraordinarily kind young woman in the ladies' loo queue at the Arts Theatre where Nick and I saw *Six* last week. She could see that I couldn't make him understand where to wait for me so she said, "I'll stay with him. You negotiate your way to the front of the queue and I'll go when you get back." And, for that matter, let's hear it for the NHS. Apart from its absurd, antediluvian, clung-to appointment/referral system, the service we've had since Nick's diagnosis has been excellent.

Sadly, the fact that so many people so willingly go the extra mile makes the exceptions stand out even more woefully. I've decided they deserve to be named and shamed so here goes.

HSBC needs to learn how lasting power of attorney works. I went to a great deal of trouble, carefully following the Office of the Public Guardian's quite complex instructions and safeguarding rules to get all the right documentation, including certified copies of the LPA document which are validated (with a special Braille-like watermark) by OPG. When I took one of these to HSBC, they said they couldn't accept a copy. They had to have the original – which is utter nonsense. They also made Nick sign a lot of papers, which defeats the object of LPA. The document I had in my hand supersedes the need for all that. The woman we saw (twice, as she insisted I go back with the original LPA document) was very pleasant and, of course, it isn't her fault that HSBC, in arrogant ignorance, has imposed this way of working on its staff.

And I'm furious with Thames Water, who write to me regularly because they want me to have one of their tiresome smart meters. I have resisted that and shall continue to do so. A recent letter commented that our water consumption is higher than average for two people. Well, of course it bloody well is. One of us is sick. He needs far more showers (three so far on the day of writing – I'll leave the details to your imagination) than the rest of us and he generates a great deal of laundry. Whoever manages, or mismanages, the sending out of irritating, insulting even, letters like that ought to be sent on an awareness training course immediately.

I'm not pleased with the National Trust either. I phoned them to renew our joint membership – or, to put that another way, to make a donation of £120. Despite my saying that he has Alzheimer's, I was told that I had to bring Nick to the phone to authorise the renewal unless I paid from a joint account. They wouldn't take the payment from my personal one. In exasperation, I paid from a joint account, although it wasn't what I wanted to do. I complained about this on Twitter which eventually led to an email from an apparently helpful NT person saying that she would make me the 'lead member' instead of him, which would solve the problem. Then the membership cards arrived – still addressed to him and with an asterisk against his name. So I shall have the same problem next year. Or maybe I won't bother. Their loss.

There's far too much of this sort of thoughtlessness about. We hear a lot about dementia awareness these days and it's good to see 'Dementia-Friendly' notices and badges becoming commonplace. But until every single organisation gets the message, there's still a lot of work to be done.

20 March 2019

Why is so much Alzheimer's research focused on the concept of diagnosing the disease earlier? It isn't as though there is any treatment which can then be applied to prevent the full-blown disease from developing.

An early diagnosis of, say, breast cancer after a routine mammogram is a completely different kettle of fish. Treatment at that stage often saves lives, which is marvellous. Until there is comparable treatment for Alzheimer's, I struggle to see the advantage (for the patient and his/her family, anyway) of knowing a lot sooner that this inexorable disease is going to kill you slowly and horribly.

Nick lost his sense of smell twenty-five years ago. I now know that is quite a common pre-Alzheimer's symptom. At the time, we naively thought it was odd but quite funny and put in smoke alarms. What good would it have done us if, back then, someone in medical authority had done tests and advised us that he would go on to develop full-blown Alzheimer's? These days, if I hear of anyone else mentioning anosmia (the posh name for being olfactorily challenged) then I keep very quiet. How can our experience possibly help?

Diagnosis is a very mixed blessing. You walk into the consulting room feeling like a normal human being with a future, a cat and a life to lead, and you come out weighed down by a massive invisible label. You have crossed that huge chasm which divides the well from the terminally ill. The Grim Reaper is waving his sickle at you and you can see him clearly. You are now a patient and your life is, at a stroke, medicalised.

And I've never forgotten, at an assessment meeting a few weeks before Diagnosis Day, the nurse turning to me and saying: "Now I have to ask you a few questions as his carer." For a minute, I couldn't think what she meant because I had never thought of myself in carer terms at all. I was, and am, just his wife. It seemed almost laughable at the time. But I too was about to be dragged, very much against my will, across that chasm to become a medical statistic – complete with hideous, unwanted new job title.

I sympathise a lot, then, with people who are clearly in the early stages of Alzheimer's or other form of dementia but who have – thus far – refused to discuss it with anyone official. They know that they can, more or less, carry on normal life for the moment and that as soon as they hand their problems over to the medics and support workers, everything will change and their lives will no longer be their own. Well-meaning 'help' will arrive in the form of occupational therapists, advisory nurses, care assistants and the like. Who can blame them for delaying such intrusion for as long as possible? I certainly don't.

None of this is, in any way, a criticism of the system. Almost every NHS employee we've seen in the last two years has been – in no particular order – helpful, kind, practical, friendly, supportive and willing to give us as much time as we've needed.

Take the GP we saw last week for a 'routine review'. We seem to see a different man or woman almost every time we attend the surgery because it's a big practice. In this instance, though, it was Dr K who happened to be the first GP we saw not long after we moved when we finally decided to 'report' Nick's multiple problems. He remembered us and was really delightful – leading the confused, wobbly Nick gently into his consulting room by the hand, carefully noting all our concerns and promising to come back to me soon with some answers. He also had an animated chat with me along the way about the Globe's *Romeo and Juliet,* which he was due to see with his wife and daughter that evening and which I am reviewing this week.

My point here is that diagnosis recast us in new roles. Nick became an invalid and I his carer. And it was instant. On 28 April 2016, we were an ordinary couple planning and looking forward to things. By the afternoon of the twenty-ninth, our whole world had shifted. I remember the consultant saying bravely at that appointment: "Nothing changes." Well, I suppose she meant well but it's a lie, because everything changes diametrically the moment you know you have this illness for which there is no cure or even any effective treatment. Suddenly your future has gone and you face only terminal decline. It's a death sentence. But, of course, no one is going to tell you that in so many words. They have to be as positive as they can.

So, personally, I am very glad we didn't get a diagnosis any earlier. It would simply have curtailed our normal life together sooner and for longer. And until they manage to develop some effective interventionist treatment, I shall continue to be sceptical about 'earlier diagnosis' as a research aim. Yes, I know that if they can get people on board long before real illness sets in, maybe they can monitor and observe the decline more closely, which might help research. Consider, though, the frame of mind of the individual whose future is being made even worse by having to live with the certainty that Alzheimer's will eventually fell them. Sometimes, ignorance – innocence anyway – is better. I'm really grateful that we didn't know until relatively recently.

27 March 2019

And how are YOU, Susan? It's a question I'm now asked all the time, usually by people with lots of kind, knowing sympathy in their eyes. They see Nick, weakened by the ever-heavier weight of Ms Alzheimer's on his back, while hearing me obliged to talk to him as if he's a biddable three-year-old. And they wonder.

The answer is that in many ways I'm absolutely fine. I'm blessed with excellent health and a brain which seems to be locked in overdrive. If people push me, I confide that I have a bit of arthritis (?) in my left thumb, which hurts, so I wear a thumb splint to play the violin and try to avoid doing up too many buttons on my clothes or Nick's – hardly a major issue.

And it's important that I stay that way. It's the crashing aircraft principle: fit your own oxygen mask before helping anyone else. If you're not fit (or breathing!), you won't be any use to anybody. So I eat healthily, watch my weight, try to build exercise into daily life, go very easy on booze and, of course, I don't smoke.

There are, however, two negative factors which are beyond my control and not, I suspect, doing me any good at all. One is sleep and the other is stress.

Nick now needs a great deal of twenty-four seven help. I have to shower him at night (a sort of hosing-down operation), assist with drying and then physically put him into his nightclothes before easing him into bed – and of course we do the whole operation in reverse each morning, including another very necessary shower. It means that I can't even start to get myself into the bath, until about forty-five minutes after I start to help him. By the time I eventually get into bed, he's probably been asleep for a while but, typically, wakes up five minutes after I've put the light out and has to be helped out to the bathroom – a routine we sometimes go through four or five times in a single night and on a bad night several times in a single hour.

Twice last week, I got less than four hours' sleep – and then only in short bursts. Nick gets very confused in the night too and will wake up and talk a lot. He wants answers and I do try, but most of what he's saying is incoherent and dream-related, so whatever it is, it isn't a conversation. But it means I'm awake. Sometimes, I give up, get up and do some work in my office next door in the hope that he'll settle. If he stirs, I can still hear him. I could sleep in another room, of course, except that I can't. There's no way he can just be left to get on with it. Half the time, he doesn't know what building we're in or where any of the rooms are. I wouldn't be able to relax for a second if I shut myself away in another part of the house. It would be like parking a baby out of earshot. Not on.

So if you meet me out – at the theatre, say, reviewing (while a carer I've paid man-sits at home) and you think I look hollow-eyed with tiredness, then you're right. Lack of sleep – and the stress it causes – is said to be very bad for your health, and if I read another article telling me that, I think I shall scream. In my situation, you have no control over the number of hours you get. I'm happy to allow seven or eight hours, but it's most unlikely that Ms A will permit me to sleep for most of that time. Roll on the three days next month when I'm going to stay with a friend in Yorkshire while our elder son takes over at home.

And it's the toll that this constant tiredness takes on the carer which isn't generally recognised by the decision-makers, although our GP quizzed me about it only last week when I took Nick for a routine 'condition and medication review'. And people I know personally, or whom I've got to know virtually or actually through these blogs, are very understanding.

It is, however, in the government's economic interests to keep people like me going for as long as humanly possible. If I weren't looking after him day and night, someone else would have to, and that would cost the country a great deal of money. Alzheimer's patients are entitled to 'free' (i.e., paid for by lifelong taxpayers like us) care via the NHS Continuing Home Care service, providing that their health problems have no other underlying cause. In practice, of course, provision is very patchy.

I was delighted to pick up a little video of Derek Thomas MP for St Ives, West Cornwall and the Isles of Scilly last week addressing parliament about the plight of people like me. He has clearly met lots of us and spoke with real authority in support of the Alzheimer's Society's new campaign 'Fix Dementia Care', following its report earlier this year.

On a happier, but related, note, I am uplifted and cheered by Hunter Davies's joyous new book *Happy Old Me,* which I've gobbled in the last few days. Like us, he and his late wife – respected novelist Margaret Forster – had been together since their teens and had been married fifty-five years when cancer got her in 2016. He is delighted to be alive and reasonably well at eighty-three, determined (like me) not to retire and busy carving out an enjoyable life for himself. It's one of the most encouraging, positive books I've read for ages, and all couched in his characteristically insouciant, self-deprecating style. Thank you, Hunter, for reminding me that there IS light at the end of the darkest possible tunnel and that it IS possible to come through battered but generally pretty okay.

3 April 2019

Well, we are now officially a 'Golden' couple. The much-anticipated fiftieth anniversary fell last Friday and we are now enjoying (or something) our fifty-first year of marriage.

I've realised for some time that this will be our last landmark anniversary, so despite Nick's vagueness about it all, it seemed a good idea to Do Something. For our twenty-fifth, we had a big party at home, and we took forty-five people to lunch in a hotel on the fortieth anniversary.

This time, I hired the eight-bedroom Tudor Wing attached to an even larger house in lovely countryside near Tunbridge Wells so that the entire immediate family could spend a long weekend together. That meant a house party with two sons, two daughters-in-law, four granddaughters and eldest granddaughter's boyfriend. My sister and her family – seven of them – joined us for Sunday lunch, along with GD3's lovely mother.

It was all pretty jolly and fairly restful for me because there were lots of other kind people around to help Nick, who could never, for example, find his way round the large premises, which variously dating from 1350, 1460 and the nineteenth century, has a lot of doorways, stairs and steps. And on Saturday morning, I was able to go to Tunbridge Wells with elder son and family knowing that Nick was being safely looked after back at base by younger son and co.

The next generation did all the catering, cooking and shopping. All I had to do was eat and drink and there was, of course, plenty of both. Some of us swam (a rather good heated, covered outdoor facility), played table tennis, pool and other games. And there was a lot of sitting, chatting with cups of tea and wonderful homemade biscuits – with everyone working hard to include Nick and jolly him on as much as they possibly could.

Although we had masses of Golden Wedding cards which I displayed at the weekend (and still have 'up' at home), most of the time Nick hadn't a clue what we were doing and why we were there. "Well done for putting up with her for fifty years," said my sister, cheerfully, when she kissed him goodbye on Sunday. Blank stare.

"So glad to share your Golden Wedding with you," said younger daughter-in-law. Flash of understanding.

"See you again at our sixtieth?" he said. Ouch. Momentary poignant pause. Does he really think we have another ten years together?

"Oh, I think you might see me before then," she said with kind presence of mind.

As I drove Nick homewards on Monday morning, I asked gently, "Do you remember what the weekend was really about?"

He thought for some time before answering. "Was it to get the family together?"

Me: "Yes, partly a bonding exercise, I suppose, but one with a very specific point. Can you recall what that was?" I prompted for a while but in the end I had to tell him. Again.

All of this raises the issue of whether it's worth celebrating an event at which one of the key participants doesn't know what's going on. Is it appropriate? Is it in questionable taste? Well, the eighteen other people who took part all had a good time, and it's important to build family memories. I love to see them all in the same place for a bit too. It brings out the *materfamilias* in me and it doesn't happen that often. The youngest two GDs (seven and four) excitedly fell in love with the gloriously Blytonesque house, which was like nothing they'd ever seen before apart from on National Trust visits, and immediately named their atmospheric attic bedroom 'The Harry Potter Room'. I expect they will remember celebrating Grandpa and Granny's Golden Wedding in that huge and mysterious house with its exciting low beams, panelling and uneven floors and hiding places for the rest of their lives, and I like the idea of that.

11 April 2019

If life with Ms Alzheimer's is a 'journey' then every week seems to bring a new staging post on the road downhill. Nick now seems to be a compulsive mover of bits and pieces around the house for no reason. I suppose it relates to some distant, foggy memory of tidying up but it's jolly irritating to live with.

The well-fitting, good-quality upstairs bathroom basin plug went AWOL weeks ago. The several cheap and nasty replacements I have bought are uselessly leaky, so now it's impossible to run and retain a basin of water. I try not to curse. I really do.

Then there was the birthday card I carefully bought for my

great-niece this week. I put it with a stamp at the top of the stairs ready to take down and write later – it disappeared. As did the towel from the downstairs loo, which I eventually found quite by chance neatly folded in the umbrella box on the shelf in the coat cupboard in the hall. Newspapers are frequently folded up and put in funny places – usually before I've read them – and I seem to spend several minutes every day hunting for the Marmite, which could be anywhere. One evening last week, in the hour between the carer leaving and my getting home from a review job, all the sitting-room coasters were carried up to our bedroom. I recently found his toothbrush wrapped in a clean face flannel and put in a drawer, and so it goes on.

I'm aware, of course, that this is a classic Alzheimer's symptom. My best friend's mother used to drive her daughter potty by hiding things such as keys around the house – or worse – throwing them away in my friend's absence. Another friend has now removed all her mum's jewellery because she's so afraid it will get hidden and/ or lost. Years ago, we laughed (sorry – I wouldn't think it remotely funny now) when a distant elderly relation died and her family found stashes of quite large sums of money hidden in unlikely places all over the house.

The trouble is that you can't reason with them, and that's hard to deal with when until relatively recently you could have a sensible grown-up conversation. I am constantly (and tetchily) saying, "Look, if I put something down in a certain place, there is a reason for it. If you don't understand the reason, don't worry about it. JUST LEAVE THINGS ALONE, PLEASE." At brighter moments, he understands this. Sometimes, he even laughs at his own eccentricities but within minutes he will have forgotten – and be at it again.

And, of course, I'm not the kindest or most patient of carers, however hard I try.

Nick is very restless these days and likes to struggle up from the table and try to carry things into the kitchen – typically before I've finished eating, so I find myself barking: "Leave that, please. I'll do it when I'm ready." And the problem is compounded by his quite often 'seeing things', which is another classic symptom. He'll mistake a pair of shoes on the floor for an animal, for instance, or if I ask him to walk out of the bathroom door, he sees/imagines a door at the other end of the very small space and heads in the wrong direction. And sometimes it's surreally, harmlessly hilarious. Younger son, Felix, in charge for a few hours last weekend, reports that when he gave Nick a ginger biscuit, the latter wanted to put a battery in it.

When people casually commiserate with all this, my usual response is to throw it off lightly by saying, "Oh well, it's just the shit life throws at you." Lately, that has become… er… a bit literal. A heartfelt thank-you to whoever invented disposable latex gloves.

And now, here comes the upbeat bit: By the time this posts, and you read it, I shall have escaped, very thankfully, to rural North Yorkshire for three nights, leaving Lucas in charge at home. The lovely friend I'm going to stay with is very good at 'respite' and I shall be allowed to sleep all night, not to have to wash and dress anyone other than myself and to have proper chats with someone who answers properly rather than ricocheting between non sequiturs. No one will hide the basin plug either.

24 April 2019

I seem to have spent the whole of the last week playing hide-and– seek with Nick. I have already mentioned the mystery of the vanished hand basin plug – which I have now, I'm happy to report, managed to replace on the third attempt with one that fits. Don't let anyone tell you these things are standard, even when they all purport to be one and a half inch.

Since then, I have removed drinking glasses from the cat's cupboard, items of fruit from the bedroom and his cardigan (more than once) from the housekeeping cupboard where the vacuum cleaner, spare light bulbs *et al.* live. Boxes of tissues and toilet rolls frequently walk round the house and goodness knows why, the other day, he took all the crackers out of their tin and put them in with the sweet biscuits.

The other form of the game is finding things for Nick that he says have 'gone' but they haven't: his toothbrush, glasses, watch, etc., are always 'disappearing' but of course, actually, they're exactly where they should be.

Then there's a new habit of forgetting to turn taps off. I now have a new last-thing routine whereby I check that the taps are all off at the same time that I make sure all the doors and windows are locked.

It all happens when he's alone. If I'm upstairs working in my office (which I often need to be) and he's downstairs, he'll potter about rather than settling to anything for more than a few minutes. Then when I go downstairs after, say, an hour (dare not leave it any longer), I never know what bits of muddle I shall have to sort out. Why, for example, has the ice cream scoop been removed from the dresser drawer and put in the hall? What's the washing-up liquid doing on the dining table? The same applies if I'm out working in the evening and there's a half-hour or so gap between the carer leaving and my getting home.

In itself, it's all very trivial stuff, but the totality is intensely tiresome and irritating. And I'm afraid patience isn't a strength of mine. I haven't succeeded in two careers and always had more than one job on the go at a time by sitting about patiently. I've done it by striding ahead at speed and being totally focused on the goal. None of that helps a jot now. It just compounds the frustration because I'm having to act a role in which I am very badly cast.

My lovely Yorkshire-based friend, with whom I had four glorious days' respite earlier this month, talked to me at length about 'seeing someone' to talk all this through. Well, I've always respected the counselling industry but hey, I come from a family in which we all put our heads down and get on with it. We're strong. We don't 'do' airy-fairy psychology. It seems to work for others but I had long been convinced it wasn't for me.

But my friend was very persuasive so when I got home I found a local practitioner – walking distance – who has strings of qualifications and accreditations, along with twenty years' experience. Last week, I had a session with her. Let's call her L.

To my surprise, I enjoyed every minute of it. To sit in L's peaceful, professionally set-up sitting room and to be allowed to pour it all out – all those unsayable things which I've been bottling up for a very long time – was absolute bliss. Real-life conversations are punctuated with interruptions and, more often than not, the other person highjacks the conversation perhaps because they feel awkward. This was quite different. It was just me and my situation for a whole hour.

And L did make some really helpful observations. She pointed out, for example, that the man I married in 1969 has already gone. The person I now live with, mostly now incapable of any form of sequential conversation, is someone completely different. I am in a sense already widowed. Now, in truth, I had already worked that out, but it was a huge relief to hear someone else overtly articulating it.

She also listened attentively to my account of what I have to do: showering (at least twice a day and often more) and cleaning up an increasingly disabled person, supervising him twenty-four seven, shouldering every domestic task, including cooking, gardening, admin and more laundry than Widow Twankey, along with a demanding job as a journalist /author. "But, Susan, no wonder you're pissed off," she said simply. "You're doing three separate full-time jobs."

Spot-on. That's it, exactly. And it isn't what I want at all. I'd quite like my life back, for a start.

L made two linked practical suggestions. She thinks I should have a proper focused discussion with both our sons (together) about possible strategies for the future. She also thinks I should check out some local care homes which might, just possibly, be useful in the future, if only for respite. It's always better to have provisional plans in place than to have to make hasty decisions when an emergency strikes. I have all this in hand.

I now realise I've been undervaluing the importance of 'offloading' your problems for most of my life. No woman is an island, as John Donne nearly said. I have made a follow-up appointment with L.

1 May 2019

I have bought a wheelchair. And if it's a bit sad to be quite excited by it and what it promises, then okay: guilty as charged.

I borrowed one at Tate Britain last month so that I could push Nick round the *Van Gogh in London* exhibition and by golly it really improved the experience for both of us. People politely parted so that we could see the paintings and captions properly. And I didn't have to worry about Nick flagging, feeling dizzy and needing to sit down. He and Ms Alzheimer's were securely contained in their temporary vehicle. Win win.

Then, a couple of days later, we met our younger son and his family at Chartwell where, again, with Nick safely installed in a National Trust wheelchair, neither he nor we had to worry about steps, slopes and standing about.

It convinced me that we could make good use of one on a daily basis. Nick now walks mostly in a very slow, short-stepped trudge. That, apparently, is a classic Parkinson's symptom and therefore part of the 'mixed dementias' our consultant now thinks he has. When he's not trudging, he loses control of his legs as if he were trying to run. And that's terrifying as I try desperately to keep him upright while his feet paddle out of control, his body veers all over the path and I struggle to steer – most of the way along Upper

Street, for example, when I (unwisely?) took him to see *HMS Pinafore* at King's Head Theatre recently. It's only a matter of time, if we continue thus, before he goes flat on his face and takes me with him. Then, if we're both injured, we really shall be in trouble.

Hence the wheelchair. I looked online but the options are as complicated as buying a car, and it's a learning curve (who knew that a 'bariatric wheelchair' is one designed for a heavily obese user?), so I went to an excellent place in Penge where very helpful staff sold me a lightweight one which I can lift and which fits easily in the car – for a hundred pounds less than anything I'd seen online.

It means we can explore the local parks and, here in south London, we're blessed with lots of lovely ones. I can also push him to one of three local shopping centres if only to have a cup of tea and come home again. It's very much what I used to do with babies and young children in prams and pushchairs – fresh air and a change of scenery even if it's only a few ducks, a pretty flowerbed or half an hour in a coffee shop. It's a relief too to be able to progress at my own speed rather than toiling along in frustration at about 1 mile an hour.

And it will be much easier when I take him with me to, say, Chichester (twice this week) or Canterbury to get him from car to restaurant to theatre. And I might experiment with taking the wheelchair into central London by train if I can work out some step-free routes; Nick spends too much time at home doing very little. If I can get him out a bit more on his new wheels then that's got to be a good thing. Activities are supposed to help counter Ms A. And although he evinces very little enthusiasm for anything these days, Nick doesn't seem to mind being pushed about.

And there's another huge bonus. I used to do quite a lot of exercise – swimming, hooping, weights, mini-trampolining, etc. – and regular middle-distance walks of five to six miles. In the last couple of years, it has all fallen away, thanks to Ms A. For a start, I have to spend almost every waking moment doing my three jobs: carer, domestic, writer. Even if I do find myself with a rare spare hour, I feel obliged to devote it to Nick, whom it's increasingly difficult to leave 'unsupervised' for more than a very short time. For a long time now, my exercise routine has been reduced to gratefully striding between Tube stations when I can and taking stairs rather than lifts and escalators.

Well, my weight is more or less okay at present but I'm jolly flabby. Not for much longer, I suspect. Pushing a wheelchair with an adult man on board – even one who tips the scales at barely nine stone – immediately finds muscles you didn't know you had. Pushing it up a slope (plenty of those in our area) really works your thighs and calves, and even proceeding on the flat makes you use your whole upper body and back. With every step, I can feel my fitness improving, and it's extraordinary how much better that makes me feel.

I'm not banking on too many more summers, but I reckon this one could be quite a lot better than it might have been.

8 May 2019

The War of Elkin's Ear broke out last week. Well, 'war' might be a bit of an exaggeration but Nick certainly looked like a bit-part actor in a field hospital scene by the time Ms Alzheimer's and Royal Sussex A&E in Brighton had finished with him on Sunday.

It all started with the TV remote control. Blooming thing went AWOL on Saturday night. Nick's incessant, obsessive, tiresome fiddling with and moving or 'hiding' things has got noticeably worse of late. I'm always reminding him to put things down or quietly replacing them where they should be. But I can't supervise every waking minute; Ms A is very sly and things have an increasing habit of simply disappearing. I don't actually watch a lot of TV but I reserve the right to do so when I want to. At present, I can't apart from on my iPad. And that's jolly annoying. It had been a difficult couple of days anyway with a series of very bad, broken nights. The lost remote was the last straw. I sounded off forcibly at Nick (I know I shouldn't but…) and on the family WhatsApp group.

Early Sunday morning, my younger daughter-in-law, Liz – who must be one of the kindest, most tolerant and thoughtful women on the planet – rang. "Susan, I think you should come to Brighton today," she said. "You need a break. We'll look after him while you go out for the afternoon – round the Brighton Open Houses, for example." So I scampered round tidying up, phoned Ocado to change my delivery slot and grabbed Nick's emergency rucksack – the grown-up equivalent of a nappy bag. Then I bundled him into the car and headed for the M23, arriving at their house about noon.

The Brighton Open Houses were lovely. I had a good look at the arts and crafts in about six of them, bought a pretty bracelet and then had a quiet cup of tea and a read in the lovely café and blissful solitude at St Augustine's Events Centre before heading back. It was really quite a therapeutic couple of hours. I felt almost calm. Back at base, Felix started to cook a vegetarian roast supper for us all. Nick kept picking up their remote and trying to tell me he'd found ours but we worked round that.

So far so good, until ten minutes before the meal (smelling good) would have been ready. Nick suddenly got up from sitting next to me on the sofa where we'd been looking at the Sunday papers. Usually now wobbly when he's vertical, he lost his footing and slipped. He seemed to slide on a newspaper one of us had left on the floor and fell into the bay window where his head hit the radiator. The sharp-ish edge of it sliced his earlobe and almost severed it. Cupping it in my hand in horror, I yelled for the chef and of course the upshot was that within a few minutes, at about 6.00, we were heading for A&E, turning off the oven and leaving long-suffering Liz to get GD4 (aged four) to bed.

Inevitably, it was a long, long evening. As always with the NHS, we had a great deal of excellent, caring, competent service from individuals, culminating in a very pleasant young Ear, Nose and Throat doctor, named Sarah, putting ten stitches in Elkin's Ear and making it whole again. The staff are brilliant. It's the system and modus operandi that could do with a shake-up. We finally ate our reheated nut roast at about midnight.

By then, it was obviously too late to drive back to London. Bless them, they gave us their bed so Nick could use the en suite, and lent us PJs. Then our lovely son rustled up cooked breakfast in the morning for a treat. We finally got home at about midday on Monday, much to the relief of our very hungry cat.

So much for my having any sort of respite – I was much more tired at the end of all this than at the beginning. The whole experience has taught me a few things, though.

I've realised that I'm still underestimating Nick's growing disability – possibly because it changes every day, mostly for the worse. He needs watching and probably assisting when he gets in and out of a seated position. QED. Most of the time, I do it, but I still forget sometimes. One of the things they tested at the hospital was blood pressure lying and standing, and it seems his BP drops when he's on his feet – hence the wobbliness. Susan, take note. And just forget all that much-bandied-about stuff which implies Alzheimer's is mostly about memory loss. It's a holistic disease with long and powerful tentacles.

I am also reminded of just how supportive our fabulous family are. That long wait at the hospital would have been much worse if Felix hadn't been with us. He could have dropped us off and come back for us when we were done, but I don't think the thought even crossed his mind. And his wife, whose evening and weekend was completely scuppered, just takes it all equably without a word of complaint. Libby, GD4, meanwhile, bought me some flowers – all her own idea, apparently – while they were in the supermarket just before we arrived. "Let's get some flowers for Granny Susan." Yes, I have a lot to be very grateful for.

15 May 2019

I suppose, at some point in the future, I shall be allowed to sleep for more than an hour or two. I yawn with excitement at the mere prospect, but I know it's unlikely to be tonight, or tomorrow night or the night after.

What routinely happens is this. I put Nick to bed, having washed, dried, dressed and tucked him in exactly as you would a child. He goes straight to sleep and I go off to have my bath after I've tidied and locked up downstairs. Finally, I get into bed beside him – still peacefully sleeping – and read for a bit.

Then it starts. The moment I put the light out and snuggle down, he's awake and chatty. There's a word for this well-recognised phenomenon. It's called 'sundowning' and is, I gather, a classic Alzheimer's symptom. What is, apparently, unusual in our case, is that the sometimes hours-long midnight monologues are more fluent than anything he ever says during the day. The man who now really struggles to work out and articulate, for instance, "Can you pass the pepper?" at lunchtime or "I can't find my glasses" when he's just taken them off will, at 1am, casually come out with the likes of "But that precludes the necessity" or "It depends on the strength of the application."

Not that what he says makes any contextual sense at all. Typically, it goes something like this: "There was a boy at Honour Oak Park

Station. We must ask the others. I don't want to see you chopped up in pieces. It's an executive decision. I'm cold. We could share the fireplace. Have you signed the authorisation? There's the other gentleman to remember. You've committed a criminal offence." And I've taken all that from notes I've made next morning. It goes on and on, often for an hour or three, all delivered in a monotonous, mid-register whisper. It reminds me very much of a poorly dramatised version of *Finnegan's Wake* without the Irish accent.

Sometimes, I try to engage with it on the basis that if he gets a response he might find some peace and we can both go to sleep. "We can talk about that in the morning. Let's go to sleep now" is a tack I often try. It doesn't work, although occasionally he gets quite shirty if I try to doze and ignore it.

"Listen to me, woman," he said fiercely the other night. It's as if someone else – the toxic being I call Ms A, maybe – is inside his head borrowing his voice, because in fifty years of married life he has never spoken to me in that tone. How appalled the real Nick – wherever he is now – would be if he were around to hear it.

When it's particularly bad, I give up, get up and leave him to it. If I go to work in my office, which is next to the bedroom, I can hear him if he moves and at least I can do something constructive with the time. I've quite often, in recent weeks, penned a review or a feature at 2am. It isn't the healthiest way to live, though.

It's hard to fathom where Nick's poor muddled mind is and what terrifying hell it must be to be locked in a world where you can't tell the difference between dreams, fantasies and worries and prosaic reality. I wonder how many hundreds of times I've said: "Listen. Trust me. There's no one else here and absolutely nothing to worry about. It's just you and me in this bed in Catford and it's three o'clock in the morning – time to go to sleep."

He pauses for a few seconds, says "Really?" in a brighter, reassured voice, takes a breath and relaunches Finnegan. I know how King Canute felt.

I'm trying to persuade the GP to prescribe some sort of sleeping pill that won't conflict with the Alzheimer's medication, but I'm not getting anywhere much at the moment. I've pointed out that Nick is tired all day – although it's hard to tell how much of that is Ms A doing her stuff and how much is down to the restless nights. More to the point is that I'm doing the caring twenty-four seven more or less single-handedly, thereby saving the support services much work and cost, and if I'm to keep that up, I need a night's sleep occasionally.

Ironically, I used to be an insomniac. Now, I can fall asleep almost instantly – if I get the chance – exactly as I used to be able to over forty years ago when I had babies to breastfeed in the small hours. I've become an opportunist kipper to such an extent that I'm usually involuntarily asleep within five minutes of getting on any sort of public transport, and I sometimes struggle for wakefulness in the theatre, which is infuriating. I also now think twice – an informal risk assessment – about driving far if we've had a really rough night, which can mean I have to cancel a work commitment.

That's one of the most pernicious things about this bloody disease. It doesn't just get the sufferer. Its knock-on effects reach further than most people – who don't have to live with it – can begin to imagine.

22 May 2019

I regard myself as a sensible person but, oh boy, have I been stupid. I've been interested in food all my life. I cook. I read recipes. For a while in the 1980s, I taught vegetarian cookery as a sideline. I read lots of books about eating and its effects. I know about nutrition and healthy eating. Yet, although I had vaguely noted that Nick is becoming seriously underweight, I hadn't considered what I should be doing about it. Now that I've confronted it, my former lack of awareness is almost unbelievable.

Some background: I have struggled with my weight all my adult life and have long adapted my eating habits to keep calories low but plates full. This is nothing to do with 'going on a diet'. It's a permanent way of living. That means cooking with very little fat or oil, bulking out every meal with vegetables (we became vegetarian in 1978) and always buying low-fat versions of anything where there's an option – cheese being an obvious example, along with ready-mades such as pesto, curry sauces, salad dressings, and so on. It also meant not buying or making cakes or puddings except on special occasions.

Well, of course I didn't cook two versions. I simply made what I regarded as a healthy meal and served it for us both. When he was well, I realise now he was so used to this routine that he thought nothing of it and he often had an extra course such as cheese and biscuits. He was fit, reasonably active and stayed the same weight for many years.

Then Ms Alzheimer's arrived and his body began to disappear. All the medical professionals comment on it and express concern. They keep weighing him.

We have recently been visited twice at home by a very pleasant, congenial, practical speech therapist to whom we were referred because Nick has a persistent, worsening cough. Nasties, such as lung cancer, have been eliminated and the consensus now is that the cough – like his diminishing voice – relates to the weakening of his swallowing reflex, which is an Alzheimer's symptom. Anne, the speech therapist, wanted to observe Nick eating so that she could make practical suggestions to ease the situation for him. Quite early in the conversation, she observed that his clothes are very loose and asked about his weight.

The upshot is – not that she would have put it in these terms – that I've been starving him for decades and now that he's ill, the effects are showing. He's unlikely, at this stage, to put weight on because, towards the end of life, as Shakespeare observed, 'shrunk shank' is natural, but in order to keep him as strong as he can be for as long as possible we must try to stop him losing any more.

And that means a big rethink. My fridge now looks like something in a student-shared house. I have two plastic pots of grated cheese labelled with our names – mine's low-fat and his is full. There's hummus in two versions. I have a bottle of top-quality walnut oil which I drizzle over his pasta or rice at table. I put what Enid Blyton would have called 'lashings of butter' on his toast. I give him best dairy ice cream, formerly an occasional treat, almost daily. I buy him those little individual steam sponge puddings you can do in the microwave. I encourage him to drink more fruit juice.

Anne also suggested I make him food that slips down very easily, on account of the swallowing problem. So now it's very soft sandwiches with cream cheese (full-fat, naturally) or gooey egg mayonnaise. And I dutifully cut the crusts off, feeling as though I've morphed into my pretentious maternal grandmother or an underling in the kitchen at Fortnum & Mason. It's a pity he has never liked soup but the cut-off crusts (I was brought up not to waste anything) work well as bread dippers for my daily low-calorie lunchtime bowl. Biscuits are a 'tough eat' too, I'm told, so I've been buying moist fruitcake and malt loaf for him – and although I've barely made a cake since my hungry sons left home, I'm resolved to go back to baking as long as I can resist the temptation to eat the results myself. I shall have to do as I always used to when the boys were small and make the sorts of cake I don't much like.

It all feels very odd because it flies in the face of everything I've done for decades. And, in a funny way, it really isn't all that healthy because he's eating, for example, less fruit and fewer vegetables, although he's probably still consuming more than the average Brit. He's certainly also having more sugar, given his cake consumption, but I suppose it's a question of balance. At this point, preventing further weight loss matters more than fretting about the finer points of his diet. We have to deal with the present. There is, after all, precious little future to safeguard against.

I really ought – given the level of my engagement with food and healthy eating – to have worked all this out for myself and done something about it before now. I must be more blinkered than I thought. Too much else to think about too.

29 May 2019

I am heartily sick of seeing attractive photographs of smiling people with Alzheimer's. You know the sort of thing. The Alzheimer's Society and comparable charities pump them out on social networks every day, along with upbeat stories about astonishing people who have just climbed Everest (or something) for charity five years after diagnosis.

Yes, I know that when a disease is incurable and inexorable, the only thing these organisations can do to support the newly diagnosed is to try to be positive. 'Let's all look on the bright side' might have been written for them. The ghastly truth, when you actually live with it twenty-four seven, is so frightful that it would scare the pants off most people if it were spelled out.

Well, I'm sorry (but not very). I don't do denial and lies. Nick – now I think technically at the 'moderate to severe stage' – is doubly incontinent. I have to hose him down night and morning and often several times in between. I never had any sort of nursing vocation, I reflect, as I wipe dollops of excrement from the bathroom floor, sponge more of the same off his legs and dispose of filthy pairs of throwaway pants. Sometimes, I can hardly believe I'm doing it. At present, our black bin is emptied fortnightly and with everything tightly wrapped that's just about okay. If they try, as some boroughs are threatening, to reduce it to three-weekly or monthly, it most definitely won't be. Nothing about any of that in those upbeat photographs, I notice.

Nick is, incidentally, now quite beyond managing any of this for himself. He can just about clean his teeth if I put the paste on the brush and lead him to the basin, although he makes a horrid, sticky mess of it. He also still shaves. Again, I run the warm water, take him there, line up the four items he needs and leave him to get on with it. I doubt that he'll be able to do it for much longer. Then what? Grow a beard? I don't think I'd be much cop as a barber.

He finds sitting down on any sort of chair very difficult to co-ordinate – simply getting his bottom above the seat and bending his knees to lower himself is a major operation. When we're out – from medical appointment to theatre to sitting on a bench in the park – other people usually help. So kind, as I've often said. He eats very messily these days, however easy I try to make it for him. He isn't in the least like any published Alzheimer's charity ad.

He is extremely wobbly on his legs and often gets 'the shakes'. Since the severed ear saga in Brighton, he has fallen in our bathroom and again on Spring Bank Holiday Monday in our garden. The latter meant the whole afternoon at a local emergency care centre because he dislocated and fractured his left-hand ring finger.

And as for all those smiling faces – often euphoric as they look at photograph albums, for example – in the pictures, the new Nick now has a blank expressionless gaze. There's a rather old-fashioned un-PC expression about someone 'not being all there'. Absolutely accurate. He definitely isn't there much – most – of the time.

Then there's the usual Alzheimer's memory/cognition stuff, which is worse every day. He remembers almost nothing. I can say, "We're going out this afternoon" ten times in a morning and he's still surprised when I tell him it's time to go. I ask him if he wants a slice of cake and he says yes. By the time I get back to the table with it, he's shambled off and, when I remonstrate, says, "I didn't know I was having cake." And the non sequiturs get worse. Inclined to follow me about anyway, he was today lurking behind the front door when I came in from watering the hanging basket by the porch. "Oh, do go and sit down," I said in irritation.

"It was for toast," he muttered.

Oh yes, the muttering. He now speaks mostly in a very low voice in between bouts of coughing. Both these, apparently, are the result of a failing swallowing reflex. Then there are frequent bouts of Jabberwocky-style nonsense words. Great stuff, this disease, is it not?

I could go on but you've probably got the gist. A spade is most definitely a spade if I'm in charge of it. Nick is now a leaky, seeping, accident-prone body with whom you can no longer have any sort of conversation, and often very irritable – not a wholesome, smiley old gent who has just forgotten a few things.

All rose-coloured spectacles in the bin.

5 June 2019

I enjoyed the recent witty, rueful correspondence in the *Daily Telegraph* about the age or stage at which you stop 'falling over' and start 'having falls'. I'm inclined to think the change takes place when you can no longer get up. But it's all academic and it doesn't make much difference what you call it. In recent weeks, Ms Alzheimer's – or one of her pals – has firmly shoved Nick into the 'having falls' category.

During the last month, he has, as I have detailed, fallen in our son's house and almost severed his earlobe, gone headlong in our own garden and broken a finger, slipped getting out of the shower and knocked me over (it would seem we even share bruises these days) and fallen a second time in the garden and grazed his arm. Yesterday, I came downstairs to find him distressed on the dining-room floor, apparently unhurt but quite unable to help lever himself up. Thank goodness for the family WhatsApp group. GD1, who's training as a nurse, made some very helpful suggestions. In the end, I went next door where Ben (not his real name) lives with his partner and his feisty ninety-four-year-old granny whom they look after. Thank goodness he was in. Not only did he drop everything to help me get Nick off the floor but he gave me his mobile in case of future problems.

"If I'm not here, I can ring my uncle up the road and he'll come down," he said. I was almost weeping with gratitude by the time he went back to his granny.

The worrying thing about all this, of course, is that we are presumably at serious risk of a much worse fall any minute. And it's pretty hard to prevent, because you can't reason with someone to whom Ms A's claws cling so tightly. I can say until I'm hoarse with repetition: "Now just sit there and look at the papers/listen to the radio (substitute as appropriate) while I go and make the bed," but within a few seconds he's forgotten what I said and is on his feet shambling about. Part of the problem, I think, is that he's suddenly – for no physical reason I can fathom – become very hunched. He's now inclined to shuffle, head and arms towards the ground like a very slow, sick gorilla. It's not, as I keep trying to explain to him and failing, how human beings are supposed to walk. It means the centre of gravity is awry and he's inclined to tumble forward.

So he really has to be watched almost continuously. I am – and this is a first – writing this blog on my iPad sitting next to him at the dining table so I can keep an eye on him as I type. It is no longer safe, other than when I know he's resting horizontal or late at night when I've got him to bed, to leave him unsupervised even for a few minutes. Realistically, I can no longer repair to my upstairs office where all my things are and where I feel instantly in work mode.

Yes – before you ask the obvious question – the local NHS 'Falls Service' have been notified of our predicament. An occupational therapist is coming from there later this week to assess him and make some suggestions about safety. Well, Lucas has already put in ramps and a second stair rail. And while I was away recently, he sensibly put some grab rails up. He knew I'd protest so he just did it as a fait accompli in my absence and he was right. The OT will probably 'prescribe' more, and I'm not looking forward to her visit.

I'm torn between trying to be sensible and caring and agreeing to the 'desecration' of the house I've worked so hard to get as I want – and how I like it – over the last three years since we downsized from Kent.

It is clearly time to get more 'help' too. I'm in the process of applying for one of those dreaded 'social services packages' to supplement the care I'm already paying for to cover my absence when I'm out working. Even the doctor at the emergency care clinic last week was surprised that I have no official help, and that was a bit telling.

A lot is said and written about maintaining the independence and autonomy of people with Alzheimer's and similar conditions. One hears a lot less about the independence of the carer. It now costs me a substantial sum in man-sitting fees every time I leave the house, and now it seems I can't even exercise my freedom to go where I want, when I want, within the house. As I often say to anyone who'll listen: All I have ever really wanted to do is to carry on working. And I get really frustrated when circumstances make that so difficult, because work is my lifeline. Nothing to do with money – it's what keeps me sane.

12 June 2019

Many women despair over snoring husbands. It leads to anguish, anger and separate bedrooms. Not me. The excellent news is that Nick has started snoring, and I couldn't be happier because it means that he is well and truly asleep. The change is all down to our lovely GP, Dr K. Although we're in a group practice, we've seen Dr K several times recently so we know him and he knows us. I now regard him as 'ours'.

I told Dr K that if he didn't help me find a way of stopping Nick and Ms Alzheimer's keeping me awake for hours every night with their nonsensical chattering and fidgeting, then he'd soon have two pretty sick patients on his hands rather than one. He has really pulled the stops out to help, consulting a specialist colleague about what drugs can be taken alongside the Alzheimer's medication and then ringing me to see how we were getting on. Anyway, at the second attempt, we have found something that works. I give Nick the capsule to swallow mid-evening. By the time he's washed, dried and tucked up in bed between ten and eleven, he drops off instantly. Within a few minutes, the snoring starts and I'm punching the air in glee. The result of this is that during the last week, I've started, after many months of badly broken nights, sleeping for six, seven or eight hours. Result? I'm a New Woman.

It's not the only thing that has improved either. Both my regular carers have agreed to get Nick showered and into bed before I get home when I'm out reviewing and they're doing a man-sitting shift. This feels like Christmas and my birthday rolled into one each time it happens. It means that instead of facing an hour's hard labour with a by-then tetchy man at the end of the day when I'm tired, I can get myself straight to bed or, if I feel like it, sit and write the review in idyllic calm.

One of my carers has also agreed to do two morning slots for me on a regular basis from this week so that I don't have to spend the first hour of the day tending to someone else's personal hygiene. I'm determined to do something useful with that time. I hope to ring-fence it for violin practice. I'm always saying that it too often gets squeezed out.

So, all in all, I'm feeling quite positive at present. It's amazing what a few decent kips can do.

Meanwhile, of course, my life may have improved a little but Nick's illness certainly hasn't and won't. Everything about Alzheimer's is hideously cruel and in our case there seem to be loads of Parkinson's symptoms as well: loss of muscle tone in various parts of the body, including throat and swallowing so that he coughs continuously, for instance. He does a lot of 'freezing' too – stopping mid-action because he can't remember what he's supposed to be doing – sitting down on a chair or walking round the bed, say – and even if he can, his brain isn't sending the right messages to his limbs.

And I strongly suspect that he's often much more confused than I realise because if he doesn't say anything, I don't know what's going on in his head. Last Thursday, not long after he woke up, I said, "Oh, by the way, there was some lovely news last night from the Wilders [not their real name]. They've got their new grandchild, a little girl." I had forgotten myself and was chatting normally.

Now, Philip Wilder, with whom Nick was at school, and his wife are some of our oldest friends. Well, he didn't say much. A few minutes later, I started the getting-up routine with him. By then, he'd clearly completely forgotten who I was. When I pressed him, he said brightly, "You're Philip Wilder." The confusion lasted much of the day. Halfway to Chichester to see and review *Plenty,* he accused me of being a doctor. He was burbling about a girlfriend he had for a few months nearly sixty years ago when he and I were still just friends too. He thought I was her. Upsetting? I don't allow it to be. I just smile and wonder what persona he'll assign to me next. But if any indication that he's slipping downhill were needed, there it is.

His walking ability is waning fast too. Thank goodness I bought the wheelchair when I did because it's proving very useful indeed and means he'll be able to get to a few more plays and concerts – not that he shows much interest, but I feel instinctively that it must be better for him to be out and about than not.

As long as he goes on sleeping so that I can too, then somehow I shall cope. Long may he snore.

19 June 2019

This is not a *cri de coeur*. It's an observation. I am wryly (grimly) amused to discover over the last week or two that there comes a point in this hideous disease when the much-promoted doorways to 'help' begin to close against you. It's a good job I'm resourceful and, by nature, a coper.

Last week, I was advised to contact the local dementia support hub on the grounds that they're 'really helpful' and 'can support you in lots of ways'. Well, I'm sure that's true if you – or your Alzheimer's person – has just been diagnosed and you're floundering. But it seems not to apply if you're (as, ever-truthful, I have worked out we are) approaching the end of stage 6 in a disease which – shades of Shakespeare's Jacques in *As You Like It* – is deemed to have seven stages.

I spoke to a very pleasant woman at the hub who mentioned most of the things I did long ago such as applying for attendance allowance, registering for reduced council tax and setting up lasting power of attorney. She then mentioned various local activities that Nick might take part in, but my mention of double incontinence was a conversation stopper. "Oh, I'm so sorry," she said. "None of the centres and clubs we work with are suitable if there are toileting issues." We ended up affably agreeing that there is nothing her organisation can do for us, although she kindly sent me some leaflets – which, inevitably, tell me very little I don't already know.

Then there was the private care agency I contacted with a view to setting up some regular morning visits. I wanted someone competent to get Nick up, showered, etc., and give me a bit of free time and space. When the two women who visited saw just how severe Nick's condition now is, they emailed afterwards to say that their carers would only be able to work with us if I was on hand to assist (and, by implication, take responsibility). Well, that, of course, is no use at all, so I told them I wouldn't proceed. Instead, one of my regular carers is going to do it.

I've also spoken to social services. A pleasant man phoned me – once I'd asked my ever-helpful GP to give them a prod because, to my astonishment, they weren't taking phone calls when I tried to approach them a week or two earlier. Hard luck if you have a serious emergency, clearly.

Now, I'm well aware that I'm going to have to pay the entire cost of any care Nick has: that's the reward for working very hard all my life, living within my income and saving money regularly. I've been paying carers I found and hired independently (very good they are too) for seven months now. When I explained this to the social services man, he suggested that I simply carry on with that because if I opt for a social services 'package', they will design and control it while I foot the bill. That was fair of him, I suppose. I do rather object to both paying and being told what to do. Whatever happened to 'He who pays the piper calls the tune'? But it felt like yet another organisation washing its hands of us.

I've also been brightly advised by several professionals (my counsellor, Nick's speech therapist, the physio *et al.*) to contact the local carers' group. "What would they be able to do for me?" I asked cautiously.

"Oh, they can support you in lots of ways. They have meetings and events for carers," comes the answer. Well, no doubt it's an excellent service for people who feel isolated, but I really don't want to create a social life out of sharing woes with other carers. Moreover, there are dozens of events in my world that I could attend every week, and I'd really like to – if only I could get away more. I haven't contacted the group.

Within the family, our fabulous sons do their best and are tremendously supportive, but neither is now keen on taking sole charge for too long because the responsibility is so great. And one of 'my' regular carers is becoming concerned that she doesn't have the training to deal with an accident on the stairs, so she's understandably reluctant to commit herself too far into the future as the whole situation spirals downwards. Fortunately, my other carer – and I shall very soon have to find and hire one or two more like her so that I have a watertight team to help me cope with the downward path – is very experienced, completely unfazed by the situation and willing and able to do anything that's needed.

For the 'future' – and who knows when that will be? – I'm planning to put a bed downstairs for Nick with a bed sensor which works like a baby alarm so I'd hear him if he tried to get out of bed. I have it in mind, when the time comes, to ask for a hospital bed, and at the present rate of decline I think it's likely to be sooner rather than later. I also intend to apply, eventually, for a not very well publicised NHS service called 'continuing home care' (CHC), which gives you daily nursing at home. I learned about this from a newspaper article and then researched it further, by the way. No professional I've spoken to has mentioned it. CHC means that you're not bed-blocking in a hospital or dumped in a care home. I'm told it's difficult to get, but I reckon I can probably fill in the forms persuasively. Words are what I do, after all.

Meanwhile, I'm chuckling ruefully. When Alzheimer's is first diagnosed, every doctor, other medical professional, friend, colleague or the person you're standing next to in the supermarket queue tells you brightly that there is a great deal of help available. Not when the going gets really rough, there isn't.

3 July 2019

When I'm trying to assess – or get my head round – the helter-skelter speed of Nick's decline, few things are more telling than the look in other people's eyes. The people who see him frequently – me, the immediate family, carers and other regular callers – are well aware of the way the man we once knew is disappearing, almost literally (weight now way under nine stone) as we watch. But it's only when Nick and I see someone we haven't seen for a while that I see that look of shocked, sympathetic horror, and I'm reminded just how far things have really gone.

Last weekend, I played in the Hayes Symphony Orchestra summer concert in a church in West Wickham – one of a number of musical events I'm involved in each year. Elder son, Lucas, came for the weekend with his wonderfully practical, kind and helpful wife, Mrs W-E. Between them, they have forty years of library employment, so they went into professional mode and put everything back in my office after its redecoration so I'm now better organised and more orderly than I've ever been. And, even more importantly, they looked after Nick while I went to the Saturday afternoon rehearsal and then brought him over to the concert.

I'd arranged a wheelchair reservation and Lucas wheeled him in. As ever these days, Nick was looking a bit irritable and slightly bemused. That habitual blank, middle-distance stare into eternity is both sad and chilling. It seems right for him to have been there. After all, he's been attending musical performances I've been part of all the years we've been together, often in the past as a front-of-house volunteer. And it was a pleasant concert by any standard. These days, I'm pretty sure he neither knows nor cares what's going on, although, as Lucas pointed out, conventional concert behaviour is deeply programmed in. He sits quietly during the music and claps at the end. None of what he heard would have been new to him anyway. He's known the very mainstream repertoire we played all his life. Besides, I've dragged him along and seated him at the back where I can see him for almost every rehearsal this term because that's still just about okay, and it saves me paying a carer. I suspect, however, that by the time the orchestra reconvenes in September, taking him with me will no longer be an option.

Also at the concert were six members – three generations – of my extended family who live nearby. Two old friends, one of whom goes right back to our schooldays, came too. It's a few months since we saw any of them in the flesh, although a lot of Facebooking goes on. And most of them read these blogs.

I was very aware of the reactions – in eight different people – when they looked at Nick, physically weak in his wheelchair and unable to string even one sensible sentence together. Each and every one of them, of course, made a point of going over to him and trying to engage with him because folks everywhere are generally extraordinarily kind and decent – and it's taken me seven decades and a nasty disease to appreciate that fully.

Nick has known most of these eight people for many years. One was a bridesmaid at our wedding back in 1969. Yet I don't think he had a clue who anyone was at all. When I went back to find my violin for the second half, Lucas was saying with a patient, slightly rueful grin: "You have two sons. I'm Lucas, the elder one, and this lovely lady next to me who cooked your lunch is my wife." Nick just said "Really?" as if he were at a drinks party making polite conversation and getting bored with it.

The looks of pity say it all. Back at the car at the end of the concert, Lucas was busy bodily lifting his father into the car (which I can't do, of course, and have to make do with tortuous guided shuffling when I'm in charge) while I was chatting to the old schoolfriend and his wife a few feet away. Suddenly I could see what they were seeing: a very sick, emaciated, confused old man barely recognisable as the feisty, opinionated, active chap they used to know. Lucas actually thought there was a noticeable deterioration even in the forty-eight hours he and Daughter-in-Law were with us over the weekend. I suspect most of 'my' concert groupies went home wondering if they'd ever see him again.

7 July 2019

Nick can no longer manage the stairs. In fact, trying to climb them, whoever is behind him helping, has become very dangerous for all concerned as he sways, staggers and freezes, unable to process verbal instructions. Big gulp and time to accept that we've now moved on to a late stage in this ghastly, plummeting illness. And it calls for new sleeping and bathroom arrangements.

Well, we're more fortunate than some. One of the things that attracted us to the 1930s three-bed semi we moved to in south London three years ago was the spacious kitchen in a large rear extension. So the original galley kitchen gives us an extra room at the side of the house with a downstairs loo behind it. It was meant to be Nick's office. Once he stopped doing office-y things, I commandeered it as a music room. Now, as his parameters close in, it is to become his sleeping area. I hesitate to call it a bedroom because it's rather more clinical than cosy.

Take back what I said recently about Lewisham Health and Social Care because they've come up trumps and provided the hospital bed I asked for. The two therapists from the Falls Service who have visited the house several times have turned out to be good advocates. They can see at a glance how serious the problem is, but beds are outside their budget. Beds are in the gift of social services, apparently. Then one of them rang me about something else and I told her that I really couldn't, under the circumstances, be faffing about with waiting lists. We don't have time to wait. I would, I said, therefore buy a bed privately. "Give me an hour before you do that," she replied. The upshot was that she spoke to someone at LHSC and they agreed to supply me with one.

Yes, it was good news but, oh golly, the implications. As my sister (who's been more or less where I am now) hinted, once you start on hospital beds and sleeping downstairs then you know Ms Alzheimer's and her pals have a new friend hovering nearby. He, or maybe she, has a hood on his head and sickle over his shoulder.

Second, there was the issue of clearing the space. My elder son and daughter-in-law happened to be here when I got the call. They worked like Trojans to get the room ready and I was very grateful. I now have a filing cabinet in the dining room, a door behind the sofa, a desk in the guest bedroom and a piano in the wardrobe – as you do. All a nuisance – and definitely not what I would have chosen in the house I worked so hard to get as I want – but preferable to the care home alternative, which almost everyone I know now keeps murmuring at me.

Third, it is a very strange feeling when you've shared a bed with someone for half a century to know that now you're not going to – ever again. It's another – very big and quite symbolic – thing gone. I remember how upset my mother was when my father's illness forced them into a similar situation. I didn't understand at the time but I do now. It's like incremental widowhood.

I'm a practical person, though. For the last ten years, Nick and I have shared a six-foot bed because I liked the ones in, for example, American hotels. It isn't quite as large as the Great Bed of Ware but you get my drift. I had long since quietly decided that once I'm on my own, I shall get rid of it, buy something more modest for myself and make more room in the bedroom, which is a lot smaller than the one we bought said bed for.

Well, I've now brought that forward. I couldn't bear the idea of rattling about in that huge bed upstairs by myself while Nick is downstairs. On the day that I got the call about the hospital bed, I popped out, while I had people in the house to man-sit, and ordered the bed and mattress I had worked out I needed. By the middle of this month, I shall be a solo sleeper in a sensibly sized bed, although I still have to rattle for a few more days until it arrives.

Clearing 'our' bedroom of his personal bits and pieces – combs, photograph of his mother, bedside oddments – and taking them downstairs felt very odd indeed. So did making the bed with only one set of pillows on it, when I first did it. I must confess that I surprised myself by having 'a moment' while I was doing it. The upside, I suppose, is that it's one more threshold crossed and one less to face later.

10 July 2019

Well, the hospital bed is unslept in. My life has suddenly changed gear and I have no idea whether it's temporary, or in any sense permanent.

Nick is in hospital and my feelings ricochet continually from liberated to miserable, from relieved to worried and from pragmatic to guilty. So when I'm asked (about every five minutes on average) how I am, there isn't really an answer that tells the whole truth.

So what happened to trigger this new phase? His mobility levels have declined dramatically in the last couple of weeks, so the final night before the expected arrival of the downstairs hospital bed, I padded him up securely and settled him on the sofa for the night. It worked fine except that in the morning he couldn't stand up or balance at all. With the assistance of a carpet fitter and a physiotherapist, both of whom happened to be in the house that morning, we eventually got him back onto the sofa from the floor he'd slithered to. Then it was an ambulance, paramedics and Lewisham Hospital, where he's now been for a week.

He's on a bright, airy, quiet medical ward and being looked after well. Earlier this week, I persuaded a staff nurse to shave him and trim his moustache – all done willingly with cheerful good humour. And he's seen a neurologist, a speech therapist, physio and lots more. Basically, they are waiting to transfer him to a 'Care of the Elderly' ward (I suppose that perfectly decent, Greek-derived word 'geriatric' is no longer PC) for a full assessment but at present there isn't a bed. Every medical pro who sees him is mystified by the rapid deterioration because this is not typical of Alzheimer's. So they are gradually concluding that there are other illnesses in the mix, including maybe Parkinson's or Parkinsonism. Life is bloody unfair, isn't it?

I, of course, am not surprised by any of this. I live with him (or did until last week) and have been saying most of what they're now saying for months. I can't tell medics their job, but curious information-seeking journalist that I am, I first mentioned 'dementia with Lewy Bodies' eight months ago in November. Now they're all talking about it. Frankly, I don't now think it matters what you call it. He is very ill and we have to manage the situation as it is. The medics are muttering about trying Parkinson's medication very cautiously with an escalating dosage, but there are potential problems with drugs not agreeing with each other, or causing dangerous side effects, so I'm really not sure whether it's a good idea or not.

So how is he in himself? Very sleepy and rarely with us. He sometimes knows who I am and can tell me my name, but don't bank on it. In A&E last week, he told the doctor that our eldest son was 'my daddy', a word I have never heard him use in nearly sixty years of knowing him. He must have slid back, at that moment, to about age eight. Most of the time now he mutters incoherently and softly – trying to communicate something, but we have no idea what. At the time of writing, he hasn't been out of bed since he left home. Nurses clean and feed him. His condition has declined even since he's been in hospital. Quality of life? None.

So what happens now? Well, I think he'll be in hospital some time while they attempt to sort out medication. Then there's a suggestion that he might go to a 'neurodegenerative rehabilitation centre' (note the contradiction in terms) for a bit before coming home to the awaiting hospital bed with a home nursing plan. I wonder. Given the speed at which he's going downhill, I'm not convinced.

Back at base, I'm trying to adjust things like food quantities for someone living alone. I did a single person's supermarket shop at the weekend and spent, amazingly, only £22. I've also put all the illness gear – packets of pants, plastic bags, wipes, special cutlery, etc., way out of sight. I can get it out again easily enough later if the situation changes. Or not. But the house looks more like home.

And I have to be honest (because that's the way I am). It is actually easier to live and work with him safe in hospital than it is when I'm constantly worrying about where he is, what he's doing, booking carers, rushing to get home to relieve them and all the rest of it. A lot cheaper too and I'm less tired. But as silver linings go, it's pretty ragged.

17 July 2019

He was seventy-three when he went into hospital and now, two weeks on, he is seventy-four. Not a great age by twenty-first-century standards.

The bedside birthday party went as well as it could. Nick drowsed and muttered occasionally while the rest of us – both sons, one daughter-in-law and two elder granddaughters – worked our butts off to be jolly and upbeat in an appropriate register. Hard work but I think we pulled it off.

First of all, let me say a huge thank-you to all the people – many of them readers of this blog – who sent cards. We had four times as many as he would usually get. We painstakingly showed him each and every one and reminded him who all these kind people were. I had something in my eye during much of this. At one point, I had to slip out into the corridor, comforted by GD2. The messages were so carefully thought-out and the cards so tactfully chosen. Of course, we all know that there won't be a seventy-fifth birthday. That's why it was so poignant.

I baked a squishy chocolate cake and took it to the hospital. After a muted rendering of *Happy Birthday*, I made sure that the other three men in the bay and their visitors all had a piece. And I was tremendously touched by two doctors, to whom I'd spoken several times previously. We met them downstairs by chance while we were waiting for GD1 and GD2 to arrive from Suffolk before we went up to the ward. "Oh, we've bought balloons and we're on our way up with them," they said. What nice people – but actually that's been true of almost every medical professional we've encountered at Lewisham Hospital.

He's now been there two weeks, having transferred to "Care of the Elderly" from Medical after the first five days. They've done a lot of tests and drawn several blanks. An MRI scan shows Alzheimer's (as did the original one at his diagnosis twenty-seven months ago) but no Parkinson's, although there may be some Parkinsonism. Neither has he had a stroke, and his heart, blood pressure, etc., are more or less normal.

So why has he gone downhill so fast? Well, it's partly bad luck and a hideous, hateful illness. The much-quoted four– to eight-year post-diagnosis survival rate is just an average. For some people it's less and for others it's more. But why – and this is what has been puzzling the medics – has the rate of deterioration accelerated so much in the last month?

The new theory – and let this be a lesson to us all – is dehydration. Nick has been pretty tiresome about drinks all his life – always demanding tiny cups and glasses and refusing to drink more than a few drips of anything. And lately it's got worse. As one of the doctors observed on the day of writing, "Lessening of appetite and thirst is part of the progression of the condition." In recent weeks, I've been struggling, really struggling, to get even half a pint of liquid into him each day.

At the hospital, they've been topping him up with an intravenous feed into a canula. The aim is gradually to bring his sodium levels down because excess sodium can add to confusion. It seems to be working, and he's now awake a little more often than he's asleep and sometimes makes a sensible comment such as a muttered, "No more now, thank you" when I'm trying to feed or water him.

When he seemed to be slightly more with me briefly this morning, I said, "Come on. This is serious. You must drink more. You know what happens to slugs if you salt them? They shrivel up and die. That's what will happen to you!"

He actually grinned (sort of) and mumbled, "That's horrible!"

I replied: "Yes, it is. That's why you must drink more both in this hospital and when you come out of here." But by then he'd gone out of focus again.

As far as I know, he hasn't been out of bed for a fortnight despite the best efforts of physiotherapists so he's pretty weak. Apparently, they (physios) will now try to sort him out ready for discharge – maybe at the end of next week. We're not going down the care home route if I can possibly help it.

The hospital bed awaits him at home with me. I have yet to discuss the dreaded 'care package' with anyone, but I envisage supplementing whatever I agree to have arranged for me with the man-sitting carers I already have so that I can still go out working. And at least I shall be able to prepare some tasty vegetable and fruit purees. He only eats a few teaspoonfuls of anything now and really doesn't like what they try to give him in hospital. His swallowing mechanism is now pretty poor, but the catering people don't seem to have got the messages about soft food – especially when you want it to be vegetarian as well.

I suspect he'll be more or less bedridden from here on. And I sincerely hope that 'from here on' isn't for too long, because his quality of life is non-existent. Who wants to live for months as a decelerating, muttering, largely prostrate body while well-meaning people shovel food in one end and clean up the other?

I often think about Nick's father, my father-in-law, George. He died less than five years ago at the age of eighty-nine. Had he had the longevity of, say, the Duke of Edinburgh or my feisty next-door neighbour, he'd still be with us now. Thank goodness he isn't. I am deeply relieved that he didn't live to see his only child as he is now.

24 July 2019

In the bed next to Nick, in the peaceful Lewisham Hospital top-floor ward overlooking leafy Ladywell Fields, is a man I'm pretty sure is a retired clergyman. He has a Bible and BCP on his locker, visibly prays, has a loud booming voice and a wife with vicar's wife-type social skills. Chatting to me last week, she looked at Nick, who was asleep as usual, and, not unreasonably, asked me what his illness was. She was surprised when I told her it's Alzheimer's. "I hadn't appreciated that it affects sufferers physically as well as mentally," she said. She isn't alone. Her husband, incidentally, aged eighty-six, has an infection and is expected to recover. Mine, of course, will not. Nick's brain is rapidly breaking down and that affects every part of the body. That's what the disease does. It's unrelenting and irreversible.

It's very odd how few people understand the progression of Alzheimer's. Yet it was very clear in that wonderful film *Iris* in which Judi Dench played the older Iris Murdoch. She became increasingly confused, rapidly more infirm, went to a care home and died after a short period of semi-consciousness in bed. I suppose memory loss is easier to comprehend and deal with. While there is no cure, it's almost taboo to dwell on the rest of it. You can almost romanticise early-stage memory loss and you can certainly joke about it, as I have often done in these blogs. Even now he mutters funny things sometimes. This morning, he was, inconsequentially, on about rawlplugs, for example.

In contrast, double incontinence, inability to swallow, feed yourself or stand up are about as unglamorous and unfunny as it comes. Someone said on the Alzheimer's Society website recently, '*When I was diagnosed, it felt like a death sentence*'. Well, yes, that's exactly what it is. No wonder so many people delay seeking help and becoming a dementia statistic. The longer you put it off, the longer you can delude yourself. Not a good idea really, but I can certainly understand why people think that way.

So Nick lies there in his hospital bed, quite peaceful and comfortable, with Ms Alzheimer's snuggled tightly under the bedclothes with him. She's sticking to him unrelentingly, but the one thing she doesn't seem to do is cause him any pain. Sometimes he's awake and from time to time he says something, or tries to. It's rarely anything I can understand or respond to and he speaks only in whispers. I think he usually recognises me even if he isn't sure who I am. As far as I know, he hasn't been out of bed for three weeks. Physios keep trying, using hoists, but since he can neither bear weight nor take instruction, it's abortive. Given that it was being unable to stand up which put him in hospital in the first place, I am at a loss to understand why anyone there thinks he's likely to be any better at it now after three weeks in bed, getting more wasted every day. This is, after all, a degenerative progressive disease. Why, therefore, keep disturbing and upsetting him?

I keep expecting to be told that he must be discharged because he's bed-blocking, but to the great credit of the staff on the ward – who are all kind, courteous, caring and friendly from the ward manager down to the silent woman who sweeps the floor but always smiles at both Nick and me – no one has yet mentioned this, except very vaguely as something for the future. In fact, whenever I ask, they tell me that there's no question of it until occupational therapists and social workers have made sure that everything is right and ready for him at home. And none of them has yet raised the subject with me. Maybe they know something I don't and there will be a call at 3am one morning telling me to get down to the hospital pronto. Or maybe this limbo will go on for months. And so we move into the fourth week... accepting, as the consultant put it this week, that 'this may be the new baseline'.

Meanwhile, I go to the hospital every day, fitting it in as best I can around work commitments. It now feels like a very familiar part of life. I even have a loyalty card for the café, where staff recognise me when I pick up a cup of tea to take up to the ward with me. I'm also au fait with Ladywell station, from where I have several times gone on into central London.

At present, I'm stoical rather than sad most of the time, although I wish very much that Ms A had allowed Nick a bit longer to enjoy the fruits of our move back to our native London three years ago. We had such plans for all the things we were going to do (visit the museums we missed in childhood, walk the Thames Path, attend lunchtime concerts at St Martin's in the Fields, etc.), but because of his illness we have done almost none of it. Earlier this year, I walked him from Angel Underground to King's Head Theatre, Islington (maybe a third of a mile) and he frightened me so much veering across the pavement that I bought a wheelchair the next day. The move has been a great success, in many ways, not least – as things have turned out – the escape from a large house with fifty-two stairs. For myself, I really love living where we now do, especially from a work point of view. The novelty of being able to meet someone for coffee at the National Theatre half an hour after walking out of my front door has yet to wear off. I just wish he'd had more chance to relish it all too.

31 July 2019

He's coming home. Eventually.

The plan is to discharge Nick to me now that he's 'stable'. He will sleep downstairs and be visited by a pair of carers four times a day. They will attend to his 'personal care' (thank goodness – less shit for me to deal with. Literally) and hoist him, using a bulky piece of kit which will live with us, into his wheelchair for part of the day. Then I/we shall be able to wheel him round the ground floor to the TV in the sitting room, the dining room to sit at table and maybe into the garden. It's not much in terms of life quality but perhaps a little better than lying in a hospital ward. And definitely better than any care home.

The $64,000 question – and I do so hope that's not literal too – is who is going to pay for the very high levels of home care he needs? Arguably, this should come under the NHS-funded Continuing Health Care (CHC) scheme, which is based on medical need. That, however, for obvious reasons, is very hard to get and something of a postcode lottery. At present, forms are being filled in and signed by all the professionals at the hospital ready to be sent to Lewisham Health and Social Care. LHSC will – if they are prepared to consider the case, and even that's not certain – then set up an assessment procedure of their own before finally making a decision. Then they have to find an agency with the capacity to provide the right level of care. If we 'pass' as it were, then it will be fully funded but – well, there are lots of 'buts'.

And none of that is going to happen in five minutes, is it? Moreover, although no one has said so, I reckon it's also all bound to take longer at this time of year because key people will be away and offices will be working with reduced staffing. I have no idea what happens next if the application is unsuccessful because the equivalent of eight carer visits today is going to cost a fortune if I have to pay for it, especially as, either way, I shall have to supplement it with the carer/man-sitters I had before to cover the time I'm out working.

Meanwhile, Nick lies, tranquilly and reasonably comfortably, in his hospital ward where staff now greet me like an old friend. They've taken to reading these blogs and some of my other stuff. It begins to feel like an extension of family. I shall almost miss it, and them, when he comes home.

I continue to marvel at the professional competence and human, humane kindness of every single NHS employee I've met at Lewisham Hospital. I just wish Jacob Rees-Mogg could spare half a day to sort out the NHS style guide because it seems to have developed a laughably impenetrable, otiose sociolect.

Nick has to be graded in twelve 'domains' in relation to the CHC application. "What?" I said, amazed, to the discharge co-ordinator, and I hope it didn't sound rude. What they mean, I eventually realised, is that they have to report on things such as mobility, cognition, speech and feeding. There are twelve of these. Now, I haven't told anyone at the hospital that I taught English for thirty-six years, have written dozens of English text books and have worked with words all my life. 'Domain' comes, of course, from the Latin word *domus*, house (hence domestic, domiciliary). These days, it also means a virtual space which houses your website, but how can it possibly mean a medical assessment category? Shades of Lewis Carroll's Humpty Dumpty, who opined that words mean what you want them to mean? What's wrong with a word such as 'area', or 'section'? Why not say that patients are assessed under twelve headings…?

If he gets enough marks (and yes, that's how it works – on a numerical points system), the application might 'trigger'. By then, I was trying not to say "What?" too often. It means that LHSC are willing to take it to the next stage, but one really shouldn't need a translation.

I also have a problem with the ever-cheerful obfuscation, upbeat language and the way NHS staff are trained/programmed never to say anything negative. Witness that careful, well-rehearsed phrase the consultant used about the 'new baseline'. Nick is a very sick man. He cannot swallow. He has lost masses of weight. He's unable to stand up or walk and he often doesn't 'speak' to me for the whole time I'm there. He's gradually getting worse, although they've rehydrated him and sorted his sodium levels. It is obvious to me (and presumably to them) how this is going to end. It's just a question of how long it will take and making the path as smooth and comfortable as possible from here to there.

Yet I often arrive to find the staff hopping up and down with excitement because Nick has muttered two or three coherent words or smiled. They're lovely people and I know they care, really care. They are trying to cheer me up, although I never go in looking miserable. But they and I are not being totally honest with each other. And I sense that if I try to call a spade a spade in my usual plain, blunt way then it makes them feel uncomfortable. Interestingly, in years gone by, I suspect it would have been the other way round.

Today, I was gleefully told before I'd even reached the bedside: "He ate half his porridge this morning and most of a cup of tea! And of course he really loves his protein booster drinks! He had almost a whole banana one earlier." Anyone who knows Nick and his – quite fussy – food predilections will know just how hilarious that is.

"Oh good!" I said, playing it their way and trying to keep a straight face. Well done, Lewisham Hospital staff, though, for trying so hard and for, unintentionally, making me smile.

4 August 2019

I'm not really a poet but just occasionally one bubbles out of me. This one had been tapping me on the shoulder demanding to be written for days.

Letting go

You lie, dying
Inch by inch,
While I am brightly, tightly alive
In my rainbow summer clothes,
Smelling of outdoors and real life.

You fingers fumble, like Falstaff's
With the soft white hospital sheet.
Your lower lip trembles as you breathe softly in your deep, ever deeper, sleep.

And the gaping gulf between us continues to widen.
The ship you're aboard is sliding slowly away from the quayside,
Leaving me on dry land, alone.

4 August 2019

I kiss you.
I murmur, "I love you"
I stroke your head, hands and arms.
I try to rouse you.

You slumber on, oblivious.
Never have I felt so close to you.
Never have I felt so far from you.

Once you could make me laugh
Or arch in ecstasy.
Now a massive hole yawns
Where communication once was.

I sit, queasy, uneasy
Watching, waiting.
Or I chat cheerfully to other patients and staff
Because they have a future
And my professional manner is a useful mask.

And then back to your bedside
For a quiet, private tear.

Don't linger, my love.
It's time to go.
Your job here is done.
I'll manage without you.

Somehow.

7 August 2019

When you are struggling with the hardest job you ever do – trying to raise a child half-decently – and you're heading for what feels like rock bottom, there's always someone nearby who tells you, "It's only a phase." Well, of course, those phases don't stop with toddlerhood and they become as clear towards the Very End as they were in the cradle. Shakespeare, famously and with his usual extraordinary power of observation, puts it like this:

Last scene of all,
That ends this strange eventful history,
Is second childishness and mere oblivion;
Sans teeth, sans eyes, sans taste, sans everything.

I now think a lot about the 'last scene of all' because I am watching it unfold daily. Nick has lain in hospital for five weeks. Hospitals are for people who can be helped to get (at least a little) better. Despite the excellent efforts of staff at Lewisham Hospital, Nick has continued to deteriorate. There is no more they can do. "We are approaching the end," the consultant told me plainly this week. The upshot is that he needs to go somewhere else where nature will simply take its course.

And unless nature takes us by surprise in the next few days, he's coming home to die. The bed is ready for him. All ideas of hoisting him in and out of it are now abandoned. We're just waiting for funding to be agreed and the care package to be set up. I am due to meet the palliative care team later this week. There may be hospice involvement.

Well, Shakespeare, you really did get it right, didn't you? Nick now refuses even to try and eat almost everything he's offered. He can hardly swallow, and even getting medication in is difficult. Once home, without an IV drip, he will be dependent on the few drops of water we can spoon in. 'Shrunk shank' is very much in evidence. Realistically, I suspect he's on track to starve to death, and given his frailty, it's unlikely to take long.

He hasn't worn his denture since they had to remove it weeks back for an MRI scan and the process was so difficult that he's been 'sans teeth' ever since. He's been more or less 'sans taste' since he lost his sense of smell twenty years ago, and I really don't know how much his blank rheumy eyes are seeing. 'Second childishness and mere oblivion' apply too since he can do less for himself than he could (presumably) as a six-month baby but seems mercifully unaware of it.

He isn't quite (yet) 'sans everything', though. It is well known that hearing is the last thing to go. This week, I have started taking my iPad and his old Bose headphones to the hospital. Yesterday, I played him the whole of the Mozart *Requiem*. I sat at the bedside quietly doing a puzzle and listening to a comic drama staff were having with another patient while he lay unmoving with the headphones on. Suddenly I thought I saw Nick's hand move but assumed I'd imagined it. Then it happened again. And suddenly his right forearm was vertical and twitching – and his mouth was moving. He was 'conducting' along to the *Sanctus*. It was a marvellous, quite uplifting few moments and wonderful for me to think that he'd briefly found a tiny shred of enjoyment and life quality. Thanks, Wolfgang Amadeus.

9 August 2019

Last Wednesday, I was called into the hospital at 2.30am. I got there in fifteen minutes from the moment I picked up the phone. Our two sons joined me an hour or two later. We listened at Nick's bedside, tense and on tenterhooks, to ragged breathing with some longish pauses between breaths through the quiet of the night until, eventually, dawn broke over Ladywell. Various medical people came in to do checks during the long night. Once it was fully light, Nick opened his eyes and then, after a while, drank a few sips of water and we realised that he was rallying – a little – and that he would probably linger for a bit longer.

Five days later and that's still the case, except that we're now firmly and definitely in the world of palliative care. The consultant came to see us on Wednesday and we all four of us agreed no more medical intervention (including cannula and rehydration drip) or observation. Instead, they will keep him comfortable and pain free, and there's an open prescription for three 'comfort' medications, including morphine, should he need it. She offered us the services of a priest and asked if there were other family members we wanted to bring in.

There is, now, no question of discharging him home. He is simply to stay where he is, on a comfy pressure mattress bed with a view over the leafy Ladywell Fields, for as long as it takes. Given that he now refuses more than a few drops of water, I don't see how that can be long. I go to bed very tired every night but unable to settle because I know as well as anyone that the most likely time for another phone call is 2am to 4am, when the body is at its lowest point in the twenty-four-hour cycle. Instead of sleeping, I lie there thinking and waiting.

Meanwhile, Nick is sometimes awake during the day. Occasionally, he murmurs at me, but it's not comprehensible, and I'm not convinced he recognises me anymore.

Strange though, how even when you're trying to survive the most stressful thing that is ever likely to happen to you – death, or imminent death, of spouse – there are still things to chuckle at.

One day early last week, an enthusiastic nurse radically pruned Nick's moustache because she said it was in the way of

spoon-feeding him. The next one didn't recognise the remnants as a moustache and shaved it off completely. Well, he's had that moustache since 1970 and his children have never seen him without it, but I decided that, in the scheme of things, it really doesn't matter and said so.

"I am not upset. Don't worry about it," I said to two (other) nurses whom I've got to know quite well.

"Well, we are!" they said and between them, created a notice to make sure it doesn't happen again. They were afraid that some nurses and assistants with limited English might not know what a moustache is, so they found and printed off an illustration to pin behind his bed. And it makes me smile every time I look at it.

I can't say too often how impressed I am by the quality of the faultlessly kind, genuine, friendly care Nick (and I) is/are getting from the staff of Ash Ward at Lewisham Hospital. The moustache saga is just a tiny example. On the morning that we made the palliative care decision, one, always warm and thoughtful, came to 'our' bedside, hugged me and said, "Listen, we're here for you guys as well as for the patient. Don't forget that." They deserve ten stars, never mind five.

As for me, I'm locked in a curious limbo world. It feels as if a train is hurtling towards me relentlessly but in slow motion. Like Olive Oyl in all those old *Popeye* cartoons, I'm tied to the track. She was always rescued at the very last minute. I shall not be.

Even now – and I've written over 90,000 words on this subject in these blogs – I sometimes struggle to get my head round the enormity of what's happening to me.

18 August 2019

Nick has now been in palliative care for what feels like a very long time indeed. I'm writing this as the twelfth day dawns. And he's been in hospital for nearly seven weeks. I've almost forgotten what normal life feels like, and everyday marriage, when we talked to each other and shared things, seems about two centuries ago.

I go to Lewisham Hospital every day, often twice. Sometimes, I'm joined by other, ever-supportive, close family members but usually it's just me. It is now four days since Nick woke in my presence or showed any sign of consciousness. He just slumbers on. He hasn't eaten anything for days and takes only tiny drops of water, usually from a little sponge. He is now thinner than I could ever have imagined anyone being. He looks like one of those profoundly shocking concentration camp photographs – literally skin stretched over bone. I suppose he's starving to death and yet he breathes on.

The agony, however, is mine (ours) and not his. He is comfortable and warm in his bed and not in any pain. Hospital staff are making sure of that. I sit by the bedside with a book or a cup of tea (I think a constant state of feeling 'tea-logged' goes with the territory), holding and stroking his bony wrist and sinewy hand under the bedclothes. It feels right and is, oddly, comforting for me. He is, I'm almost certain, not even aware I'm there or who I am.

You're an absolute bastard, Ms Alzheimer's. You have robbed him (and me) – at such a speed that even doctors are surprised – of everything he enjoyed and was looking forward to in his early seventies. But even that wasn't enough for you. Now that he's dying, you've won and there's nothing anyone can do about it. You're gleefully prolonging it for as long as you possibly can, sod you.

On the other hand, maybe it's our own wholesome lifestyle coming back to hit us on the nose. One of the nurses, whom I feel I know quite well, returned to work on Thursday after seven days off duty. "Well, I didn't expect to see you still here!" she said with her usual warm twinkle.

"We didn't expect to be here," I replied, to which she said cheerfully, "It must be all those healthy veggie casseroles you've fed him for the last forty years." It almost makes me wish I'd given him a lifelong diet of chips and deep-fried stuff. Perhaps then his heart would have given up by now.

People often ask how I am in this horror story. Well, most of the time, I manage to hold it together and conduct normal conversations with people, but I'm extremely brittle if someone says the wrong thing. I also find it difficult to deal with ordinary tiresome trivia such as some jobsworth being officious, or Brexit, or remembering what I've promised to do. And reminders can reduce me to a shuddering wreck: Wagner's *Prelude* and *Liebestod* on Radio 3 last week, for instance. It was one of Nick's favourites and it is, of course, an utterly gut-wrenching farewell so it's apt.

It is also very tiring and stressful to be constantly on the alert, waiting twenty-four hours a day for That Phone Call. Inevitably, I'm sleeping badly.

And so it goes on. And on.

21 August 2019

Till death us do part. That's what we promised at St George's Church, Forest Hill back in 1969, and we both kept that promise. Our marriage ended fifty years and five months later, when Ms Alzheimer's took her final fatal bite.

Nick died at dusk on Tuesday, 20 August in Lewisham Hospital. His given names were Nicholas Donald George but almost everyone, including his children, called him Nick. Alzheimer's is an utterly hideous, degenerative, terminal disease which, in Nick's case, galloped at an obscene speed. He died only two years and four months after diagnosis. He was just seventy-four.

These days, apparently, you can negotiate the cause of death with the doctor, which seems odd to me. Who's meant to be the expert? Anyway, they rang the following day and spoke to my elder son, Lucas, saying: "We'd like to put Alzheimer's down for the death certificate. Would that be all right?" I heard him take the call. More patient than me, he politely agreed. I would probably have said: "Well, of course it's all right. What else were you thinking of putting? Yellow fever?"

So how am I doing now that I'm a very new widow? I seem to be okay-ish. Both sons, who are just as bereft as I am, of course, have been tremendously supportive. I'm relieved that Nick finally managed to go the week after Felix's family holiday in Devon and the week before Lucas's in Wales so that neither of them had to cancel and one or other of them has been there for me throughout.

I struggle a bit with what I'm feeling, what I'm meant to be feeling, and what I might soon be feeling, because this is terra nova and the mind can play strange tricks. At the moment, I am, it seems, getting back to normal life, doing what needs to be done – including, at last, some Work Work (as Nick and I used to call the stuff which pays the bills as opposed to doing the ironing or shopping) – and catching up with a few of the things I haven't been able to do for months such as practising my violin and seeing friends. I tell myself very firmly that Nick no longer exists (other than in our memories). What is, at the time of writing, lying in the morgue at Lewisham Hospital is not Nick. It is just a few bits of leftover skin, bone and other body parts. And, obviously, the three of us are funeral planning and sorting out post-death admin but not too frenetically.

I weep a bit over the kind, thoughtful cards and letters which arrive every morning. And the Facebook and Twitter support has been utterly, movingly astonishing. Otherwise, I'm not falling apart. I suspect I did much of the grieving process, including anger, months ago.

My sense of the ridiculous is returning too. Nick, I reflect, would have enjoyed the sitcom of his own death. Lucas, Felix and I were sitting with him with the screens drawn. I'd been at his bedside for most of the previous thirty-six hours, having popped home only once for a quick change of clothes. The boys had done shifts. So we were pretty peckish. An hour or two earlier, Felix had nipped out and bought pizzas because we had no idea how long we were going to be there. When Nick took what became his last breath, I was holding his right hand with my left with a pizza box on my lap, a mouthful of mushroom pizza and another piece in my right hand. Very romantic. Not quite how it is in the films. You'll be relieved to know I never finished what was in the box.

For three weeks before his death, one of Nick's neighbours in the ward was Peter (not his real name). Suffering from frontal-lobe dementia and consequent disinhibition, he shouted all the time, constantly yelled inappropriate things, openly masturbated and tried to grope the unflappable nursing staff. It was sad and I was desperately sorry for Peter's wife and family but it was also hilarious. As Felix said, it was like falling asleep and waking up in a *Carry On* film. On the afternoon of Nick's death, Peter disappeared. In his place arrived a very sick man who vomited noisily and frequently and whose lungs had to be audibly sucked out. All this was going on, a few feet away, as we sat with Nick, watching and listening to those last tortured breaths, the intervals growing ever longer. "Oh, I asked the nurse about Peter. They've moved him to another part of the ward," I whispered to the boys against the sound of yet another bout of retching.

"Please, can we have him back?" said Felix laconically, reducing Lucas and me to fits of giggles.

Meanwhile, the man in the bed immediately next to Nick, well enough to read the *Daily Mail* avidly every day, was chatting to his wife on the phone, telling her cheerfully – and to our amused horror – that it was getting a bit dark in the ward because both the new arrivals opposite were black men. "No, we're not outnumbered yet," he continued. "The chap next to me is still with us. His wife stayed all night last night and I think she'll be here again tonight."

She wasn't. I was, as things turned out, home by 10pm.

8 September 2019

It is now eighteen days since Nick's death on 20 August. And I find myself in the strange terra incognita of early widowhood. It's a time of discovery in several ways. First, Louis Armstrong was right. It is indeed a wonderful world. Never mind scumbag politicians, silly strikes or even terrorists. The vast majority of people are kind, caring, thoughtful and good. I have had over forty cards and letters and literally hundreds of emails and social networking messages. I have never felt more warmly supported.

On the other hand, dealing with others isn't always easy because this is such a Big Thing. If I meet a casual acquaintance when I'm out working who says, "How are you?" and obviously doesn't know, it's hard to know how to answer because if I tell the blunt truth, she or he is immediately very embarrassed. But if I say, "Fine, thanks," and move on, the next day they will hear what has happened from someone else and think it was very odd that I didn't mention it. So I usually end up with something like: "Okay-ish but not the best of summers. Sorry, you'll wish you hadn't asked but the truth is…"

Then I have to get accustomed to living alone – in the house we moved to three years ago with high hopes of a long and happy time here together. Most of the time, it's all right. I have, effectively, lived solo here since Nick was admitted to hospital on 3 July, apart from odd nights that sons have stayed and two weeks when my regular visitor (an old schoolfriend who lives abroad) was here for her summer residency. So I've had time to get – sort of – used to it. I have the radio on almost all the time (Nick hated that unless he was actually sitting, listening to it) for company and the cat is earning his keep. Darker evenings may be harder. We'll see.

There is always plenty to do after a death, and Lucas and Felix and I are working through it all. Between us, we've now done all the important notifying and we've hired a local solicitor to help with probate which, for a couple of boring legal reasons, has not turned out to be quite as straightforward as it should have been. We've dealt with possessions too and restored the house to normal.

I also have a busy work diary – I reviewed five shows last week. At the point when Nick died, I was just one week off two big deadlines which I'd been trying not to think about. In the event, I got that work done and submitted on time so that was satisfying, a relief and oddly therapeutic because it felt like Real Life of which I had had very little for many weeks. Work will be what saves me, I think.

And of course there are things I don't miss at all: worrying every single moment I'm not in the house, dealing with incontinence and disability and, latterly, spending hours every day, anxious and tense, at Lewisham Hospital, and so on and on.

I can now eat what and when I like too. I'm so revoltingly practical and sensible that I now have a freezer full of home-cooked single portions of all my favourite dishes – some of which, such as mushroom stroganoff and Lebanese moussaka, Nick wasn't fond of, so, in practice, I used not to have them very often. Now I can.

Inevitably, there's plenty I do miss, though: the warmth of his hand, his smile if he heard an especially lovely bit of music, the sound of his footsteps around the house and lots, lots more. And, once upon a time, he did all my paperwork, managed the dishwasher and put the bins out. Fifty years is a long time to share your life with someone.

I struggle a bit with what I'm actually feeling and what I'm meant to feel at this moment. I suppose everyone's different. I knew almost from the moment Nick was diagnosed in 2017 that this disease was going to consume him quickly. And if I have a strength, it's being able to look the truth straight in the eye – and then plan on the basis of reality, however awful it is. I have therefore thought a great deal about how things would be, and what I would do, after his death. I've been 'acquainted with grief', as *Messiah* puts it, for a long time. And I think that preparation is helping now. I also know – unequivocally and with total certainty – that, hideously cruel as it was and much as I loved him, Nick had lost all quality of life and his death was a relief for him as well as for us.

None of that, of course, means that I'm not brittle and, inevitably, it takes very little to reduce me to tears – but usually not for long. Sometimes, I get involved in work or something else and don't think about any of it for a whole half-hour. Then I remember and press it like a sore spot to see if it still hurts. It does. Obviously.

I also have very painful back problems which started about a month before Nick died and have worsened since. Of course, it can't be coincidence. My body is protesting about what it, and I, have been through in recent months. In some ways, this is, at present, causing me more 'grief' than anything else, but I have sought expert advice and am doing all the right things.

I've been told, by several people, that it's common to hit rock bottom at about three months. That takes me to the end of November – the beginning of the panto season when I am usually pretty busy. Maybe this year will be different. Don't know. This new life of mine is like being in a completely foreign country where I don't understand the language or what's going on. Best just to take each day as it comes and 'let the grief in' (as a wise friend advised last week) when I need to, I suppose.

14 September 2019

What are you supposed to feel at the funeral of a dearly beloved partner which whom you have shared over half a century of your life? Devastated, is the answer in my case. All the strength, urbane front and cheerfulness that I've paraded for the last three weeks suddenly evaporated as I stared weeping at the beautiful wicker coffin, topped with white lilies, which I'd chosen. The enormity of my loss suddenly hit me like a sledgehammer, and the one person who could, once, have comforted me wasn't there.

But funerals are about shared grieving, letting go – and, of course, celebrating a life well lived. It was, therefore, utterly wonderful to see, in the congregation, so many people from so many aspects of the life Nick and I enjoyed together for so long: a unique, eclectic and rather special group. I was flanked by my sons, and three of our four granddaughters (GD4, aged four, had gone to nursery as usual) and our daughters-in-law. The rest of the extended family – including some gloriously extended bits of it – was very well represented. Also present were three of my editors and one of the carers who helped me look after Nick at home during the last months before he went into hospital. Then there was an old school friend of Nick's and his wife, along with a former student of mine and her infant son, my younger son's lifelong friend, two neighbours and a friend of a (very old) friend who happens to live locally. They had come from all over the country. There were, inevitably, many more people who couldn't – for personal, professional or geographical reasons – be with us on the day. Right up to the last minute, I was getting lovely messages from Italy, America, Australia, Yorkshire, Somerset, elsewhere in London and many more places.

The service was magnificently led by a school friend of mine, one of the first women in the country to be ordained.

I'm not a conventional religious believer and neither was Nick. Although we met at a church youth club and both came from churchgoing families, we rejected the doctrines and trappings before we were out of our teens. Nonetheless, these days, I can go along with some sense of a force of love and goodness in the world, and it was very much in evidence at Nick's funeral. I could feel it palpably buoying me up as I mopped the (many) tears.

I loathe the clinical tastefulness of crematoria. They exist for one purpose only: processing the dead. And I wanted something warmer and more rounded than that for Nick. So we went back to St George's Church, Forest Hill, where we were married in 1969. Structural problems led to the demolition of the old Victorian barn of a building fifteen years or so ago. The airy modern church built on the same site but incorporating the original stained glass rose window is stunningly beautiful, and it felt absolutely the right place to be. Inevitably, there were at least eight people present who were at our wedding fifty years ago, including the best man and all three bridesmaids. Rather a lovely bit of continuity.

I asked people not to wear black and the sun was shining merrily, so the atmosphere was light and bright.

We played four pieces of classical music which Nick might have chosen himself and included some silences for reflection. Felix read a Hilaire Belloc poem. Bernard, Nick's first cousin, who was best man at our wedding, read a Christina Rossetti poem and

Lucas delivered a beautifully thought-out eulogy that really paid tribute to Nick's varied life, along with anecdotes about spilled honey, dishwashers and socks drawer filed in colour order.

The trick, of course, is to try to stop thinking about illness, Ms Bloody Alzheimer's and the ghastliness which beset the last few months and to make your mind leapfrog back to happier times. The montage of photographs Felix set up on a loop at the reception (I hate the word 'wake') was a brilliant idea. I had forgotten Nick showing us on a visit to Dover Castle that, yes, he really had learned – at a yoga class – to stand on his head. There were pictures of him at all ages and stages – often with cats and/or babies. Or me. Or his parents. Or with one of the many cars he owned over the years. It made a good focus and talking point.

So now I'm a widow and my new life starts here. It's unknown territory and I don't know how it's going to pan out. I shall carry on working. I've never wanted to retire and I want it less than ever now. Working makes me feel part of the real world and reminds me that I still have a purpose in life. I also have some holidays planned and lots of invitations to spend time with friends and family.

The psychological effect of a funeral is odd, though. It's like a door finally, finally slamming. It's bleak. Nick ceased to exist on 20 August and I was very rational about that. I now realise, though, that in a sense he wasn't quite gone during that limbo period. He is now.

So this is the last of these Alzheimer's blogs. Thank you for staying with me for so long. Over and out.